Quantitative Analysis for Economics and Business

Quantitative Analysis for Economics and Business

Using Lotus 1-2-3

Guy Judge
Principal Lecturer in Quantitative
Methods and Econometrics
Portsmouth Polytechnic

Harvester Wheatsheaf

New York   London   Toronto   Sydney   Tokyo   Singapore

First published 1990 by
Harvester Wheatsheaf,
66 Wood Lane End, Hemel Hempstead,
Hertfordshire, HP2 4RG
A division of
Simon & Schuster International Group

Printed and bound in Great Britain by
BPCC Wheatons Ltd, Exeter

British Library Cataloguing in Publication Data

Judge, Guy
    Quantitative analysis for economics and business:
    using Lotus 1-2-3.
    1. Economic analysis. Quantitative methods.
    Application of microcomputer systems. Spreadsheet
    packages.
    I. Title
    330′.0724

    ISBN 0–7450–0513–6
    ISBN 0–7450–0666–3 pbk

---

3 4 5   94 93 92 91

To Pauline, for her forbearance

Contents

Preface

This book has grown out of a series of lectures, handouts and practical exercises which I have used to teach a course called 'Economics Workshop' on the BA Economics degree at Portsmouth Polytechnic, beginning in 1986. The aims of that course were as follows:

1. To enhance the integration between the quantitative methods and economics courses and thus to demonstrate more clearly the relevance of the techniques and methods of quantitative analysis to the study of economics.
2. To ensure that all students undertake some practical work in applied economics, requiring them to analyse real data.
3. To encourage students in the use of computers and information technology in order to improve their productivity both during their course of study and afterwards in employment.
4. To develop a more student-centred approach to learning. (It was not expected that very much staff time would be saved in the process, because of the time needed for the preparation of exercises and assignments, but it was felt that student motivation and satisfaction could be improved by making a move in this direction.)

In planning the course it became apparent that a spreadsheet package such as Lotus 1-2-3 should be given a central role. The benefits of using Lotus 1-2-3 for quantitative analysis are outlined in the Introduction, where it is suggested that although different spreadsheet packages have many common features, Lotus 1-2-3 (Release 2.01) is particularly suited to use by economists. This is because, as well as incorporating graphics, it has matrix and regression commands available.

In writing this book I had a difficult decision to make. Should I limit my coverage to this one particular package, leaving the reader to work out how the instructions would have to be modified to work with other packages, or should I attempt to give a more general description of the use of spreadsheets for quantitative analysis in economics which could then be applied to any spreadsheet package? In the event I have chosen the former approach because it is hard to explain what steps need to be taken at each stage of the analysis without relating the description to a particular package. However, if you have a different spreadsheet package at your institution it should be possible for you to reinterpret many of the examples and applications described in this book so that they can be used with that package. The basic principles of operation are common to all spreadsheets and you should have no real difficulty in modifying the instructions given here so that you can use them with other packages such as Quattro, VP-Planner or SuperCalc (although only the first of these includes matrix commands).

At the time of writing, Release 3 of Lotus 1-2-3 was still not available. It is now expected to be launched in June 1989. Consequently all references in this book are to Release 2.01 of the package. However, it will be possible to proceed to Release 3 without difficulty because the Lotus Development Corporation is ensuring upwards compatibility of worksheets prepared under Release 2.01. Any time you spend studying this book will not be wasted if your institution buys Release 3 of Lotus 1-2-3!

This book also assumes that you will be running the package under the MS–DOS/PC–DOS operating system on an IBM PC or compatible computer. These machines will have a disk drive to read and write files to a 5¼″ floppy disk so you will be able to store worksheet and graph files on your own disk. Newer machines, such as the IBM PS/2 series, use smaller 3½″ disks. Some computers may have Release 4.0 of MS–DOS which has pull-down menus to replace the commands typed in at the keyboard. These developments are unlikely to affect the majority of readers just yet and are beyond the scope of this book.

For those readers who have never used a PC before, some background information on personal computer systems and operating system commands is given in Chapter 1, which also describes how to load Lotus 1-2-3. The remaining chapters of the book concentrate on how 1-2-3 can be used for quantitative analysis in economics.

Guy Judge
Portsmouth

References

Lotus 1-2-3 Release 2.01 (Lotus Development Corporation, Cambridge, MA, 1985).
Quattro (Borland International, Scotts Valley, CA, 1987).
VP–Planner (Paperback Software International, California, 1986).
SuperCalc4 (Computer Associates International, New York, 1986).

Acknowledgements

I owe debts of gratitude to a great many people, without whose help in some way this book would not have been written.

First, although I have never met them, I must thank Dan Bricklin and Robert Frankston, the authors of the world's first spreadsheet package VisiCalc, which was first available in 1978. Along with Mitch Kapor, who designed the first version of Lotus 1-2-3, these men have made possible facilities which it is so easy to take for granted.

Next, I must thank my colleagues at Portsmouth Polytechnic who have helped me with the Economics Workshop course and have given me support and encouragement during the writing of this book: Saxon Brettell, Pat Cooper, Mike Dunn, Sheila Dutton, Dave Fysh, Martin Holmes, Ed Kopinski, Tad Podolski, Andy Thorpe, Richard Welford and Dave Whitmarsh. I must also recognise the role played in shaping the book by the students who have taken the course, particularly Barry Andrew who read and commented on an early draft of some chapters. Colleagues at other institutions who have heard (and in one case co-presented) my papers on the use of Lotus 1-2-3 and have made helpful suggestions include George Blazyca (Thames Polytechnic), Bob Jones (Trent Polytechnic), Jean Soper (Leicester University) and Peter Taylor (Bristol Polytechnic).

The staff at Harvester Wheatsheaf have provided the professional expertise necessary to turn my computer printouts into book form, and Peter Johns maintained just the right balance of restrained interest and concerned chivvying to ensure that the book was eventually completed.

As is customary, I acknowledge that any remaining defects are entirely my responsibility.

Trademarks

'Lotus' and '1-2-3' are registered trademarks of the Lotus Development Corporation.

'IBM' and 'IBM PC' are registered trademarks of International Business Machines Corporation.

'Microsoft' and 'MS–DOS' are registered trademarks of Microsoft Corporation.

'Quattro' is a registered trademark of Borland International.

Introduction

What is this book about and whom is it for?

This book is about the use of Lotus 1-2-3 for quantitative analysis in economics. It is aimed at first- and second-year degree-level students in economics (and related subjects such as business studies). However, it might also be of interest to academic, professional and business economists who could benefit from using 1-2-3 in their teaching, research or consultancy work, but who require information on how the package can be applied. It is assumed that the reader has taken, or is taking, courses in quantitative methods which include introductions to descriptive and inferential statistics (including regression analysis) and some mathematical topics (including matrix algebra and difference equations).

The book shows how Lotus 1-2-3 can be used as a convenient yet powerful tool for quantitative analysis in economics. Three types of quantitative analysis are dealt with: statistical (or data) analysis, problem-solving or decision-making analysis, and model analysis and simulation.

Chapter 1 provides some general background information to prepare readers for what follows, and then Chapter 2 establishes the main concepts and functions of 1-2-3 in the analysis of a simple business application. The next three chapters deal with index numbers (Chapter 3), time series (Chapter 4) and the analysis of cross-section data (Chapter 5), showing how using Lotus 1-2-3 can facilitate data analysis and help users to gain a better understanding of the techniques involved. There are then two chapters which show how 1-2-3 can be used in decision-making applications. Present-value and other interest-rate calculations relevant to investment decisions are illustrated in Chapter 6, and Chapter 7 shows how 1-2-3 can be used to solve resource-allocation problems which can be expressed in the form of a linear program. Again, in both these chapters the aim is as much to use the package to help the reader improve his or her understanding of the concepts and techniques as to provide a straight problem-solving facility. Chapters 8 and 9 illustrate the use of 1-2-3 for regression, giving a key role to graphical analysis in model selection and validation. Chapters 10 and 11 demonstrate the use of 1-2-3 in modelling economic interdependence. Chapter 10 shows how to use 1-2-3 for the analysis of dynamic interdependence with applications to two difference-equation economic models. In Chapter 11 the matrix commands of 1-2-3 are used in an application of (static) input–output analysis. Chapter 12 suggests some of the many other types of application which are possible using Lotus 1-2-3 and briefly describes some of the other program features not covered elsewhere in the book.

What is Lotus 1-2-3?

Lotus 1-2-3 is an applications package designed for the IBM PC and compatibles which is widely used in business. Indeed, the program has been the best-selling computer software package of all time, and Lotus has estimated that in 1988 there were around ten million 1-2-3 users worldwide.

The package is based on spreadsheet principles and allows users to enter and manipulate quantitative information (and accompanying text) in the rows and columns of a worksheet. (We use the word *spreadsheet* to refer to the package which produces the framework of rows and columns, while a *worksheet* is defined by the contents of the cells as built up by the user.) Each cell in a worksheet is referred to by a letter indicating the column location and a number indicating the row position. Thus B4, for example, identifies a cell as being in the fourth row of the second column.

A cell can contain a formula which refers to the contents of some other cell or cells, using standard mathematical operations. For example, when cell B3 contains the formula +B1/B2 the computer will show the value 3 at this cell position on the screen if cell B1 holds the number 6 and cell B2 holds the number 2. The formula itself is displayed at the top of the screen when this cell is highlighted (see Table 0.1).

It is straightforward to build far more complicated formulae than this and the package contains a great many 'built-in' functions which can assist in the construction of formulae. For example, @LN(B1) could be used to find the

Table 0.1 Part of a worksheet showing the formula for the current cell (B3) and the resulting value displayed in the cell

B3: +B1/B2

								READY
A	B	C	D	E	F	G	H	
1	6							
2	2							
3	3							
4								
5								
6								
7								
8								
9								
10								

natural logarithm of the contents of cell B1 (provided, as in this case, that the contents of this cell is a positive number).

Why use Lotus 1-2-3?

Five factors make a spreadsheet package like Lotus 1-2-3 an invaluable tool for quantiative analysis in economics (or indeed in any other subject where quantitative analysis is used):

1. The spreadsheet approach to entering data and defining formulae is so easy that users can begin to construct productive worksheets with very little initial training or assistance.
2. Spreadsheet packages allow huge worksheets to be created and quite complex models can be constructed. In Lotus 1-2-3 (Release 2.01), for example, up to 8192 rows and 256 columns are available to hold quantitative or textual information (although when information has been entered into a large number of cells the computer's memory will begin to fill up and the operation of the package will slow down).
3. Manipulating information with a spreadsheet is very easy. The package is *menu-driven* with commands arranged in *tree* or *hierarchical* form. To issue a command the user simply calls up the menu by pressing the / (slash) key and selects the chosen command by moving the cursor to highlight the command and then presses the *<Return>* key to confirm the choice. If at any stage a user gets lost, pressing the *<Esc>* (Escape) key takes them back a stage up the menu structure. Extensive on-screen *Help* facilities are also available. When a similar type of formula is needed in a number of cell positions it is not necessary to enter each one separately. A **Copy** command allows a formula to be copied from one cell to another and even makes automatic adjustments to the formula to reflect the relative position of the new cell in the worksheet.
4. Because the package defines formulae in relation to cell addresses it will automatically *recalculate* the result if the contents of any underlying cell is changed. This enables users to conduct *what-if* experiments to discover the effect on the results of changes in key values. Because recalculation is virtually instantaneous, spreadsheets allow users to undertake all kinds of modelling exercises and to improve their understanding of a method or technique by experimenting with different values and examining the results.
5. A feature which makes Lotus 1-2-3 particularly useful for quantitative analysis is its built-in *graphics* facilities. Using the graphics commands within the menu structure, several types of graph can be constructed based on the contents of particular cells in the worksheet. For example, line graphs can show time-series plots of variables or illustrate a functional relationship between variables whose values occupy different columns of

a worksheet. The computer looks after the scaling automatically (although the computer's choice can be overridden if desired) and titles and labelling can be inserted without difficulty. (One slight annoyance is that, unlike the worksheet itself, a graph cannot be immediately printed out, but must first be saved as a file to be printed later using the *PrintGraph* part of the package.) However, just like the formulae, screen graphs respond instantly to changes in worksheet values so that a visual assessment of the influence of particular values can be made.

Taking these factors together, a spreadsheet package like Lotus 1-2-3 is seen to be an ideal tool to use in quantitative analysis. Computation is straightforward and reliable, but does not require sophisticated programming skills. Recalculation is quick and easy if new data becomes available or if the user wishes to see the effect on the results of a change in some of the values. The graphics capabilities mean that the results or the impact of changes become more meaningful and can be seen quickly. Overall, the package is a flexible and powerful tool for the manipulation of quantitative information, yet it is easy to learn and to use.

Further comments on the choice of 1-2-3

Although Lotus 1-2-3 is the most popular spreadsheet it is far from the only one available. However, 1-2-3 was chosen as the subject of this book and is recommended to be used by economics students for two reasons. Firstly, because it is the package which students are most likely to have to use after graduation, teaching them how to use the package provides them with transferable skills which are valuable quite apart from their utility in studying economics. Secondly, 1-2-3 has features which are particularly useful in economic analysis and which are not always present in other packages. These features are as follows:

1. Regression commands. Release 2.01 includes commands for the regression analysis of data held within the worksheet. Although the regression output produced by 1-2-3 is fairly rudimentary, the ease with which these results can be augmented within the worksheet or illustrated graphically makes 1-2-3 a convenient vehicle for simple regression applications. It can also be used for improving the understanding of the technique and associated concepts (see Chapters 8 and 9).
2. Matrix commands. Release 2.01 of Lotus 1-2-3 added some commands for simple matrix manipulations. These commands greatly increase the potential of the package and are used in Chapter 11, which deals with input–output analysis.
3. Links with other packages. Because Lotus 1-2-3 is used so widely many other packages (including a number that economists might wish to use)

provide specific facilities to read Lotus 1-2-3 files. (An example is the econometrics package RATS from VAR Econometrics.) This means that 1-2-3 can be used to set up databases containing information which may be needed later in a study, even if the 1-2-3 regression commands themselves are recognised as being inadequate for this analysis. It is often easier to create and maintain databases using 1-2-3, extracting data for use with other packages as required, than to keep the files in any other way. Output from other packages can also sometimes be read into Lotus worksheet files, providing a convenient method of constructing reports and other documents. In this way Lotus 1-2-3 can be used as a bridge linking inputs and outputs from several packages which are individually incompatible. This provides yet another justification for making Lotus 1-2-3 your spreadsheet choice. (See Chapter 12 for details of how to transfer files between 1-2-3 and other programs.)

Some comments on the coverage of this book

No attempt has been made to discuss all the functions and features of Lotus 1-2-3 in this book. There are many other books on the market which provide full descriptions of 1-2-3 functions. Perhaps the most comprehensive of these is LeBlond and Cobb (1985). In common with most of the other books currently available on 1-2-3, their book provides only a cursory treatment of the matrix and regression commands. Indeed it is clear from the authors' remarks that they do not expect many people to want to use these features. This is because their book is aimed mainly at business users who are unlikely to give these features high priority. Conversely, in this book there is no discussion of the database management commands within 1-2-3 which are given a whole chapter in the book by LeBlond and Cobb. Our lack of attention to the database commands is not because they will never be of use to students of economics, but because within a textbook devoted to the use of 1-2-3 for quantitative analysis they must be excluded because of space constraints. (The name 1-2-3 refers to the three types of applications which have been brought together in the package, namely spreadsheet, database and graphics.)

References

RATS [Regression Analysis of Time Series] (VAR Econometrics, Minneapolis, 1986).
G. T. LeBlond and D. F. Cobb, *Using 1-2-3* (Que Corporation, Indianapolis, 1985).

Chapter 1

Preparing to use Lotus 1-2-3

Purpose: To prepare the reader to be able to use Lotus 1-2-3 (or a similar spreadsheet package) by providing some general background information on personal computer systems and basic spreadsheet concepts and operations.

Preview: Section 1.1 provides a description of personal computer systems and their components for the reader who will be using a PC for the first time to run Lotus 1-2-3. Section 1.2 goes on to discuss the disk operating system (DOS) which controls the operation of a personal computer system, identifying key points for new users. Section 1.3 describes how to load Lotus 1-2-3 and introduces some fundamental spreadsheet concepts and operations.

Concepts introduced in this chapter:

Personal computer systems: keyboard – QWERTY keys, function keys, numeric keypad, special keys; monitor – monochrome and colour monitors, on/off switches and brightness controls; system unit – microprocessor chips, coprocessors, primary storage capacity and RAM, hard and floppy disk drives, graphics adapters; printers – dot-matrix, daisy-wheel, ink-jet and laser; obtaining graphics and colour printouts; additional input and output devices; mouse, plotters.

MS-DOS: files; directories; commands; 'booting' the system; formatting a disk; filenames; file extensions; drive specifications; changing the default drive; displaying the contents of a directory; subdirectories; making and changing directories; erasing, renaming and copying files; note on the care of disks.

1-2-3: system disk; the 1-2-3 access system; initial worksheet screen display; cell pointer; moving the cell pointer using the arrow keys and the F5 (GOTO) key; entering text, numbers and formulae; calling up the main menu using the / (slash) key; using the **Copy** command; editing cell entries and the F2 key; calling up Help with the F1 key.

Preamble: Readers who have used a PC before with some other type of applications program such as a wordprocessing package may want to go straight on to Section 1.3. However, readers who have not used a PC before are strongly advised to read through Sections 1.1 and 1.2 before attempting to use Lotus 1-2-3.

1.1 Personal computer systems for running Lotus 1-2-3

Lotus 1-2-3 was written to run on an IBM PC. The letters 'PC' here stand for 'personal computer' and one of the great attractions of this kind of computer is that it can be used independently, with all the separate parts of the computer being located together in one place, giving a user complete control of all its functions. If a printer is attached to the computer then when the analysis is complete a hard-copy printout of the results can be obtained straight away.

To use Lotus 1-2-3 you must have a suitable PC, with or without a printer (the *hardware*), and a copy of the 1-2-3 program itself (the *software*). You will also need your own floppy disk on which to store your worksheet and graph files. Standard floppy disks for PCs are 5¼ inches across and are encased in a protective cover.

The computer you use to run Lotus 1-2-3 will be an IBM PC of some sort, or a PC 'compatible' such as a Compaq PC, an Epson PC or an Amstrad PC. Although these machines are compatible (in the sense that they can run the same software) the various models do differ in their general appearance, in the components which they use, and in some ways in the quality of their performance.

Your computer could have two *disk drives* for *floppy disks*, or it might have a *hard disk* along with just one floppy disk drive. Computers require a *disk operating system* (DOS) to supervise the overall operation of the computer system. For example, you issue DOS commands to see what *files* you have on a disk, to erase unwanted files from a disk, to copy files from one disk to another and to see to other disk 'housekeeping' tasks of this type. The operating system used on PC machines is called *MS-DOS* (PC-DOS is virtually the same). An introductory guide to MS-DOS is given in the next section. The rest of this section describes the hardware of a PC system in more detail, looking in turn at the *keyboard*, the *monitor*, the main *system unit* (which contains the microprocessor which actually does the computing), the *printer* and a variety of further *input* and *output* devices which may be attached to the system.

The *keyboard* is the device used to type in data or to issue instructions to the computer. The standard IBM PC keyboard is built around a conventional 'QWERTY' typewriter set of keys with the letters arranged in three rows (beginning with the letters Q,W,E,R,T and Y at the top left). Above them is a row of number keys and these and some other keys give a variety of punctuation marks and other symbols, some of which are accessible by pressing a key together with the <*Shift*> key (sometimes marked by a large upward arrow on the key).

On the far left of the keyboard is a block of *function keys*(labelled F1 to F10). These keys are programmable and the computer will perform a particular task when one of them is pressed, depending on the context. For example, within Lotus 1-2-3 the key labelled F1 can be pressed at any stage to give access to the program's Help screens (see Appendix D for a full list of the function keys in 1-2-3).

On the right of the keyboard is a *numeric keypad* of nine keys. Just to its left is the <*Return*> key (sometimes with the symbol ⮐ on it). This is one of a number of special keys which it is necessary to know about. When you type in data the inputs will not be entered into the computer's memory until this key has been pressed. Other important special keys include the <*Escape*> key (usually with just the letters *Esc* on it) and the <*Caps Lock*> key. We shall look at the function keys and the special keys in more detail as we need them. For now do not worry if your keyboard layout differs from the one described in this book. Computer manufacturers use several different keyboard layouts and we shall not attempt to describe all the variations. Sometimes you will find the function keys are in a separate line along the top of the keyboard. There may also be a separate set of *arrow movement* keys with the symbols ←, →, ↑ and ↓. On standard keyboards these are built into the numeric keypad.

Your link with what is going on in the computer is the *monitor* (sometimes called the visual display unit (VDU) or cathode ray tube (CRT), or just the screen). The characters you type in at the keyboard (i.e. letters, digits or other symbols such as £, %, etc.) will be displayed on the monitor screen, as will be the results produced by the computer. Your computer may also be capable of displaying graphs, although this will depend on it having an appropriate *graphics adaptor* (see below). Even if your computer cannot display graphs on the screen it is still possible to use Lotus 1-2-3 to create graphs which can be saved and printed out later. (There is a separate program called *PrintGraph* within 1-2-3 for printing graphs – see Chapter 2.) However, it is obviously much easier if you can see the graph on the screen as you are creating it so that you can check it, and if necessary modify it straight away.

If your computer has a monochrome monitor you will only be able to obtain black-and-white images (or perhaps green and white or even amber and white). To enable you to see colour displays the computer must have a *colour graphics monitor*, even if you have a colour graphics adaptor. Although there are some advantages in having colour displays for graphs so that plots of different series can be shown in different colours, this may be a luxury that you will have to do without for reasons of economy in the purchasing of computing equipment.

Two last points to note about monitors are that some have a separate on/off switch and most have a brightness control which can be adjusted to give a screen display which you find comfortable.

The keyboard and the monitor are only input and output devices. The heart of the computer is the *microprocessor*, an integrated circuit or 'chip' which is attached to a printed circuit board and which is housed within the main *system unit*. The microprocessor is what provides the computer with its ability to perform arithmetic, comparisons and general control operations. The speed of a microprocessor is measured in megahertz (MHz) or millions of cycles per second, and this gives an indication of how quickly it will be able to carry out its operations. The IBM PC XT and many PC compatibles use the Intel 8088 chip which gives speeds of around 4.77 MHz. The IBM AT uses the faster 80826 chip, performing at around 8 MHz.

In comparing computers you will also find that they differ in the amount of *primary storage capacity* or current memory that they have available. The *random access memory* (or RAM) is that part of the computer's memory which is available to users for storing programs and data. It should be distinguished from the *read only memory* (ROM) which contains pre-wired functions which cannot be changed, but may be called upon, for example, to get the computer running when it is first switched on. In computing, memory is measured in bytes, kilobytes (K) or megabytes (Mb) (1K = 1024 bytes, 1Mb = 1000K) and the value will indicate how much information can be stored. To run Lotus 1-2-3 a minimum of 256K RAM is required. This is not likely to be a problem since most PCs on the market today have as much as 640K RAM.

The main system unit will also house the *disk drives* for the computer. If your computer has two (twin) floppy disk drives they will be referred to as drives A and B. If it has a hard disk this will be referred to as drive C (and the single floppy drive with it can be called either A or B). The disk drive enables you to transfer programs and data to and from the current memory from the *secondary storage* facility provided by the floppy disk or hard disk.

Whenever a computer is switched off, all the information in the current memory is lost. Consequently any data that you wish to keep must first be saved onto a floppy disk or to the hard disk. In order to run a program like Lotus 1-2-3 it will have to be loaded into the computer's memory from secondary storage. When you buy Lotus 1-2-3 it comes on floppy disks and if you have a twin disk drive system you will load the package each time from these disks. If your computer has a hard disk it is easier to install the program onto the hard disk and then load it from there each time you use it (see Section 1.3 for instructions on how to load Lotus 1-2-3).

PC computers require that their *operating system* (MS-DOS) has been loaded at the beginning of each session. On a hard disk machine this will be done automatically when the machine is switched on, but with a twin floppy disk machine this must be done as part of the 'booting up' procedure when you switch on (see Section 1.2).

Each floppy disk drive has a slot large enough to accept a 5¼″ floppy disk and a door or catch to close and hold the disk in the drive. When a computer is retrieving (reading) information from a floppy disk or saving (writing) it to a disk a light will come on by the disk drive.

WARNING You should never remove a disk while this light is on, nor should you switch off the computer while a floppy disk is in a disk drive as this can corrupt the information stored on the disk.

Floppy disks have a memory capacity of around 360K when used with PCs. Before they can be used to hold data files they must be *formatted* (see Section 1.2).

A hard disk is contained inside the main system unit and is not removable. You will not be able to see it or the hard disk drive in which it sits. However, you will be able to tell whenever the computer is reading or writing to a hard disk because a light will flash on the system unit close to where the hard disk is located. Hard disks vary according to how much storage capacity they provide. Usually they come in blocks of 10 or 20 megabytes.

A further complication is that your twin floppy disk computer might have a *hard card* which has been plugged into an expansion slot within the system unit. Such a hard card functions exactly like a hard disk – indeed it is simply a removable hard disk on a card. It can be used to upgrade a twin floppy disk machine like the IBM PC XT.

In the discussion of the monitor above, it was noted that the computer must have an appropriate *graphics adaptor* present if it is to be able to display Lotus graphics on the screen. Such an adaptor may have been built in to the machine as standard, or it may have been fitted on a card into one of the expansion slots inside the system unit. The graphics adaptor may be limited to providing only monochrome graphics displays (as in the case of the Hercules graphics card) or it may be able to display colour graphics (assuming that the computer also has a colour monitor). There are several different standard types of colour graphics adapter, with the *CGA* (*Colour Graphics Adapter*), and *EGA* (*Enhanced Graphics Adapter*) being the best known. The EGA card provides more colours and higher-resolution graphics than the CGA. Both will still work with monochrome monitors, displaying varying degrees of grey shading in place of different colours.

Although a *printer* is not necessary for you to be able to run Lotus 1-2-3 on your PC, you will need one if you require a hard-copy printout of the worksheet information or of any of the graphs which you create. You may be lucky and have a printer attached directly to your computer, giving you a truly personal computer system, or you may have to share a printer with other users. In some cases a printer will be linked to several computers via a *switching* unit. Only one person will be able to use the printer at a time and he or she must first ensure that the unit is switched through to the correct computer. Another possibility is that in a suite of computers some will have printers and others will not, so that you actually have to switch machines in order to obtain a printout. In this situation you will have to ensure that your work has been properly saved on a floppy disk before moving to the machine with the printer.

A variety of types of printer can be used for printing Lotus 1-2-3 worksheets or graphs. Typically it will be some kind of *dot-matrix* printer which forms characters from a collection of dots in appropriate positions within a small box on the paper. Such a printer will also be able to print high-resolution, hard-copy graphics images such as those produced by the *PrintGraph* program within Lotus 1-2-3. A *daisy-wheel* printer, commonly used in word-processing applications because it produces letter-quality printed output, cannot be used for printing graphs and so is not suitable for 1-2-3 users. It gets its name because it has a small 'daisy'-like rotating wheel on which are mounted 'petals' with typewriter-style heads. Fully formed individual characters are printed when the heads hammer the ribbon against the paper. Both dot-matrix and daisy-wheel printers are *impact* devices. They work by hitting needles or heads against a ribbon and onto the paper.

Another type of printer is the *ink-jet* printer. These high-quality printers propel electrostatically charged drops onto the paper to create characters and lines. Higher-quality printed output can be obtained by using a *laser printer*. This operates rather like a photocopier but uses a laser beam light source. There are also newer *liquid crystal display* (LCD) printers which are similar to laser printers but use a different light source for the imaging process.

It is also possible to change the size of the printed characters when printing 1-2-3 worksheets. This is done by changing the *set-up string* in the *Print* menu (see the *1-2-3 Reference Manual*, p. 100). Special Lotus 1-2-3 'add-ins' such as the utility *Sideways* are also available, which as its name suggests, enables you to print worksheets sideways on, with a choice of nine different sizes (see Chapter 12).

Some additional input and output devices could possibly be linked to your computer system. The Amstrad PCs, for example, have as standard an input device called a *mouse* which is attached to the system unit through a *port* on the left-hand side alongside the place where the keyboard is plugged in. A mouse is a push-button control device which, when used with a menu- or icon-driven program, can eliminate the need for typing in commands at the keyboard. (An *icon* is a small picture representing the item to be selected.) The user moves the mouse around the desk top until the pointer is at the chosen position on the screen and then 'clicks' the mouse to transmit a message to the computer. Although it is possible to use a mouse with Lotus 1-2-3 running on a PC under MS-DOS, there are no real advantages in doing so. However, applications programs and operating systems will become increasingly 'icon' based in the future, making the mouse as important an input device as the keyboard.

An alternative method of obtaining good quality graph plots from Lotus 1-2-3 is to use a *plotter* instead of a printer. A plotter uses pens rather than a print wheel or print head to mark the paper, and by using several different colour pens a coloured graph can be produced. Such an output device is unlikely to be available for class use, but can be controlled by the *PrintGraph* program within the Lotus 1-2-3 package (see the *Reference manual*, p. 292).

It is also just possible that your machine has an additional external floppy disk drive. For example, one can now buy drives for 3½″ disks which can be attached to a PC to give a bridge to PS/2 machines.

1.2 An introductory guide to MS-DOS

The role of a disk operating system is to manage the flow of information around the various parts of the computer system and to keep track of what is stored in the computer's memory and on disk. Information is stored on disk in *files* which are organised in *directories* and *subdirectories*. For example, when you save a Lotus 1-2-3 worksheet it will be saved as a file.

In MS-DOS you can issue instructions relating to files or directories by typing in DOS *commands*. These commands will contain DOS *keywords* such as **COPY**, **ERASE**, **TYPE**, etc., as well as the names of the files or directories to which they are to apply. DOS commands must conform to a required structure or *syntax*, otherwise an error message will be displayed. A command is not sent to the computer until the <*Return*> key is pressed, so any errors spotted before then can be corrected by using the *backspace* key which deletes the last character typed. (If an incorrect command has already been executed, just type in the correct command after the error message.)

Some of the most frequently required DOS commands and their format will be described later in this section. A longer list is given in Appendix E at the end of the book.

There are also processes which can be activated simply by pressing certain important keys. For example, you can print out what is on the screen (assuming that a printer is connected and switched on) by pressing the <*Shift*> and <*PrtSc*> (short for *Print Screen*) keys together.

Booting the system

Before you can do anything with the computer at all, DOS must be loaded. This is easy if you have a machine with a hard disk since all you have to do is to switch on the computer. However, if the machine you are using has only two floppy disk drives you will need to load DOS from a floppy disk containing the DOS commands (this is somtimes called *booting*, as the machine gets itself going using a *bootstrap* program in its ROM). The procedure is as follows:

1. Put the DOS disk into drive A (the one on the left or at the top, depending on the machine).
2. Make sure that the label is facing upwards and is on the edge nearest to you.
3. Close the disk drive door and switch on the machine – the switch is usually on the right-hand side of the system unit.

The computer will whirr away for a few seconds as checks are carried out on its circuitry and memory. Then the light will go on by drive A as the machine loads in DOS from the floppy disk.

DOS has been revised several times and each time you start up the system the version number that you are using will be displayed. On some versions you will at this stage have the opportunity to reset the date and the time shown on the computer. Just follow the instructions, or if you do not wish to change the date or time you can simply press the *<Return>* key.

When A> is displayed on the screen you can remove the DOS disk from the disk drive. The A> is a prompt for an input and the letter A indicates that the disk drive A is currently the *active* drive.

With a hard disk machine when the computer is switched on it automatically searches for MS-DOS on the hard disk. The prompt C> will be displayed when all checks are complete. When booting a hard disk machine make sure that there is no disk in the floppy disk drive, as the computer checks there first. An error message will result (unless the disk in question also contains the DOS files).

When either the A> or C> prompt is displayed, the computer is ready to be used and you can load Lotus 1-2-3 (see Section 1.3).

At this stage you might also want to think about the procedure for ending a session and switching off the computer. If you are still within the 1-2-3 package you should first save the current version of your work as a file and then exit from 1-2-3 (as will be described in Section 1.3). This will take you back to the DOS prompt. Remove all floppy disks and put them back in their envelopes. Only then should you turn off the computer at the switch on the main system unit. If necessary turn off separate switches on the printer and monitor as well.

Formatting a floppy disk

When using package programs like Lotus 1-2-3 you usually have your own data disk in drive B so that you can *save* and *retrieve* files to and from the disk. However, such a disk must first have been correctly *formatted* so that it can store data passed to it from the computer's memory. (You only have to do this once for any disk, the first time you use it and before you try to save any files on the disk.)

Formatting gets a disk ready to receive information. It checks the disk for bad spots and lays down *tracks* on the disk in a pattern appropriate to the computer being used. (*Note*: a disk which has been formatted for use on another non-compatible computer such as a BBC B will have to be reformatted if it is to be used with a PC. In reformatting a disk you destroy all information previously stored on it, so be careful to check that a disk is blank or has only files which are no longer required before you format it.)

The procedure for formatting a disk is as follows. First, make sure that DOS has been loaded, so that either the A> or C> prompt is displayed on the screen. (If you have a twin floppy disk system you will need to keep the DOS disk in drive A while the formatting takes place. The command **FORMAT** is an example of an *external* DOS command which can only be executed from the DOS disk itself. All the other commands described in this chapter are *internal* commands which are kept together in a file called *command.com* which is automatically loaded into the computer's memory on 'booting' up.)

Type format b: and enter this DOS command by pressing the <*Return*> key. (*Note*: FORMAT B: would have the same effect. DOS does not distinguish between upper- and lower-case letters.) The following message will then be displayed

> *Insert new diskette for drive B:*
> *and press ENTER when ready*

Now place your blank disk in drive B (close the drive door) and press <*Return*>. The message *Formatting* will be displayed. After a few seconds a message will appear:

> *Formatting . . . Format complete*
> *362496 bytes total disk space*
> *362496 bytes available on disk*
> *Format another (Y/N)?*

Type N and the DOS prompt will return.

WARNING Do not attempt to format a hard disk!

Filenames

Whenever a new file is created it is given a filename. Each file on a disk must have a unique or different name. It is a good idea to use a name which reminds you of the contents of the file so that you can recognise it when you need it. Filenames are from one to eight characters long and can be made up of any letters or numbers and some other symbols such as brackets. No spaces, commas, full stops or colons are permitted, but brackets can be included. The following examples are all valid filenames:

A
REPORT1
SALES87
GJMAY88
FIG3(2)

whereas these are not:

REPORT 1	spaces not allowed
1988FORECASTS	filename too long
GJ,MAY1988	comma not allowed
FIG3:2	colon not allowed

Filename extensions

Files may also have an *extension* added to the name which can be used to indicate the file type. This extension has up to three characters, and is joined to the main filename by a full stop. The following are examples:

REPORT1.WK1
SALES.PIC
AUTOEXEC.COM

In fact, if you create files from within Lotus 1-2-3 the program will automatically add the extension WK1 to worksheet files and PIC to graph files.

Some extensions have special meaning to DOS. For example, the extension COM identifies a file as a *command* file which contains a program which DOS runs when the filename is typed. Note that if you use some DOS commands with files (for example, if you use the renaming command) you will have to give the full filename, including its extension.

Drive specifications

DOS will also have to know which drive to look on to find a file. If you wish DOS to look on a drive other than the current *default* drive (which is the one shown by the prompt) then the filename must be preceded by the appropriate drive name, followed by a colon. This is the drive specification. Thus a full *file specification* may look like this:

B:REPORT1.WK1

Changing the default drive

To make a different drive the default (current) drive you just type in the drive specification you want. For example, if the prompt is currently C> but you want to switch to drive B then you type B: and press <*Return*>. *The computer will respond with* B>.

Displaying the contents of a directory

You may often wish to see what files you have stored on a disk. For example, suppose you have saved some 1-2-3 worksheet files on a floppy disk and you want to see what they are without going into the 1-2-3 program itself. You can do this using the DOS *directory command* **DIR**. Assuming that the disk with the files on it is in drive B, there are two ways that this can be done. One way is to transfer control to drive B (from either drive A or drive C) by typing B: and pressing <*Return*> as described above. Then just type DIR followed by <*Return*> (DIR is short for Directory – remember upper- and lower-case letters have the same effect). The command **DIR** lists all the files in the current directory. Something like the following will appear on the screen:

Volume in drive B has no label
Directory of B:

REPORT1	*WK1*	*33714*	*27–11–87*	*15:22*
SALES87	*WK1*	*22711*	*6–04–88*	*10:49*
GJMAY88	*WK1*	*4865*	*11–05–88*	*14:50*
PROFITS	*PIC*	*10036*	*11–05–88*	*14:57*

4 File(s) 289792 bytes free

From this it can be seen that the disk contains four files with the names REPORT1, SALES87, GJMAY88 and PROFITS. The second column indicates what type of file they are. In fact the first three are 1-2-3 worksheet files and the last is a 1-2-3 graph file (which has the extension PIC). The next column tells you how much space (in bytes) each file takes up on the disk (you are also given an indication at the bottom of how much space is still free on the disk). The last two columns give information on the date and time when the files were saved or last edited.

Exactly the same directory list could have been obtained without switching the default drive to B. At the A> or C> prompt just type dir b: and press <*Return*> and the same information will be provided.

If the disk contains a large number of files the list might scroll off the screen before you have had a chance to make a note of the early ones. There are three ways of avoiding this. The first is to get the computer to *pause* using the /p option. For example, with B as the default drive type dir/p. DOS will cause the first 23 entries to be displayed, followed by a message inviting you to *Press a key when ready*. To see the next screenful you can press any key, repeating until all the filenames have been shown.

Another way of stopping the list disappearing off the screen is to freeze the display using the combination of the *<Control>* and *<NumberLock>* keys. This might be useful if you have already given the command **DIR** without the pause option and the list is starting to appear on the screen. To freeze the display hold down the keys *<Ctrl>* and *<NumLock>* together (*<Ctrl-S>* also works). This will halt the scrolling until you press any other key to allow it to continue.

A method of showing a long list on the screen in more compact form (without the dates and times columns) is to use the */W* (*Wide*) option. This is probably the most convenient method of seeing a long list of files and requires you to type (at the B> prompt) dir/w (or dir b:/w at the A> or C> prompt).

Note: Lotus 1-2-3 will save and retrieve files from within the package itself. You can also obtain a list of the 1-2-3 files in a directory from within the 1-2-3 package (see Chapter 2).

Subdirectories [This passage may be omitted on first reading]

Just as with any physical collection of files it makes sense to group similar files together, so too with computer files it is advisable to use DOS to arrange and structure files in *subdirectories*. For example, suppose your disk is to contain both Lotus 1-2-3 worksheet files and files created with some word-processing package. You can use DOS to create subdirectories on the disk into which the appropriate files can then be saved.

What you would have would be a *tree* or *hierarchy* of files, beginning with the main or *root* directory. Within this directory you could create two subdirectories called LOTUS and WORD (see Figure 1.1). If you wanted to keep Lotus worksheet and graph files separate you could have a further level of subdirectories within LOTUS, called, say, WORK and GRAPH.

If you type in the command **DIR** at the root directory you will get a list only of subdirerctories at this level (plus any files which are in the root directory itself). Files which are in a subdirectory at a lower level in the tree will not be listed. To see what files are in a subdirectory you must either use DOS to

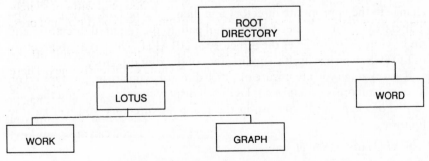

Figure 1.1 An example of a disk directory structure

issue the *change directory* command then type DIR or you must specify an appropriate *path* to the directory as part of the **DIR** command. First, however, the appropriate file structure will have had to have been created using the **MakeDirectory** command (you can type mkdir or md for short).

Using the example in Figure 1.1 as an illustration you might proceed as follows. First, make sure that the default drive is the one you wish to work on, let us say drive B. So the prompt should be B>. Type cd\ and *<Return>* just to make sure that you are at the root directory level. (*cd* or *chdir* are shortened versions of *change directory*, and the backslash symbol on its own here indicates that you want to go to the root directory.) Now type md lotus and press *<Return>*. Then type md word and press *<Return>*.

You are still in the root directory so if you type DIR, DOS will list these two new directories (plus any files that were already in the root directory). Assuming that you began with a blank but formatted disk you will get something like the following:

Volume in drive B has no label
Directory of B:

LOTUS   <DIR>   31–07–88   11:47
WORD   <DIR>   31–07088   11:47
*   2 File(s) 360448 bytes free*

Now to create subdirectories within LOTUS. First type cd lotus and *<Return>* to change directories and then

md work *<Return>*
md graph *<Return>*

The directory structure has now been created. To get back to the root directory at any time just enter cd\. To get to any subdirectory the full path must be shown. For example, to change to the graph subdirectory within the lotus directory you would need

cd \ lotus \ graph

To list the files within any directory or subdirectory you can either first change to the appropriate directory and then just type DIR, or you can type a directory command specifying the full path to the required directory; e.g. dir b: \ lotus \ graph gives the directory of GRAPH, which is a subdirectory of LOTUS, which is itself a subdirectory of the root directory.

If at any stage you are unsure of which directory you are in, just type cd on its own (and press *<Return>*). DOS will display the directory and the path to it. For example, if you are in the graph subdirectory you will get the following:

B: \ LOTUS \ GRAPH

If you are in the root directory you will just get *B:*.

Erasing and renaming files

Sometimes you might wish to erase a file from a directory because it is no longer required. The **ERASE** command can be used to erase one or more files from the current directory.

The format is erase followed by the filename, including any extension (note the space between the command **ERASE** and the file name).

For example, in drive B to erase the file REPORT1.WK1 you will need

B>erase report1.wk1 <*Return*>

To erase a number of files with similar names you can use the *wildcard* characters * and ? The asterisk is used to represent a whole set of characters in a filename, while the question mark can be used for single characters which vary. For example, if you wish to erase all the worksheet files in a directory you could type

B>erase *.wk1 <*Return*>

which erases all files with the extension wk1, no matter what the filename.

Suppose, however, that you only wish to erase those worksheet files with the word REPORT at the beginning of the name (e.g. REPORT1.WK1, REPORT2.WK1, etc.). Here you would put

B>erase REPORT?.WK1 and <*Return*>

WARNING Be careful before you erase files using wildcards because you could erase more files than you intend. It is advisable to display the names of all the files in a directory before you erase whole groups of files in this way.

Note that you can also use the wildcards with the directory command to list only those files within a directory with a certain type of name. For example, B>*dir report?.**.

If you want to erase every file in a directory you can use erase *.*. In this case DOS will ask *Are you sure (Y/N)?* before going ahead. If you have not checked the directory it is advisable to reply N and to check before confirming this command.

A useful command to help you to single out files which you want to keep is the **RENAME** command. You can change the name of a file either for this reason or because you wish the file to be given a more appropriate name.

The format is rename oldname newname <*Return*> (*ren* can be used as a shortening of *rename* and note the spaces beteen the commands). For example,

B>ren report3.wk1 findings.wk1

You might also want to copy files from one disk (or directory) to another as part of a tidying up exercise. You can change the name of the file at the same time if you wish. For example, to copy a file named SALES.WK1 from a disk in drive A to a disk in drive B with the same name put (at the A> prompt) copy a:sales.wk1 b: *<Return>*

To change the name at the same time you would give the new name after b:. The file to be copied is referred to as the *source* file and the file to be copied to is known as the *target* file. The source and target destinations can be more complex, including path names to subdirectories, e.g.

A>copy a: \ lotus \ leontief.wk1 b: \workshop\ sheet 4

Many other DOS commands are available for manipulating files (see Appendix E). For a full coverage of the topic see Wolverton (1985).

Final note on the care of disks

Floppy disks should be treated with care. Hours of work may be wasted if a disk containing important data files is lost or corrupted. Some suggestions are given below (see Burns and Eubanks, 1988, pp. 48–51, for a long list of dos and don'ts).

1. Always make backup copies of important files on another disk to reduce the chances of losing your work.
2. Hold a disk by the corner and take it in and out of disk drives carefully.
3. Do not attempt to remove a disk from a disk drive when the warning light is on.
4. Do not switch off the computer with a floppy disk still in a disk drive.
5. Always store the disk in its protective envelope when it is not in use.
6. Protect disks from heat, strong sunlight and smoke. Cigarette ash and smoke particles are especially likely to damage disks. Make sure you do not spill coffee or other liquids on them!
7. Keep disks away from machines or devices which produce magnetic fields. For example, be careful not to take disks through library security systems or to leave them near photocopiers or microwave ovens. You can also cause damage to disks by taking them through the underground railway system.

(*Note*: I trust that the above list will not be interpreted as a list of excuses for late submission of work caused by 'accidental' damage to a disk!)

It is also suggested that disks containing important files which you wish to retain should be protected by placing a small piece of tape (not Sellotape) over the write-protect notch on the disk. When this notch is covered new data cannot be written onto the disk, although the computer will be able to read files on the disk.

Label your disks clearly. Only use felt-tip pens to write on the disk labels.

Users of hard disk machines are advised to 'park' the heads on the hard disk at the end of each session and especially before the machine is moved at all. This is to avoid the head scarring the surface of the hard disk with the subsequent loss of files. Again, regular backup to floppy disks can reduce the effect of any mishap.

1.3 Loading Lotus 1-2-3 and some first steps

The procedure for loading Lotus 1-2-3 will differ according to whether you are working with a twin floppy disk computer system or a hard disk machine. If you have a floppy disk computer you will load the program from a floppy disk labelled 'System Disk', whereas if you have a hard disk machine 1-2-3 will be called up from a directory on the hard disk. In either case you can approach the program through what is called the *1-2-3 Access System*, or you can go straight to the spreadsheet part of the package, missing out the Access System. The reason for the Access System is that the full package is too big to fit onto a single floppy disk (in fact when you buy it it comes on six disks, although one of these is just a Backup System disk). The files covering the spreadsheet part of the package (including those giving help screens and enabling you to construct a graph based on worksheet information) are on the 1-2-3 system disk. However, the files enabling you to obtain a hard copy printout of graphs are on a separate disk labelled *PrintGraph Disk*. If at a particular session you are likely to want to move backwards and forwards from creating worksheets and graphs using the spreadsheet part of the package to printing graphs using the *PrintGraph* part of the package then it is probably best to use the Access System which makes this easier. If not, then you can go straight to the program you want by typing in the appropriate command.

Note: In what follows it is assumed that the program has been installed correctly for your machine, i.e. information has been provided to the program about the system configuration, type of printer, graphics adaptor card, etc. If you have any difficulties in loading the program ask a technician or lecturer for help.

Loading 1-2-3 on a floppy disk machine

Start up your computer with the DOS disk and when you get the system prompt remove the DOS disk and replace it (in drive A) with the 1-2-3 System Disk. Type lotus and press <*Return*>.

The 1-2-3 Access System menu will then appear on the screen with the cursor highlighting *1-2-3* in the menu at the top of the screen (see Figure 1.2).
To load the spreadsheet program just press the <*Return*> key again to choose *1-2-3* from the menu.

If you wanted to use the *PrintGraph* program you would have to use the right arrow key to move the cursor to highlight the word *PrintGraph* in the

```
1-2-3  PrintGraph  Translate  Install  View  Exit
Enter 1-2-3 -- Lotus Worksheet/Graphics/Database program
```

```
                    1-2-3 Access System
               Lotus Development Corporation
                      Copyright 1985
                    All Rights Reserved
                        Release 2

The Access System lets you choose 1-2-3, PrintGraph, the Translate utility,
the Install program, and A View of 1-2-3 from the menu at the top of this
screen.  If you're using a diskette system, the Access System may prompt
you to change disks.  Follow the instructions below to start a program.

o  Use [RIGHT] or [LEFT] to move the menu pointer (the highlight bar at
   the top of the screen) to the program you want to use.

o  Press [RETURN] to start the program.

You can also start a program by typing the first letter of the menu
choice.  Press [HELP] for more information.
```

Figure 1.2 The Access System menu on loading Lotus 1-2-3

menu and then press *<Return>*. Lotus 1-2-3 is a menu-driven program and
you use the arrow keys to highlight the required option.

When you quit *1-2-3* or *PrintGraph* you will be returned to the Access
System menu, allowing you to go on to a different part of the package. To
leave the Access System highlight the word *Exit* in the menu and then press
<Return>. The computer will go back to the DOS prompt A>.

A quicker alternative which misses out the Access System is available.

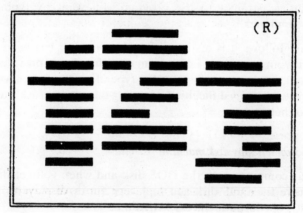

Copyright (C) 1985
Lotus Development Corporation
All Rights Reserved
2200033-3233712
Release 2

Figure 1.3 The 1-2-3 copyright message

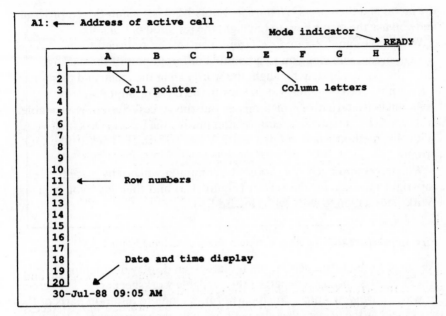

Figure 1.4 Initial worksheet screen display in Lotus 1-2-3

Just type 1-2-3 and press *<Return>* after putting the System Disk in drive A. With this method when you leave 1-2-3 you go straight back to the DOS prompt.

Whichever approach you choose the computer will briefly place the 1-2-3 copyright message on the screen (Figure 1.3) and then give you a blank Worksheet screen to work with (Figure 1.4).

Loading 1-2-3 on a hard disk machine

It is assumed that the Lotus 1-2-3 program has been installed on the hard disk in a directory called LOTUS. If some other name has been used for the directory, then substitute that name in the *change directory* (**CD**) command described below.

Start up the computer and wait until the C> prompt is displayed.

Type cd \ lotus to change to the LOTUS directory.

Now type lotus and press *<Return>*

The 1-2-3 Access System menu will then appear on the screen with the cursor highlighting *1-2-3* in the menu at the top of the screen (see Figure 1.2).

To load the spreadsheet program just press the *<Return>* key again to choose *1-2-3* from the menu.

If you had wanted to use the *PrintGraph* program you would have to use the right arrow key to move the cursor to highlight the word *PrintGraph* in the menu and then press <*Return*>. Lotus 1-2-3 is a menu-driven program and you use the arrow keys to highlight the required option.

When you quit *1-2-3* or *PrintGraph* you will be returned to the Access System menu, allowing you to go on to a different part of the package. To leave the Access System highlight the word *Exit* in the menu and then press <*Return*>. The computer will go back to the DOS prompt A>.

A quicker alternative which misses out the Access System is available. Just type 1-2-3 and press <*Return*> after putting the System Disk in drive A. With this method when you leave 1-2-3 you go straight back to the DOS prompt.

Whichever approach you choose the computer will briefly place the 1-2-3 copyright message on the screen (Figure 1.3) and then give you a blank Worksheet screen to work with (Figure 1.4).

First steps with 1-2-3

As noted in the Introduction, the initial screen display of columns A to H, rows 1 to 20 is only a small part of the available worksheet area. The screen provides a *window* onto a small part of it, moving to different parts of the worksheet as the *active cell* is changed. Initially the active cell is A1 and this is indicated at the top left of the screen where the cell address of the active cell is always displayed. The active cell is also highlighted by the *cell pointer*. There will also be a flashing cursor in the middle of the cell to tell you that the computer is ready for you to type something in. You can also see this from the *mode indicator* which is on the top right-hand side of the screen and should be showing the *READY* message.

If you type something at the keyboard it will first be displayed at the top of the screen in the space above the worksheet area itself. Only when you press the <*Return*> key will this be transferred into the active cell. This space above the worksheet is called the *control panel* and it is where 1-2-3 command menu will appear when you press the / (slash) key. Do not do that just yet. First see what happens when you type in some text.

Type My first worksheet (use the <*Shift*> key to get the upper-case M).

As soon as you start typing, the mode indicator will change to *LABEL*. This indicates that you are entering text of some kind for labelling your work. The text appears in the control panel, followed by the flashing cursor.

When you have finished typing, press the key marked <*Return*>. The text will be transferred to cell A1 in the worksheet and the mode indicator returns to *READY*. The text also appears at the top of the screen next to the address of the current or active cell. Notice that it is preceded by a single quotation mark. This indicates a text (non-numerical) entry.

Now the initial worksheet has cells which are nine characters wide (cell widths can be changed from this default value – see Chapter 3). However, the text that you typed in has overflowed into the cell to the right of A1, i.e. B1. This will always happen with text unless the cell is already occupied by something.

Now move the cell pointer by pressing the down arrow key. The cell pointer moves to A2. Move it down once more so that cell A3 is the active cell. Now move to cell B3 by pressing the right arrow key. Practise moving the cell pointer around using the arrow keys.

If you move seven more places across to the right, the screen will move with you, shifting across the worksheet to show column I with column A disappearing from view. Similarly, if you move down beyond row 20 the screen will scroll downwards. If you try to move to the left when you are in column A or up when you are in row 1 the computer will 'beep' at you to tell you that you are at the edge of the worksheet area. You can move up or down a whole screen at a time using the keys labelled *<PgUp>* and *<PgDn>*. You can move a whole screen to the left or right by pressing the *<Tab>* key. This often has the label ⇆. When shifted this key moves you to the left, and unshifted it moves you to the right.

Wherever you are you can always get back to cell A1 by pressing the key marked *<HOME>*. Do this now.

In fact you can 'jump' to any cell using the function key F5. Press this key and you will see a message in the second line of the control panel: *Enter address to go to: A1* (the mode indicator also changes to *POINT*).

You do not want to go to cell A1 – you are already there. Instead type E6 (the mode indicator changes again to *EDIT* because you are editing information). Now press *<Return>*. The cell pointer jumps to cell E6. Practise moving to some other cells in this way.

Now see what happens when you enter a number. Go to cell B2 and type 6. As soon as you type 6 the number appears in the control panel and the mode indicator changes to *VALUE*. Press *<Return>* and the entry is placed in the cell.

Move the cursor down to cell B3 and type 2. This time, though, do not press the *<Return>* key. Instead press the down arrow key. The value will be entered in cell B3 and the cell pointer will move to cell B4. In this way you can enter and move with a single keystroke. This is a very handy feature when you are entering large quantities of data.

Now enter a formula. Suppose you require cell B4 to contain the result of dividing the contents of cell B2 by the contents of cell B3. The simple formula B2/B3 will do that, but it must be preceded by a + sign to signal to the computer that you are entering a formula and not a label (text). Press the *<+>* key (shifted =) and notice that the mode indicator changes to *VALUE* (the result of the formula will be a value). Complete the formula +B2/B3 and press the *<Return>* key. Notice that it does not matter whether you use upper- or lower-case letters in the formula – the package converts them to upper-case letters whatever you type.

The formula +*B2/B3* now appears at the top of the screen in the control panel next to the cell address B4, while the result of the formula is shown in the cell itself.

Now go to cell C2 and type in the number 10. Then enter the number 5 in cell C3. Suppose we require a similar formula in cell C4 to the one we have in B4, that is one which divides the number in the row immediately above it into the number in the row above that. (We require cell C4 to hold the formula +C2/C3.) Rather than just typing in this formula you can make use of the very powerful 1-2-3 **Copy** command. This will copy a formula already in the worksheet to another cell or range of cells, making an automatic adjustment for the relative change in the cell positions.

Move to cell C4 and call up the command menu by pressing the slash key (/). The mode indicator changes to *MENU* and the top of the screen shows the main menu with the following commands:

Worksheet Range Copy Move File Print Graph Data System Quit

You want to use the **Copy** command so use the right arrow key to highlight *Copy*. Notice that as the different commands are highlighted the other line in the control panel will show different things, indicating what the command is used for or what options that command has. When the *Copy* command is highlighted this line just says *Copy a cell or range of cells*. Press the *<Return>* key and you will be asked to

Enter the range to copy FROM:

The computer prompts you to enter cell C4. This is not the cell you wish to copy from, so type the address of the required cell, namely B4, and press *<Return>*.

The computer then asks for the range to copy *TO:*. Again, because the active cell is C4 this is offered to you. As this is the cell where you want the formula to be copied to you can just press the *<Return>* key. The formula +C2/C3 appears in the control panel and the result (*2*) is shown in cell C4.

This very powerful Copy command will be used frequently in this book and (as the prompts might suggest) can be used to copy a formula from a whole *range* of cells to another part of the worksheet.

When you are working with the menu do not worry if you make the wrong choice by accident as you can always retrace your steps up the menu tree by pressing the *<Esc>* key. (The only exception is the **System** command which takes you back into DOS. But here you just need to type EXIT to get back to where you were in the worksheet.)

You can also change cell inputs quite easily. If the input is still in the control panel and has not yet been passed into the worksheet by pressing the *<Return>* key, you can use the *<Backspace>* key to delete the last character typed. Then retype and enter by pressing *<Return>*. If the entry is already in a worksheet cell you can simply type the correct value or text in that position and then <*Return*> to overwrite the previous input. Go to cell B2 and type 8 and then <*Return*>. The value 8 appears in this cell, overwriting the previous value of 6. Notice that the result of the formula in cell B4 adjusts automatically. This feature is very useful and will be exploited in a number of ways in this book.

A third way of changing cell inputs is by using the EDIT key F2. This is particularly useful for altering text or a long formula. Go to cell A1 and press the function key F2. The mode indicator switches to *EDIT* and the contents of cell A1 is reproduced in the second row of the control panel, followed by a flashing cursor. You can change the text to My very first worksheet (that is, you can insert the word 'very' before the word 'first') as follows. To get to the correct position use the left arrow key until the cursor is flashing under the letter 'f' in 'first'. Now type very (followed by a space). Then press <*Return*> and the edited text will appear in the worksheet. You can also use the backspace key to delete unwanted characters in edit mode. Try changing the text input back to its original form.

If ever you are unsure about what you are doing you can get help from 1-2-3's on-line context-sensitive *Help* facility. You do this by pressing the function key F1. Make sure that the mode indicator shows *READY* and try it. The screen will show you what types of action are possible in this mode. You can get further details by using the arrow keys to highlight particular topics and pressing <*Return*> to see the follow up screens. Press the <*Esc*> key to get back to the worksheet.

Similarly, if you have called up the main menu and you are not sure what a particular command does, you can highlight it and then press the HELP key (F1) to obtain further information. For example, to find out something about how 1-2-3 handles files, highlight the command *File* in the main menu and press <*Return*>. Then press F1 and you will be given information on saving and retrieving files. When you have had a good look through the Help screens covering File commands, get back to the worksheet by pressing the <*Esc*> key again.

It is worth experimenting with the Help screens while you are using 1-2-3 as you can discover a lot about the package from them.

Leave 1-2-3 by selecting *Quit* from the main menu. Make sure all floppy disks have been removed from the computer and switch off the machine.

In the next chapter you will begin to put Lotus 1-2-3 to work. Good luck and happy spreadsheeting!

Exercise 1

Boot up your computer to load DOS. Then load Lotus 1-2-3. When the worksheet grid appears type Exercise 1 in cell A1. (Press <*Return*> to enter this text into the active cell.)

Use the down arrow key to move the cell cursor to cell A3 and enter the text Using 1-2-3 as a calculator.

Go to cell B5 and type 6−3/2<*Return*> and note the result. Then go to cell B6 and type (6−3)/2 <*Return*> and again note the result.

Be sure that you understand why the answers are different.

Go to cell B7 and enter +B5/B6 <*Return*>. Go back to cell B5 and type 15 <*Return*>. Note what happens to the display in Cell B7.

Experiment with the following additional calculations, where

+   is the addition operator
−   is the subtraction operator
/   is the division operator
*   is the multiplication operator
^   is the exponentiation operator.

Cell	Formula
D5	1+2*(5−2)
D6	64^0.5
D7	64^(1/3)

References

1-2-3 Reference Manual, Release 2 (Lotus Development Corporation, Cambridge, MA, 1985).

V. Wolverton, *Running MS-DOS* (Microsoft Press, Redmond, USA, 1985).

J. B. Burns and D. N. Eubanks, *Microcomputers: Business and Personal Applications* (West Publishing Company, St Paul, MN, USA, 1988).

Disk Operating System Version 3.00 *User's Guide* (IBM Corporation, Portsmouth, 1984).

Chapter 2

Beginning to use Lotus 1-2-3:
a simple business application

Purpose: To consolidate and extend the reader's understanding of basic 1-2-3 concepts and procedures and to show how the package can be applied in a simple business application. To discuss issues of the planning and construction of a worksheet. To show how a worksheet can be used to provide a template for repeated use, to answer 'what-if' questions and to generate graphs.

Preview: In Section 2.1 Lotus 1-2-3 is put to work in the solution of a simple business problem. It is shown how to plan and construct a 1-2-3 worksheet which can be used as a template for any year's figures. The steps required to save and retrieve a worksheet as a file are described. In Section 2.2 the worksheet is used to process one year's cost and revenue figures and it is shown how to obtain a printout of information from the worksheet. Section 2.3 shows how to use 1-2-3's graphics commands to produce a pie chart based on data held in the worksheet and describes how to obtain a printed copy of the graph. Section 2.4 shows the power of a spreadsheet for conducting hypothetical 'what-if' experiments by changing individual cell values and being able to see immediately how this affects the results.

Although the problem described in this chapter is fictitious and rather oversimplified, it is similar in structure to some business problems encountered in the real world. It also points towards how 1-2-3 can be utilised in more complex forms of quantitative analysis.

1-2-3 features introduced in this chapter: The   key for repeating characters; user-defined formulae and built-in functions – the @SUM function; the **Copy** command; specifying a range of cells by anchoring and expanding the cursor; specifying a file directory; saving and retrieving worksheet files; right-justifying text; the EDIT function key F2; printing from a worksheet; introduction to 1-2-3 graphs – constructing a pie chart using the **Graph** command; saving a graph; printing a graph using the *PrintGraph* program; the GRAPH function key F10.

2.1 Putting Lotus 1-2-3 to work to create a template

Suppose a company which manufactures and sells three products has information available on the costs and revenues relating to each of these products for the four quarters of 1987. The managing director wishes to produce a table similar in form to that given in Table 2.1 so as to show the totals for each product and each quarter, and for all products for the year as a whole.

Table 2.1 Costs and revenues for the hypothetical firm

```
               ECONOMICS WORKSHOP plc

        PROFIT FIGURES (IN £) FOR        1987
```

	QTR 1	QTR 2	QTR 3	QTR 4	TOTAL
REVENUE:					
PRODUCT 1	100	100	100	100	400
PRODUCT 2	200	250	300	250	1000
PRODUCT 3	300	400	300	200	1200
TOTAL REVENUE	600	750	700	550	2600
COSTS:					
SALARIES	200	200	200	200	800
RENT	150	150	150	150	600
PRODUCT 1	50	50	45	50	195
PRODUCT 2	40	40	35	40	155
PRODUCT 3	45	45	40	45	175
MISC	35	30	55	55	175
TOTAL COST	520	515	525	540	2100
			GROSS PROFIT		500

This is just the kind of problem for which Lotus 1-2-3 was designed. Using Lotus 1-2-3 to perform this kind of analysis offers several advantages over the paper, pencil (and rubber!) approach (even with a calculator), as we shall see.

We shall first set up a worksheet *template* containing a title, row and column headings and other labels, along with the formulae to work out the row and column totals. At this stage the numbers will not be entered into the worksheet. The worksheet will then be saved as a file so that it can be retrieved to be used with any year's figures.

Load the 1-2-3 package as shown in Chapter 1.

When the blank worksheet screen appears start to enter row and column labels and an overall title as follows:

Move to cell C1 and type ECONOMICS WORKSHOP plc; then press *<Return>*

ECONOMICS WORKSHOP plc appears at the top of the screen in the control panel next to the address of the active cell (i.e. C1).

Notice that although each cell is only nine characters wide the text you have entered spills over into the next cell.

Now move the cursor to cell B3 and enter the text:

PROFIT FIGURES (in £) FOR

(Do not specify any particular year since this will only be entered with the cost and revenue figures for such a year.)

Next go to cell A7 and type REVENUE: and then <*Return*>. (When you are typing all capital letters you can have the <*Caps Lock*> key on. Remember to press this key again when you wish to revert to lower-case letters.)

Then enter the following labels (remember you can use the arrow keys to enter the text and move to the next cell):

Cell	Label
A8	PRODUCT 1
A9	PRODUCT 2
A10	PRODUCT 3
A12	TOTAL REVENUE
C5	QTR 1
D5	QTR 2
E5	QTR 3
F5	QTR 4
G5	TOTAL

Now draw in a dotted line across the screen as follows. Go to cell C6 and key in \ (the backward slash key) followed by the hyphen symbol -. Press the <*Return*> key. You should find that the \ key repeats the character following it (in this case -) to fill the cell. Repeat this for cells D6, E6, F6 and G6.

Now go to cell C11 and use the backslash followed by the equals sign (=) and again for cells D11 to G11 to draw the double dotted line across the screen.

Now enter the costs labels as follows:

Cell	Label
A15	COSTS:
A16	SALARIES
A17	RENT
A18	PRODUCT 1
A19	PRODUCT 2
A20	PRODUCT 3
A21	MISC
A23	TOTAL COST

Now you should know how to get the second double dotted line. Go to cell C22 and enter \= and repeat for cells D22 to G22.

The last text item is to go in cell E25, i.e. GROSS PROFIT. Do not worry if when you go to this cell the rest of the display disappears off the screen. The window will move down but you can easily move up again either by going directly to a cell or by using the up arrow key.

Now if you were only going to set up a table for a single year the next step would be to enter the numerical values for costs and revenues for that year into the table. However, since the requirement is for a general table – a template – which can be used for any year, leave the numbers until later.

Although there are no numbers in the table as yet, this need not prevent you from entering formulae which will ensure that the appropriate row and column totals will be calculated whenever data for a particular year are entered. In effect you are constructing a 'shell' into which the figures for any year can be fitted.

Go to cell C12 and type +C8+C9+C10 and then <*Return*>. This tells the computer to calculate the value in cell C12 by taking the sum of the values in cells C8, C9 and C10. At this stage you should see a zero in cell C12 because C8, C9 and C10 are empty.

This is an example of a user-defined formula. You can define cell values with quite complicated formulae if necessary, but notice that such formulae must always begin with a plus (+) or minus (−) sign. This first character tells the computer to expect a formula and not text.

In fact, certain types of formulae which are frequently required, such as the summation of a set of cell values, are built in to Lotus 1-2-3. So when you go to cell D12 you can enter the formula using a built-in function (signalled by the @ symbol). Go to cell G12 and type @sum(D8.D10) and <*Return*>.

In putting in the other revenue column sums you can use the **Copy** command. Just as cell D12 contains the sum of the values in three cells above it, you require similar sums in E12, F12 and G12. The **Copy** command enables you to put into a cell a formula which is copied *relatively* from another cell.

Go to E12 and press the slash key (/) to access the main menu of commands. Choose *Copy* by moving the cursor across to highlight this option and press <*Return*> (or you can just type the first letter of your chosen command – in this case C).

When you are asked the range to copy from, give D12. When you are asked the range to copy to, give E12.G12.

You will find that appropriate formulae have been entered into cells E12 to G12. Move the cursor along to these keys to see the formulae in the control panel at the top of the screen.

Now put in the cost column totals. In cell C23 put @sum(C16.C21). Then go to cell D23 and call up the main menu and choose *Copy*. Give the range to copy from as C23. This time when the computer prompts you for the range to copy to, instead of typing in the cell addresses at the keyboard, try the cell anchor and expanding cursor approach. Press the full stop key to anchor the cursor at cell D23 (which begins the range). Then press the right arrow key three times so that the cursor expands to highlight the strip of cells D23 to G23. The range will also be identified correctly in the control panel. Press *<Return>* and the formulae will be copied across.

Now enter formulae for the row totals. Go to G8 and put @sum(C8.F8). You can do this using the expanding cursor instead of directly typing in the cell range. Type @sum(and then use the arrow key to move the cursor to the beginning of the range, i.e. C8. Now type a full stop and move the cursor to the end of the range F8. The cursor will expand and the correct range will be identified in the control panel. Close the brackets in the sum formula and *<Return>*. Now use the **Copy** command with the range to copy to set as G9.G10.

You can copy the formula again with the range to copy to set as G16.G21 because the same relative addresses are required in the formulae for these cells. Lastly move to cell G25 and enter +G12−G23. This will calculate gross profit as total revenue minus total cost.

Before you enter any numbers you should save this worksheet template so that it can be retrieved again for use with any year's figures. Go to cell E3 so that when the file is retrieved the cursor will be in the cell ready for the first data input.

Make sure that your (formatted) data disk is in drive B. You will be saving the worksheet as a file on your data disk. First check that the file will be sent to a disk in the required drive. Press / to get the main menu. Select *File* followed by *Directory*. If the current directory appears as A:\ (or any directory other than B:\), type B:\ in its place (just B: is enough, in fact). (If B:\ is already shown just press *<Return>*.) This ensures that your worksheet file will be saved on the data disk in drive B. Press *<Return>*. The red indicator light next to drive B will come on briefly, accompanied by a whirring sound as the computer checks that you have a properly formatted disk ready to receive any files.

Then call up the main menu again and once more select *File*, but this time choose *Save*. In the control panel at the top of the screen you will see the following:

Enter save file name: B:*.wk1

All 1-2-3 worksheet files have the extension wk1 and all you need to do is to type in your cosen file name without the extension. This will be added automatically by 1-2-3. Type PROFIT. This will replace the **.wk1* at the top of the screen and when you press *<Return>* the file will be saved. It does not matter whether you use upper- or lower-case letters for the name. They are interchangeable and 1-2-3 converts all file names to capitals. You will see the light go on above drive B again as the file is written to you disk. The mode indicator *READY* at the top of the screen is briefly replaced by a flashing message *WAIT* until the process is complete.

Whenever you want to retrieve this file from your data disk during a Lotus 1-2-3 session, first make sure that your data disk is in drive B and the file directory is set to B. Get the main menu by pressing the / key and select *File*, followed by *Retrieve*. Highlight the name of the file that you require and press *<Return>*. Your worksheet will be brought back into the computer memory and displayed on the screen.

2.2 Using the template and printing information from the worksheet

Your worksheet PROFIT should still be on the screen. If not, retrieve it as explained in the previous section. Move to cell E3 and type 1987.

Now enter the following figures into the appropriate cells:

C8 to F8

100   100   100   100

C9 to F9

200   250   300   250

C10 to F10

300   400   300   200

Notice that as you proceed the appropriate row and column totals are filled in.

Next enter the following:

C16 to F16

200   200   200   200

C17 to F17

150   150   150   150

C18 to F18

50   50   45   50

C19 to F19

40   40   35   40

C20 to F20

45   45   40   45

C21 to F21

35   30   55   55

All the column and row sums should now have been computed, as well as the gross profit figure which appears at the bottom.

Before you get a printout of this table you can improve its appearance in one small way by lining up the column headings with the figures. Lotus 1-2-3 automatically places numbers at the right-hand side of a cell, but the default for text is to position it so that it starts at the left edge of a cell. In this case it would be neater if the headings in cells C5 to G5 had their text 'right justi-fied'. You can achieve this by preceding the text input by the open quotation mark ". You could simply go to cell C5 and retype this cell entry. You need never worry about correcting a cell entry in 1-2-3, you can simply type the new entry over the top of the old one. But there is an alternative which is probably easier when you only wish to make a minor change to an existing cell entry. You can use the EDIT facility, which is activated by pressing the function key F2. So go to cell C5 and press the F2 key. The cell contents *QTR 1* are displayed at the top of the screen in the control panel, followed by a flashing cursor. Notice that the text is preceded by the single quotation mark '. Preceding text by this character will *left justify* it in a cell, but since this is the default it would not be necessary to type it. Use the left arrow key to move the cursor until it is underneath the ' and then press the key marked <*DEL*>. The ' character now disappears. Type " (shifted 2) in its place and then <*Return*>. You will find that the text has been shifted across to line up with the figures in column C. Do the same for the headings in columns D to G. Then press <*HOME*> to go back to the top left of the worksheet.

If you have a printer available you can now obtain a printout of your work. Make sure that the printer is switched on and is 'on-line'. If you are sharing the printer the switch should be set to connect your machine to the printer. Press / to get the main menu and select *Print* followed by *Printer*. You must now identify the part of the worksheet that you want to print. Select *Range* and type in the required range of cells, e.g. A1.G25 for the whole of your current worksheet. (You can move the cursor over the worksheet to identify the start and end cells – anchor the cursor at A1 by pressing the full stop key, then move to G25 and press <*Return*>. The whole area covered by A1 to G25 should then be highlighted.)

The printer submenu should now be displayed. Select *Align* followed by *Go* to have your worksheet information printed.

2.3 Introducing graphs

A tremendous advantage of using Lotus 1-2-3 for quantitative analysis is that you can use the package to construct various types of graph based on worksheet entries. In this section you will discover how to construct a pie chart to show the contributions to revenue by product for Economics Work-shop plc. The pie chart will give a 'slice' to each product showing the share of the total as a percentage.

Call up the main menu and select *Graph*. Now press <*Return*> and select *Type*. Then choose *Pie*. (The other types of graph available will be discussed in later chapters.)

Move the cursor to select *A* and press <*Return*> to set the data range for the pie chart. In some ways pie graphs are the simplest of the 1-2-3 graphs because there is only one data range to be set, namely the range holding the numbers from which the pie is to be constructed. Here that is G8.G10, so enter this range and press <*Return*>.

If you now select *View* from the *Graph* menu you will find that a basic pie chart has been produced, indicating the percentage contributions of each product to revenue. However, the graph is not labelled in any way, nor does it have an overall title.

Press <*Return*> to go back to the *Graph* menu and press X to set a range to contain the segment labels. This will be A8.A10, so enter this range and press <*Return*>. View again and you will find that the slices have been labelled appropriately. Press any key to get back to the worksheet. You will have the following submenu on the screen:

First Second X-Axis Y-Axis

The last two options are irrelevant for a pie graph, but you can use the first two to give the graph a title.

First will be highlighted so press <*Return*>. The computer now prompts you to *Enter graph title, top line:* so enter Pie chart showing revenue by product. When you press <*Return*> you will go back to the *Graph* menu. Choose *Titles* again and this time *Second*. Enter Economics Workshop plc 1987.

Now choose *Quit* to go back up a level in the menu tree (<*Esc*> will do as well) and select *View* again.

One more improvement can still be made by showing the different segments shaded differently (if you have colour the slices can be shown in different colours). The package has a set of codes for different colours or shadings and these will be fed into the graph menu as the B range. Eight different colours or shadings can be produced using the codes 1 to 7 and 0 (which leaves the area blank). Leave the menu for a moment (press the <*Esc*> key a few times) so that a range with these codes can be set up. The codes will be held in the range I8.I10. This is near enough to the actual values so that you can see them both together, but does not intrude upon the table.

Go to cell I8 and enter *0*.

In cell I9 put 101 and in cell I10 put 2. (Adding 100 to the code for a slice causes that slice to be 'exploded' away from the rest of the pie.)

Now call up the *Graph* menu again and enter I8.I10 as the *B* range. *View* again and you should see something like Figure 2.1 on the screen (although the lettering will not look as nice).

As has been pointed out already, with Lotus 1-2-3 it is not possible to get a printout of the graph directly from within the worksheet. The graph must first be saved as a PIC file and then it can be printed out using the *PrintGraph* program. So call up the main menu and select *Graph* followed by *Save*. You will be prompted to enter a graph filename. Put PIE87 and <*Return*>. The graph will then be saved on your disk with the extension PIC. Before you leave the worksheet to go to *PrintGraph* make sure that you save it again, so

Pie chart showing revenue by product
Economics Workshop plc 1987

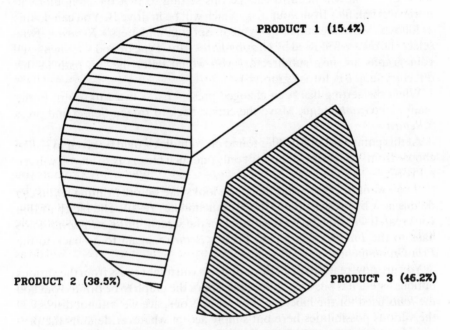

PRODUCT 1 (15.4%)

PRODUCT 2 (38.5%)

PRODUCT 3 (46.2%)

Figure 2.1 Pie chart created from the PROFIT worksheet

that your recent additions to it are not lost. If you give the name PROFIT87 again, the program will ask you if you want to replace the existing file of that name. If you choose *R* for *Replace* it will overwrite the previous file. If you want to keep that file as it is you can *Cancel* and type in a different name. Now leave the worksheet program as described in Chapter 1.

If you are ready to print the graph (it is assumed that you have a printer connected to the system) you will need to call up the *PrintGraph* program. (*Note*: It is assumed that the program has been configured to operate with the printer available. If you have any problems consult a technician or lecturer. If you are working alone see the Lotus publication *Getting Started 1-2-3 Release 2*.) You can call up the *PrintGraph* program in two ways, either via the Access System menu or, more directly, from DOS by typing pgraph (short for *PrintGraph*). Taking the latter approach, if you have a hard disk machine you will need to be in the LOTUS directory. If you have just come out of the 1-2-3 worksheet program this will be the case. With a twin floppy disk machine you will need to have the floppy disk labelled *PrintGraph* in drive A.

The following menu will appear on the screen:

Image-Select Settings Go Align Page Exit

If the *Graphs Directory* on the right (under *HARDWARE SETUP*) does not show *B:* you will need to change this setting so that the computer can retrieve graph files from your disk, which will be in drive B. You can do this as follows. Move the cursor to highlight *Settings* and press *<Return>*. Now select *Hardware* followed by *Graphs-Directory*. Type B: and *<Return>*. (If your graphs are in a subdirectory you would enter the full path to this directory, e.g. B:\lotus\graphs.)

When the setting has been changed press *<Esc>* twice to return to the main *PrintGraph* menu. Move the cursor back to *Image-Select* and press *<Return>*.

At this point a list of PIC files found on your disk would be given to you to choose from. Of course, at present only one such file exists so all you will see is PIE87.

If you want to check what the graph looks like before printing it you can do this now by pressing the GRAPH function key (F10). The pie chart that you created will then be reconstituted on the screen. Press *<Return>* to go back to the *Image-Select* menu. Press *<Return>* again to go back to the *PrintGraph* menu.

You are now ready to print the graph. As you might guess from the various options listed, it is possible to alter the size of the graph to be printed out and the *fonts* used for the labelling. For reasons of space we will not discuss all the various possibilities here but simply accept whatever defaults the program has currently set up. For a discussion of these options see the *Reference Manual*, Chapter 5.

Check that the printer is switched on and then choose *Align* followed by *Go*. After a short delay the graph will begin printing. Depending upon your printer (and on the *PrintGraph* settings), the graph may be printed quite quickly or it might take five minutes or more. When the printing stops, *Exit* from the *PrintGraph* program. If you return to the *Access* menu choose *Exit* to go back to DOS. Remove all floppy disks from the disk drives and switch off the computer and printer.

Note: The Quattro package has one major advantage over 1-2-3 in that it can print graphs directly from a worksheet. Some of the graphs in this book have been produced in this way from 1-2-3 worksheets.

2.4 A simple 'what-if' exercise

One of the major benefits of the spreadsheet approach is that it gives you the possibility of examining the effects of changing individual cell values and immediately seeing the impact that this has on all other values. You can try such a 'what-if' exercise with the PROFIT87 worksheet. Load 1-2-3, retrieve the file and make some changes to the data entries as follows. Go to cells C16 to F16 and change the values to 300 (You can use the **Copy** command to copy numbers or text as well as formulae.) This will naturally have no effect upon revenues, but it will feed through into all the cost column totals and to gross profit, all of which will be recalculated automatically. In this way you can experiment to see what effect various changes in cost will have on profits. The 1-2-3 template can be used not only to hold past data but also as a framework for future projections or planning exercises. Once the template has been set up, a businessman could examine the potential effects of changes in revenue or costs at the touch of a couple of keys.

Exercise 2

The table below gives Consumers' Expenditure figures for the UK in 1982 by component category. Set up a worksheet template into which you can read any year's figures with appropriate row and column headings, a title and formulae to compute the various totals. Save the empty worksheet as a template. Enter the 1982 figures and get a printout. Use 1-2-3 to construct a pie graph showing the share of each component in the total for the year.

Refer to the latest edition of *Economic Trends Annual Supplement* to find data for a more recent year. Enter that data and obtain worksheet and graph printouts.

Consumers' Expenditure in the UK (£million, current prices)

| Component | Year 1982 Quarter | | | | |
	1	2	3	4	Total
Food	6102	6511	6319	6632	25564
Alcohol & tobacco	3848	4234	4634	5441	18157
Clothing & footwear	2232	2446	2570	3516	10764
Energy products	3992	3322	3254	4421	14989
Other goods	3691	3878	4014	4950	16533
Durable goods	3681	3297	4143	3727	14848
Rents, rates, etc.	5199	5468	5581	5674	21922
Other services	10238	10887	12234	10992	44351
Total expenditure	38983	40043	42749	45353	167128

(*Source: Economic Trends Annual Supplement*, 1984)

Reference

Getting Started 1-2-3 Release 2 (Lotus Development Corporation, Cambridge, MA, 1985).

Chapter 3

Index number calculations with Lotus 1-2-3

Purpose: To discuss problems of index number construction and use, and to show how Lotus 1-2-3 can provide a convenient framework for their calculation and analysis.

Preview: In this chapter some of the problems of index number construction are examined. It is shown how Lotus 1-2-3 can provide a convenient framework for their calculation and analysis. Section 3.1 outlines the basic principles of index numbers with the aid of a simple example. In Section 3.2 the example is reworked using Lotus 1-2-3 to show the benefits to be derived from using a spreadsheet. In Section 3.3 it is shown how it is possible to use Lotus 1-2-3 to construct a bar chart to illustrate the results obtained. Section 3.4 shows how to use 1-2-3 to analyse a more extensive and realistic set of data using index numbers. Finally, Section 3.5 shows how index numbers may be implicit in expenditure series which are given at both current and constant price levels, demonstrating how the implicit index can be recovered in a spreadsheet. The section also covers the problem of how to obtain a single base series from shorter series with differing bases, using 1-2-3 for the rebasing calculations.

1-2-3 features introduced in this chapter: Use of arrow keys in entering a formula, resetting cell widths, writing 1-2-3 command sequences compactly; the use of the 'tilde' ˜ symbol; the @SQRT function; bar charts; 'legends' in graphs; centring text input with the ˆ symbol) the **/Range Format** command; the **/Data Fill** command; the **/Worksheet Insert** command.

3.1 Basic principles of index numbers

The concept of an index number is one of the most important in economics. Anyone attempting any work in applied economics should have a good understanding of the principles of index numbers and a practical knowledge of how to work with them.

The object of an index number is to represent in a single series (the index) movements in a whole set of underlying series. For example, one might want to know how the price of fish has changed from one year (say 1980) to another year (1985). The index would assign the number 100 to the *base year* and its value in 1985 would show how fish prices changed *relative* to the base value. For example, if the index in 1985 was to take the value 130, this would imply that fish prices have risen by 30% over the period. If instead it was to take the value of 90, this would imply the prices (on average) were only 90% of their 1980 levels, i.e. prices had fallen by 10%.

Here we are concerned not only with the interpretation of index numbers but also their construction. Unfortunately this is not a straightforward matter. To continue with the example of a price index for fish, there are many different types of fish and the prices vary considerably between types. For example, the price of cod in Great Britain in 1980 (expressed in £ per tonne) was 562.48, whereas the price of sole (in the same units) was 2677.78. By 1985 the prices had become (respectively) 776.06 and 3345.56. Even if these were the only types of fish available, we would still not have sufficient information to provide a satisfactory answer to the original question. It would not be enough simply to average the two 1985 prices and compare them with the average of the 1980 prices, i.e. to calculate.

$$[(776.06+3345.56)/2]/[(562.48+2677.78)/2]$$

which would give a result of approximately 1.272 (or 127.2% when multiplied by 100).

This simple index number is deficient because it does not take account of the differing importance of the fish types when assessing prices. In fact, landings of cod (in 1980) totalled 102.1 thousand tonnes, whereas those of sole amounted to only 1.8 thousand tonnes. In 1985 the figures were 87.9 thousand tonnes and 2.7 thousand tonnes respectively. It is clear that the increase in the price of cod (from £562.48 to £776.06 per tonne, i.e. nearly 38%) was of far greater importance than the change in the price of sole (from £2677.78 to £3345.56, i.e. just under 25%). In calculating the price index for 1985 some way should be found to reflect the much greater significance of cod price changes as implied by the differences in the quantities landed. An obvious solution would be to use the quantities of fish as *weights* in the calculation, that is the index would be found as the ratio (times 100%) of

(price of cod in 1985 × quantity landed of cod) + (price of sole in 1985 × quantity landed of sole)

to

(price of cod in 1980 × quantity landed of cod) + (price of sole in 1980 × quantity landed of sole)

There is still a problem, however, since we have not stipulated whether the quantities to be used in the calculation should refer to the base year (1980) or to the current year (1985). In fact, arguments for each alternative could be given. The advantage of working with base-year weights would be that if a series of index numbers was required (say from 1980 all the way through to 1985) only one set of quantity information would be required. And yet, it might be argued, the base-year quantities could become out of date. Indeed, although cod was still landed in far greater quantities than sole in 1985, the quantity of cod had actually fallen somewhat, whereas the quantity of sole was up by 50%. The alternative, then, is to use current-year quantities as weights. Certainly the results obtained using the different weights can differ (although in this case not by much). Using the base-year weights (this kind of index number is sometimes called a *Laspeyres* index number) we find

$$\text{Laspeyres price index} = \frac{[(776.06 \times 102.1) + (3345.56 \times 1.8)]}{[(562.48 \times 102.1) + (2677.78 \times 1.8)]} \times 100\%$$

$$\simeq 136.96\%$$

Using the current year quantities as weights (this kind of index is sometimes called a *Paasche* index number) we find

$$\text{Paasche price index} = \frac{[(776.06 \times 87.9) + (3345.56 \times 2.7)]}{[(562.48 \times 87.9) + (2677.78 \times 2.7)]} \times 100\%$$

$$\simeq 136.31\%$$

Although the results are very close, the Laspeyres index has slightly overstated the importance of the rise in the price of cod, because it has not allowed for the fall in quantity which has occurred. Conversely, the Paasche index slightly understates the change in the price of cod because it looks only at the final-year quantities. In an attempt to avoid both types of distortion one usually obtains an average of the two indices. However, because index numbers are ratios, it is appropriate to use the geometric rather than the arithmetic mean. An index computed in this way is known, appropriately enough, as a *Fisher* index number:

Fisher index = $\sqrt{(\text{Laspeyres index} \times \text{Paasche index})}$

The value obtained here is 136.63%

Whichever of these three numbers you prefer to take, they all lie between 136 and 137 and this is considerably different from the figure of 127% found using the simple index number. As can clearly be seen, weights are important in index number calculations.

We could have looked at the same data from the opposite direction to obtain index numbers of quantity, using the prices as weights. As before, an index number which uses base-year weights is called a *Laspeyres* index, one which uses current-year weights is a *Paasche* index, and the geometric mean of them is a *Fisher* index. When applied to the fish data the following results are obtained (to two decimal places):

Laspeyres quantity index = 91.05%
Paasche quantity index   = 90.61%
Fisher quantity index   = 90.83%

For the record, a simple quantity index calculated by just adding the quantities landed of the two types of fish in 1985, dividing by the sum of the quantities landed in 1980 and expressing the ratio as a percentage produces a figure of 87.20%. Here the increase in the landings of sole are not given as much 'weight' as their economic importance deserves.

3.2 Using the spreadsheet to compute index numbers

Up until now we have not made any use of the Lotus 1-2-3 spreadsheet in this chapter. The calculations could have been carried out using a pocket calculator, and the original data and the results have not been organised in a very structured manner. However, if one had been required to compute index numbers similar to this covering all the 28 types of fish identified by the Ministry of Agriculture, Food and Fisheries statistics (available each year in the *Annual Abstract of Statistics*), and if one wished to do this not just for one year in relation to 1980, but for a number of years, say from 1981 to 1985, then one would find that Lotus 1-2-3 offers a very effective means of organising the calculations. Rather than rush straight on to a problem of this size we first show in this section how the calculation completed so far could be laid out in a spreadsheet. We shall extend the problem to cover all 28 types of fish in Section 3.4.

Load Lotus 1-2-3 and create a new worksheet as follows

In cell A1 type

FISH: Prices and landings of cod and sole in Great Britain

and in cell A2 enter

Source: Annual Abstract of Statistics 1987 p187

In cell A3 put

units: price = £/tonne, quantity (landings) = thousand tonnes

In cell A4 put \− and copy this across to the range B4.H4.
In cell C5 enter the label COD (begin with a double quotation mark to right justify it). Similarly, put "SOLE in cell E5.

Now enter the following labels:

Cell	Label
A6	"YEAR
C6	"Price
D6	"Quantity
E6	"Price
F6	"Quantity

Then enter the following values:

Cell	Value
A7	1980
A8	1985
C7	562.48
C8	776.06
D7	102.1
D8	87.9
E7	2677.78
E8	3345.56
F7	1.8
F8	2.7

These are the basic data. Draw another dotted line across the screen by copying the range A4.H4 into the range A10.H10. In cell C11 enter a subtitle Expenditure Aggregates.

In Section 3.1 when we calculated the different index numbers we were in effect taking ratios of various expenditure aggregates, some actual and some hypothetical. For example, the Laspeyres price index for 1985 is the actual expenditure on fish in 1985 divided by the hypothetical expenditure made up of 1980 quantities at 1985 prices (×100%). Similarly, the Paasche quantity index would be found by dividing the actual 1985 expenditure by the expenditure which would have occurred had the 1980 quantities been purchased at the 1985 prices (×100%).

To facilitate the calculation of the index numbers themselves we will first assemble these aggregates as building blocks.

In cell A13 put the label SUM P(1980)Q(1980) =. Then add the other expenditure labels as follows:

Cell	Label
A14	SUM P(1985)Q(1985) =
A15	SUM P(1980)Q(1985) =
A16	SUM P(1985)Q(1980) =

Then draw another dotted line across the screen in row 17. The formulae for these aggregates will be placed in cells D13 to D16 as follows:

CellFormula
D13+C7*D7+E7*F7
D14+C8*D8+E8*F8
D15+C7*D8+E7*F8
D16+C8*D7+E8*F7

In entering a formula like the one in D13 you can use the arrow keys to point to the cells in the formula, rather than typing in the addresses at the keyboard. First press the <+> key to signal that a formula is to be entered. Then use the arrow keys to move the cursor to cell C7 (which contains the 1980 price of cod). When this appears as the active cell enter a * symbol (to indicate that it is to be multiplied by something). The cursor flips back to cell D13. Now use the arrow keys to move the cursor up to cell D7 (which contains the 1980 quantity of cod). The formula is extended to include this cell value and so far should read +C7*D7. Now press the <+> key again so that you can add in the expenditure on sole. Again the cursor flips back to cell D13. Use the arrow keys to move it to cell E7 (which contains the 1980 price of sole) and press the <*> key. Complete the formula by moving the cursor to cell F7 (which contains the 1980 quantity of sole).

The formula is now complete so press the <*Return*> key. (If you have any difficulty entering the formula this way you can simply type it in at the keyboard.) The value 62249.21 will now appear in cell D13, while the formula used to calculate it is at the top of the screen.

Now enter the formulae for cells D14 to D16. Do not be concerned that these figures are not quite the same as those we found on the calculator (where one extra digit appeared after the decimal place). In fact, the computer is holding this extra digit but it cannot be shown because the cells are not wide enough. With values, unlike text, the cell contents do not automatically spill over into the next cell.

You can widen the cell so as to show the extra figure. With the cursor over one of the cells in column D call up the main menu (press the </> key). Select *Worksheet* followed by *Column* and then *Set-Width*. Type 10 to replace the default value of 9 and press <*Return*>. The column widens to show the extra figure and this is signalled in the control panel where the *width indicator [W10]* appears next to the address of the active cell.

Incidentally, the step just described could have been written more compactly by /WCS10⁻. These are the keystrokes necessary to produce the effect, where the symbol ⁻ (tilde) is used in Lotus 1-2-3 to indicate that the <*Return*> key should be pressed.

Now we must obtain the index numbers themselves. Put a subheading in cell B18: Price and Quantity Index Numbers, and enter labels as follows:

Cell	Label
C20	"PRICE
F20	"QUANTITY
A21	"YEAR
A22	"1980
A23	"1985
B21	"Laspeyres
C21	"Paasche
D21	"Fisher
E21	"Laspeyres
F21	"Paasche
G21	"Fisher

(If you are lazy, the range A21.A23 can be copied from A6.A8 and the range E21.G21 can be copied from B21.D21.)

In entering these labels the worksheet will scroll upwards with rows 1 to 3 disappearing from view as rows 21 to 23 come onto the screen. Now enter these formulae:

Cell	Formula/Value
B22 to G22	100
B23	+100*D16/D13
C23	+100*D14/D15
D23	@SQRT(B23*C23)
E23	+100*D15/D13
F23	+100*D14/D16
G23	@SQRT(E23*F23)

The formulae in cells D23 and G23 make use of another *built-in function*, the @SQRT function. As you can see, such functions can be applied to formulae themselves and not just to individual cell values. The results confirm our findings and emphasise that (looking at just these two types of fish) prices rose by nearly 40% while landings dropped by between 9 and 10%.

At this stage go back to cell A1 and save the worksheet under the name FISH. Incidentally, when working on a large worksheet it is a good idea to save and resave what has been done at regular intervals in case there is a power cut or some other disturbance which could cause your work to be lost.

3.3 Bar charts to show price and quantity relatives

Before extending the analysis to all 28 types of fish we will use the spreadsheet to work out the simple price and quantity *relatives* for cod and sole, and then construct a *bar chart* to illustrate the results.

A price (or quantity) relative is just an index number showing the current price (or quantity) of an individual item relative to its base value in percentage terms. For example, when it was stated in Section 3.1 that landings of sole had increased by 50% from 1980 to 1985, another way of expressing this would have been to say that landings of sole in 1985 stood at 150% of their base year value (=100*quantity in 1985/quantity in 1980).

Retrieve the FISH worksheet and move down to row 25. Draw a dotted line across the screen and enter the subheading in cell B26:

Price and Quantity Relatives

Then enter labels as follows:

Cell	Label
C28	"COD
F28	"SOLE
A29	"YEAR
C29	"Price
D29	"Quantity
E29	"Price
F29	"Quantity
A30	1980
A31	1985

In cells C30 to F30 enter the value 100 (to complete the table). In cell C31 enter the formula +100*C8/C7 (you can move the cursor to the cells you need with the arrow keys as shown above).

Now in cells D31 to F31 you can use the **Copy** command to enter:

Cell	Formula
D31	+100*D8/D7
E31	+100*E8/E7
F31	+100*F8/F7

Call up the main menu and select *Graph*, followed by *Type* and then *Bar*. Enter the A range as C31.D31 (this contains the price and quantity relatives for cod in 1985). In the *B* range put E31.F31 (the price and quantity relatives for sole in 1985).

Now choose *X* and enter the range C29.D29. The *X* range contains the labels for a bar chart. If you now *View* the graph you will see two bars together on the left of the screen showing the price relatives and two bars on the right of the screen showing the quantity relatives.

As yet the graph does not have any labelling, nor would someone looking at the graph know what products the price and quantity bars refer to. Press *<Return>* and select *Options*.

Choose *Legend* and set the legend for the A range as Cod.

Then set the legend for the B range as Sole.
Give the graph the following titles:

First Line: Fish price and quantity relatives (1985)
Second line: [1980 = 100]

When you *View* the graph again it should look like Figure 3.1 (although it will not have such attractive fonts).

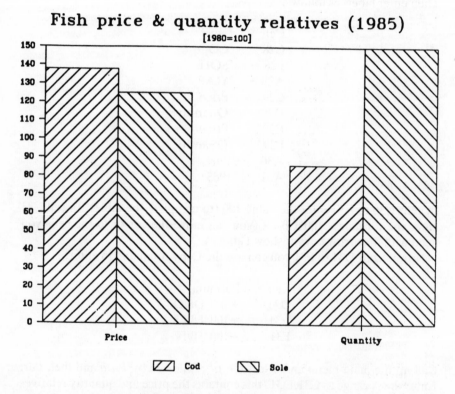

Figure 3.1 Bar chart created from the FISH worksheet

Save the graph to print out later (as shown in Chapter 2) and resave the enlarged worksheet.

You can now clear the worksheet from the screen by issuing the command sequence /**Worksheet Erase Yes**. This will not erase the worksheet file from the disk, merely clear your inputs from the computer's current memory so that you can begin a new worksheet. You can either go straight on with this (as described in Section 3.4) or you can quit 1-2-3, remove the disks and switch off the computer if you are ready for a rest.

3.4 Full price and quantity index numbers for fish

Table 3.1 shows screen dumps at an intermediate stage in the construction of a worksheet to calculate fish price and quantity index numbers for 1985 (based on 1980) and using information on all the 28 types of fish given in the *Annual Abstract of Statistics*. In fact, that publication does not actually give a separate price figure but quotes the values of fish landings (i.e. the quantities multiplied by the prices). It is simple enough to use 1-2-3 to recover the prices and columns D and G have been set aside to hold these numbers.

Table 3.1 Screen displays from the worksheet file BIGFISH

```
A1:   [W15]  'BIGFISH :
                                                                    READY

            A          B         C        D         E         F         G
 1    BIGFISH :   worksheet on price and quantity index numbers applied
 2                to fish landings
 3
 4               1980                          1985
 5               Landings    Value     Price    Landings    Value    Price
 6    Type of·fish (thousand  (th)    (/tonne) (thousand   (th)    (/tonne)
 7                tonnes)                        tonnes)
 8    Catfish       1.1        358    325.45       1.4       755    539.29
 9    Cod         102.1      57429    562.48      87.9     68216    776.06
10    Dogfish      12.2       3361    275.49      12.2      4150    340.16
11    Haddock      84.7      34069    402.23     132.1     67649    512.10
12    Hake          2.2       1831    832.27       2.5      3602   1440.80
13    Halibut       0.2        389   1945.00       0.1       365   3650.00
14    Lemon sole    5.4       4839    896.11       5.7      7130   1250.88
15    Plaice       26.1      12931    495.44      20.3     13732    676.45
16    Redfish       1.4        266    190.00       0.2        75    375.00
17    Saithe       14.5       4540    313.10      13.8      3725    269.93
18    Skate & ray   6.1       2619    429.34       6.8      2944    432.94
19    Sole          1.8       4820   2677.78       2.7      9033   3345.56
20    Turbot        0.7       1402   2002.86       0.5      1946   3892.00
24-Aug-88   11:02 AM

                                                                    READY

            A          B         C        D         E         F         G
21    Whiting      52.5      15774    300.46      41.8     16953    405.57
22    Roes          0.5        324    648.00       0.4       362    905.00
23    Other demersal 64.7    11383    175.94      59.9     21256    354.86
24    Herring       3.1       1195    385.48      92.1     11063    120.12
25    Mackerel    253        24068     95.13     172.7     18522    107.25
26    Other pelagic 46.7      3246     69.51      15.3      1542    100.78
27    Cockles      15.2        807     53.09       7.8       476     61.03
28    Crab          9.7       3967    408.97      12.7      8073    635.67
29    Lobster       0.7       3295   4707.14       1.1      7616   6923.64
30    Mussels       9.1        460     50.55       5.8       467     80.52
31    Nephrop      12.1      13094   1082.15      20.4     27453   1345.74
32    Oysters       0.6       1001   1668.33       0.4       734   1835.00
33    Shrimps       1.2        998    831.67       0.8       712    890.00
34    Whelks        1.2        259    215.83       1.6       355    221.88
35    Other shellfish 18.8    8364    444.89      18.8     13656    726.38
36    All fish
37    Total       747.6     217089  22484.70     737.8    312562  32214.59
38    Average      26.7    7753.178  803.0252     26.35  11162.92 1150.521
39    Source : Annual Abstract of Statistics 1987 p187
40
```

Begin a new worksheet and type in the entries as shown in the table. Notice that column A has been widened to 15 characters so as to accommodate the longer names. Columns B and E should also be widened, this time to 10 characters.

The labels for columns, C, D, F and G have been centred in the cells rather than right justified. To do this you begin the text with the ˆ (caret) symbol instead of the ' or ".

Next obtain the price figures by dividing column C by column B and column F by column E (rows 8 to 35 only), putting the results in columns D and G. The easiest way to do this is to enter the formula +C8/B8 in cell D8 and then copy down the column. Similarly put +F8/E8 in cell G8 and copy down that column.

Next get the computer to work out the price and quantity relatives. Enter labels as follows:

Cell	Label
I5	Price
I6	relatives
J5	Quantity
J6	relatives

In cell I8 enter the formula +100*G8/D8 and copy this down the column (range I9.I35). In cell J8 enter the formula +100*E8/B8 and copy this to J9.J35.

The appearance of these columns is rather messy, with the number of figures shown after the decimal place varying from none (e.g. J13) to five (I17). You can tidy up the presentation by using the command sequence **/Range Format Fixed** and entering a value of 2 (give the range as I8.J35). All the numbers in these columns will then be shown to just two decimal places with the decimal points neatly aligned.

In calculating the expenditure aggregates we shall approach the problem in a slightly different way to the one used in Section 3.2, also adopting a different layout (this is in accordance with the fact that in this worksheet the types of fish are shown down the rows rather than being placed in different columns as they were in the FISH worksheet). Enter labels as follows:

Cell	Label
M2	Calculation of
M3	Expenditure Aggregates
L5	"P80Q80
M5	"P80Q85
N5	"P85Q80
O5	"P85Q85

Now copy column C (rows 8 to 35) into column L (rows 8 to 35). Since these are the original values there is no need to work them out again. In cell M8 put the formula +D8*E8 and then copy down this formula into the range M9.M35. These numbers show how much would have been spent on each different type of fish if the 1985 quantities had been valued at 1980 prices.

In cell N9 put the formula +G8*B8 and then copy this down into the range N9.N35. These numbers show what the expenditure would have been on each type of fish if the 1980 quantities had been valued at 1985 prices.

Now go to cell K37 and put the label "SUMS. In cell L37 enter the formula @SUM(L8.L35) and copy this across to M37.O37. In cell J39 enter Index numbers for 1985 (1980 = 100) and then further labels as follows:

Cell	Label
L40	Price
M40	Quantity
J41	Laspeyres
J42	Paasche
J43	Fisher

Then enter the formulae:

Cell	Formula
L41	+100*N37/L37
M41	+100*M37/L37
L42	+100*O37/M37
M42	+100*O37/N37
L43	@SQRT(L41*L42)
M43	@SQRT(M41*M42)

To complete this section you can construct a bar chart to show how the prices of different types of fish have changed between 1980 and 1985, including in the chart a figure for the average price of fish as calculated by the Fisher price index. (A similar chart could be constructed to show how the quantities have changed.) First we need to place the value for the Fisher price index in cell I36, i.e. at the bottom of the column showing the price relatives. We cannot use the **Copy** command because this would simply adjust the formula in cell L43 for the movement up seven rows and three columns to the left. Instead, use the following series of key strokes (with I36 as the active cell):

/Range Value L43¨¨

You will find that the value contained in cell L43 (127.7499, etc.) has been copied to cell I36.

Now go to cell A36 and enter the label All fish. The range A8.A36 will be used to label the bar graph (although not in the same way as in Section 3.3). Enter the command /**Graph Type Bar A I8.I36**¨. Then select *Options* followed by *Data-Labels A A8.A36*¨.

When given the choice of where to place the labels choose *Above*.

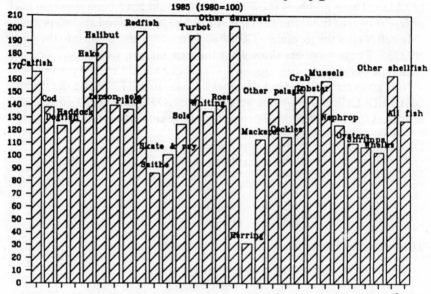

Figure 3.2 Bar chart of the BIGFISH worksheet

Then *Quit* and enter the *Titles*:

First line: Relative price of fish by type
Second line: 1985 (1980 = 100)

Quit again and *View* the graph. It should look something like Figure 3.2.

If you think that the data labels are too untidy for a diagram with this number of bars, an alternative would be to identify each type of fish by a number and provide a separate table in the worksheet to interpret the numbers.

3.5 Implicit index number series and rebasing index numbers

Statistical sources often show an expenditure series both at current prices and at the constant prices of some base year. For example, Table 3.2 shows United States GDP figures (established as an expenditure aggregate) at current and at 1980 prices.

Such a table has implicit information about price changes (in this case the GDP deflator) which can be recovered. Since all that it is necessary to do is to divide the current price series by the constant price series and multiply by 100, a spreadsheet is a particularly convenient method of obtaining the results. This is because the formula need be typed in only once with the **Copy**

Table 3.2

```
        A         B         C         D         E         F         G         H
 1  TABLE 3.2 : worksheet showing the calculation of implicit index numbers
 2  Data set : United States Gross Domestic Product (Expenditure basis)
 3             in $million
 4  Source    : O.E.C.D. National Accounts
 5
 6                      current    1980      GDP
 7                      prices    prices    deflator
 8      Year                                (1980=100)
 9      1976            1709900   2309888     74.03
10      1977            1907532   2436814     78.28
11      1978            2145697   2552007     84.08
12      1979            2388402   2618122     91.23
13      1980            2606625   2606625    100.00
14      1981            2934911   2695473    108.88
15      1982            3045279   2615238    116.44
16      1983            3275728   2692153    121.68
17
18
19
20
24-Aug-88   11:29 AM
```

command being used to generate results for the rest of the years. Before doing that for the data in Table 3.2 let us be clear what kind of index we will get.

A current price figure is in the prices of that particular year – for example 2934911 was the size of US GDP in 1981 (in $ million), measured at 1981 prices. However, if quantities had been valued at 1980 prices the table shows that the expenditure would have been 2695473 ($ million). In effect this latter figure is a hypothetical aggregate such as those computed earlier in this chapter. It is the equivalent of SUM P(1980)Q(1981) over all items of domestic expenditure. By dividing SUM P(1981)Q(1981) by this figure and multiplying by 100 we can calculate the Paasche price index. Similar results can be obtained for any other year, with the 1980 figure just being 100.

Begin a new worksheet and copy Table 3.2 into the appropriate cell positions. In entering the dates you can try out another 1-2-3 trick – the /**Data Fill** command. Go to cell A9 (where 1976 is to appear) and select *Data* from the menu, followed by *Fill*. Give the range as A9.A16 with *Start:* 1976 *Step* 1 and *Stop* 1983.

You will find that all the dates are filled in for you. This is very convenient when a long series like this must be entered with each value differing from the previous one by a constant step (usually of one).

Label column E as follows:

Cell	Label
E6	^GDP
E7	^deflator
E8	'(1980=100)

Put the formula +100*C9/D9 in cell E9 and copy down to the range
E10.E16. Tidy up the presentation using the /**Range Format Fixed** command
(choose two decimal places for the range E9.E16), and the calculation is
complete. The figures should show prices rising consistently over the period
with the GDP deflator at just under 75% of its 1980 value in 1976 and at
around 122% of its 1980 value in 1983.

Next we turn to a way of dealing with an irritating but frequently encountered situation – looking for a continuous index number series, but finding
only short series with differing bases. For example, suppose you were trying
to match up your recently computed index with some results from an earlier
study. However, you find to your dismay that the earlier series has 1975 as
the base period. Suppose that the figures are as follows:

Year	GDP deflator (1975=100)
1971	76.52
1972	79.82
1973	84.32
1974	91.70
1975	100.00
1976	105.69

Here we are lucky, because although the deflated series use different base
years they have one year in common, 1976. We can rebase one series and
join it to the other. Suppose we decide to work with 1975 as the base. The
1980 series shows that from 1976 to 1977 prices rose by a factor of 78.28/
74.03. To obtain the 1975-based value of the series for 1977 we simply
multiply the 1976 figure by this factor, i.e. we have 105.69*(78.28/74.03).
The series can be extended in a similar way, year by year.

First we must insert these 1975-based figures into the worksheet. Go to cell
F9 and issue the command /**Worksheet Insert Row** and give the row range as
F9.F13. Lotus 1-2-3 squeezes in five extra rows below row 8. In column A fill
in the dates 1971 to 1975 and then in column F put the following:

Cell	Input
F6	^GDP
F7	^deflator
F8	' (1975=100)
F9	76.52
F10	79.82
F11	84.32
F12	91.70
F13	100.00
F14	105.69

It would be a good idea at this stage to widen column E to 10 characters
and to change the format of F9.F21 to show two decimal places. Now you are
ready to rebase the series.

In cell F15 enter the formula +F14*E15/E14. Now copy the formula to
F16.F21.

The second part of the series has been rebased and the 1975-based series
has been extended up to 1983. If you had chosen to express all the figures at
1980 prices, the earlier figures would have been divided by an appropriate
fraction, going back to 1971.

This completes our discussion of index numbers and how Lotus 1-2-3 can
be of assistance for calculating and working with them. For a more detailed
discussion of index number problems you can refer to Allen (1975).

Exercise 3

(a) Table 3A gives data on fish landings and values in Great Britain for the
years 1981 to 1984. Extend your worksheet BIGFISH to include these data

Table 3A Landings of fish in Great Britain: landed weight and value

Type of fish	Landed weight (Thousand tonnes)				Value (£ thousand)			
	1981	1982	1983	1984	1981	1982	1983	1984
Catfish	0.9	1.1	1.3	1.3	308	398	494	589
Cod	112.9	111.1	109.7	88.4	59806	70122	70928	63731
Dogfish	10.9	9.7	10	10.6	3110	3045	3099	3236
Haddock	100	129	122.6	107.4	38117	50299	57351	64161
Hake	3.8	2.9	2	2.3	4302	3740	2162	2462
Halibut	0.1	0.1	0.2	0.1	256	363	360	318
Lemon sole	4.5	5	5.9	5.7	4837	5060	5493	5958
Plaice	25.1	24.2	20.9	21.3	12760	13768	13714	14005
Redfish	0.5	0.4	0.3	0.4	100	96	73	98
Saithe	13.7	15.8	12.2	11.7	3781	4627	3387	2671
Skate & ray	5.7	6	6.4	6.7	2631	2718	2852	2749
Sole	1.7	2.1	2.2	2.4	5258	5498	5826	6636
Turbot	0.6	0.5	0.5	0.5	1350	1294	1419	1651
Whiting	42.9	40.7	51.8	54.9	12621	11562	16325	21583
Roes	0.5	0.1	0.4	0.4	286	329	261	277
Other demersal	74.8	82.4	70.5	69.2	12321	13501	14313	17266
Herring	34.5	45.7	52.2	69.5	4545	5504	6694	8778
Mackerel	197.2	184	174.5	185.2	19434	19170	18532	18660
Other pelagic	34.1	28.1	19.1	8.2	2303	2010	1506	1023
Cockles	10.4	8.3	5.8	5.4	592	458	327	309
Crab	9.7	8.6	11.3	13.9	4257	4245	6372	8366
Lobster	0.8	0.8	1	1.2	3806	4181	5697	7489
Mussels	2.5	4.4	5.9	4.3	229	461	468	312
Nephrop	14.4	15.4	17.1	18.1	14112	17798	20230	21291
Oysters	0.6	0.4	0.3	0.4	1116	925	636	770
Shrimps	1.4	1.6	1.1	0.7	1097	1147	739	562
Whelks	1.5	1.6	1.3	2.1	351	380	226	450
Other shellfish	21.6	18.9	23.1	21.5	8845	9090	12323	13855

Source: Annual Abstract of Statistics, 1987, p.187

Table 3B Consumers' expenditure in the UK by commodity group (£ million)

Commodity group	Total Consumers' Expenditure		Consumers' Expenditure on tobacco products	
Year	Current prices	1980 prices	Current prices	1980 prices
1975	65338	125113	2735	4995
1976	75818	125504	3092	4821
1977	86679	124868	3628	4602
1978	99873	131742	3885	4982
1979	118426	137612	4234	4960
1980	137234	137234	4821	4821
1981	152544	136936	5515	4471
1982	167362	138201	5881	4128
1983	182877	143781	6209	4082
1984	195711	146888	6622	3943
1985	213208	152038	7005	3837

Source: UK National Accounts (Blue Book), 1986

and use Lotus 1-2-3 to obtain price and quantity indices for fish (based on 1980) for the years 1981 to 1984. Write a report discussing the results.
(b) Set up a worksheet and use the data from Table 3B to construct price index numbers for tobacco and for all goods and services (1980=100). Obtain an index showing changes in the *relative* price of tobacco goods (=100*nominal price index/price index of all goods). Report on your findings.

References

R. G. D. Allen, *Index Numbers in Theory and Practice* (Macmillan, London, 1975).
G. Judge and D. Whitmarsh, 'Fishing for figures: The use of index numbers in evaluating industrial performance', *Teaching Mathematics and its Applications*, Vol. 6, No. 1, 1987, pp. 37–42.

Chapter 4

The seasonal adjustment of economic time series with Lotus 1-2-3

Purpose: To describe the decomposition approach to the seasonal adjustment of economic time series and to show how Lotus 1-2-3 can be used for
this type of quantitative analysis.

Preview: This chapter examines seasonal (and other) patterns in economic
time series data and considers the reasons for seasonally adjusting such data
(Section 4.1). The classical decomposition model is outlined and it is shown
how Lotus 1-2-3 can be used to complete the necessary calculations (Sections
4.2 to 4.5) and, through an analysis of the residuals, a means of validating the
model is provided (Section 4.6). In Section 4.7 possible refinements to the
method are considered. The benefits of a visual examination of graph plots
are stressed throughout and the use of the 1-2-3 Line Graph is described.

1-2-3 features introduced in this chapter: Line graphs; automatic and manual
scaling; skip factors; the **/Graph Name** command; the @AVG function.

4.1 Seasonal and other patterns in time-series data – the need for seasonal adjustment

A time series is simply a set of observations of a variable observed over time
at regular intervals. The periodic frequency of observation could be once a
year (annually), once every three months (quarterly), once a month
(monthly) or even once a day (daily). Such series often exhibit regular
patterns linked with the time periods. For example, annual data on industrial production might show regular cyclical ups and downs every four or
five years as the economy first expands and then contracts (the cyclical
pattern is usually around an upward trend rather than a constant average
level). Quarterly and monthly data often have a noticeable seasonal pattern
with 'highs' occurring regularly in certain months or quarters and 'lows' in
other periods.

Table 4.1 shows some figures from a series with just this kind of pattern.

Table 4.1 New registration of cars (monthly averages in thousands)

Year	Q1	Q2	Q3	Q4
1980	164.4	123.1	137.0	82.0
1981	138.8	124.3	138.2	96.9
1982	139.2	122.8	158.3	107.9
1983	165.6	141.5	183.2	111.8
1984	167.0	146.7	167.8	104.9
1985	167.3	144.7	187.5	114.5

Source: Economic Trends Annual Supplement, 1987, p. 34

The table gives the new registrations of cars in the UK by quarter (monthly averages in thousands) for the years 1980 to 1985.

Although the figures towards the end of the series are above those for the equivalent quarters in 1980, there does not appear to be any pronounced upward trend in the data. What is clearly visible just from looking at the table, however, is the marked seasonal pattern in the data, with the fourth quarter typically the lowest figure in any year and the third quarter the highest (although the first-quarter figures are sometimes quite close). Any trend or seasonal variation in a time series can be more obvious from a graphical representation of the data and we shall first use 1-2-3 to construct such a graph.

Where seasonal patterns are present it is often helpful to adjust the data in some way so as to remove these fluctuations. This is done so that any deviations from past trends that occur in new values can be more easily recognised.

The simplest approach is to model the series as being generated from the combination of four factors; a trend (T), the seasonal factor (S), a cyclical factor (C) and random irregular movements (R). (The cyclical factor is included where it is felt that the series might be tending to move up and down in line with the business cycle. Since this cycle tends to recur only about every four or five years it is usually ignored for short data series as is the case in our example.)

If each of these factors can be isolated (or 'decomposed') from the others then we can obtain the seasonally adjusted series by removing this factor, leaving just the trend and random shifts. The first step is to estimate the trend and this is obtained either as a moving average (as we do here) or where appropriate by approximating the trend as some function of time – in the simplest case it would be assumed to be a linear function.

Such a model could also be used for forecasting, with the trend being projected forward into the future, suitably modified for any seasonal patterns which have been established.

All the necessary calculations can be done using Lotus 1-2-3 and the seasonally adjusted series can be included on the time-series graph plot for comparison with the unadjusted series. The adequacy of the model can also be assessed by examining the residuals which should reflect only random movements. Again the graph-plotting routines of 1-2-3 can be used for a visual check.

4.2 Constructing a worksheet for the seasonal adjustment of a series

In this section we begin by using Lotus 1-2-3 to construct a graph showing the time-series plot of our data. This should always be the first step of any time-series analysis since it can at once give a researcher clues as to the nature of the series and suggest any points which depart from the general pattern. Such points could indicate some special factors which applied in a particular period (for example, a strike or bad weather) or they could show up a typing error in entering the data into the worksheet.

Load Lotus 1-2-3 and begin a new worksheet. Enter the labels and data as shown in Table 4.2.

In column A we give the observation number (1 to 24) while in column B the year and quarter of each observation is identified. We have included both

Table 4.2 Initial layout for the car registration worksheet

	A	B	C	D	E	F
1	CARS : worksheet for the seasonal adjustment of time series					
2	New registrations of cars (monthly averages in thousands)					
3						
4	Period	Quarter	Cars			
5	1	1980 Q1	164.40			
6	2	Q2	123.10			
7	3	Q3	137.00			
8	4	Q4	82.00			
9	5	1981 Q1	138.80			
10	6	Q2	124.30			
11	7	Q3	138.20			
12	8	Q4	96.90			
13	9	1982 Q1	139.20			
14	10	Q2	122.80			
15	11	Q3	158.30			
16	12	Q4	107.90			
17	13	1983 Q1	165.60			
18	14	Q2	141.50			
19	15	Q3	183.20			
20	16	Q4	111.80			
21	17	1984 Q1	167.00			
22	18	Q2	146.70			
23	19	Q3	167.80			
24	20	Q4	104.90			
25	21	1985 Q1	167.30			
26	22	Q2	144.70			
27	23	Q3	187.50			
28	24	Q4	114.50			
29						
30						

ways of referencing the values since each offers certain benefits. Sometimes we will just want to think of the data as a series of 24 observations following one after the other. On other occasions we will wish to identify the specific year or quarter concerned.

Column B must be input as text so begin each entry by pressing the <"> key. You can enter the figures in column A in several different ways. Try using the /**Data Fill** approach.

Now call up the menu and select *Graph*. The type of graph we want is a line graph, so choose *Type* followed by *Line*. Next you need to tell 1-2-3 the range of cells to use for the X-axis so choose *X* from the menu now on the screen. When prompted to enter the X-axis range, key in A5.A28 and press <*Return*>. You only have one data series to plot at present and this will be identified as the A-range, so move the cursor along to *A* and <*Return*>. You will be prompted to enter the first data range and you should give this as C5.C28 and <*Return*>.

You can now choose *View* and you should see the car registration series plotted against the time period. Although the axes have numbers on them showing the scale, they are not labelled in any other way. To give the graph a title and to label the axes press <*Return*> again and you will come back to the *Graph* submenu.

This time choose *Options* and then *Titles*. For the first line of the title put: New registrations of cars (and then press <*Return*>). Select *Titles* again and then *Second*. For the second line type in: monthly averages in thousands.

Now put in titles for the X- and Y-axes.

For the X-axis put: Period 1980:Q1 − 1985:Q4
and for the Y-axis: Cars (in thousands)

When you look at the graph again it should resemble Figure 4.1. (Remember, to see the amended graph you can either select *View* from the *Graph* submenu as before or just press the GRAPH function key F10 straight from the worksheet.)

Notice that the Y-axis has been automatically scaled by 1-2-3 so as to make the greatest possible use of the screen space. The graph does not begin at the origin, but just below the smallest data value at 80. If you do not wish to use this scaling you can override the Automatic Scaling. Use /**Graph Options Scale YScale Manual** and then set your chosen upper and lower limits. As you will see if you do this, you can also choose your own scaling for the X-axis if you wish. If you do not want the scale to label every unit change in the variables you can specify the 'skip' factor you would like. For example, instead of having every observation indicated on the horizontal axis you could have a skip factor of 4 so that the start of each individual year is picked out clearly.

As anticipated, there is an obvious seasonal pattern in the data with a

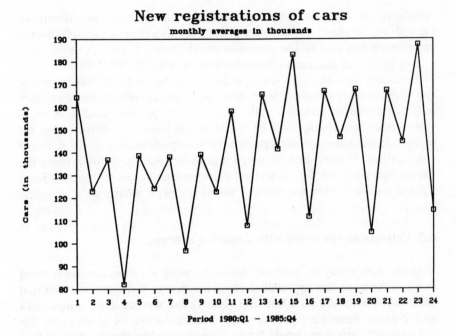

Figure 4.1 Line graph of the CARS worksheet

'saw-tooth' pattern showing the series dipping down every fourth quarter but rising again in the following quarter. In the second quarter the graph drops down again but in the third quarter the graph climbs once more (this includes the increase in August when the new registration letter is introduced).

From the relatively short set of data on view we cannot tell whether there is any real upward trend or whether the year-on-year movements are part of some cycle which recurs perhaps every four years. Whatever the nature of this factor, we shall try to smooth the series by finding a moving average. For simplicity we shall then presume that this can be identified with the trend, ignoring the complication of a cyclical component.

Before you go on you should save this graph so that you can recall it again if necessary. If you were to save the worksheet as it stands then the graph you have just created would be saved with it so that when you retrieve the worksheet file you could view it again. However, you can only have one such 'current graph' at a time with a worksheet. You will be creating further graphs as the analysis proceeds. How can you save several graphs so that each can be recalled when required?

The answer is you must use the **/Graph Name Create** sequence of commands. You will be prompted to enter a graph name. Since this is just the car registration series call the graph CARS. Enter this name and press

<Return>. If you now add to or change the current graph in any way, or even if you remove it completely, you can always recall CARS by the command /**Graph Name Use**, and selecting the graph CARS. A whole set of graphs to accompany a given worksheet can be created like this and any one of them can be recalled for viewing at the touch of a few keys. Make sure that you remember to resave a worksheet after any modifications have been made, either to the contents of the cells or to the graphs based on them. If you do not, these changes will be lost when you leave 1-2-3 at the end of the session. Remember too that it is not possible to print out a graph from within a worksheet. It must first be saved and then it can be printed using the *PrintGraph* program. So call up the *Graph* submenu again and choose *Save*. Type in a name for the graph (e.g. CARS) and press *<Return>*.

4.3   Estimating the trend with a moving average

You are now ready to estimate the trend using a four-quarterly moving average. You use this approach because inspection of the graph shows that there is no obvious smooth function which could be fitted to the data to pick up the trend. Since each year contains one representative of each quarter, any seasonal variations should tend to cancel out when the averages of four such values are taken. So if you take the values in cells C5.C8 and average them you get a figure for the middle of the year, stripped of any seasonal ups or downs. If you move on a period, leaving out the first quarter of 1980 but including the first quarter of 1981, you should still have one representative of each quarter and the average of this block of four cells could be taken to measure the trend of the series one quarter on from the middle of 1980. By dropping a value at the beginning and adding in the next value in the series in this way you can move through the series averaging blocks of four, giving a series purged of seasonal effects. Such a series would also have removed from it most of any random disturbances to which the original series might have been subjected. Since some such disturbances will be positive, some negative, some close to zero and some further away from zero, and since each random disturbance is assumed to be independent of its neighbours, when you take a four-quarterly moving average you should largely remove the random factor as well as the seasonal factor.

However, there are two problems which you must be ready for. Firstly, the moving-average series will be shorter than the original series; and secondly, the simple moving average as described above will not be 'centred', that is lined up exactly with one of the original time periods. When you average the first four observations the figure obtained falls halfway between the second and third quarters of 1980. The next moving-average figure would fall halfway between the third and fourth quarter of 1980, and so on. You can overcome this problem by averaging successive pairs of these in-between averages to obtain a centred moving-average series. The average of the first two uncentred figures would then line up with the third quarter of 1980, the average of the second and third uncentred figures would line up with the fourth quarter of 1980, all the way along until you reach the second quarter of 1985. There will be no centred moving averages for the first two quarters of 1980 – as you have seen, the first figure you can get is for the third quarter. Similarly, at the end of the series you must stop with the second quarter of 1985 because there are no new values to bring into the moving average when you drop the 1985 Q1 figure.

In using Lotus 1-2-3 it will not be possible to place the uncentred moving averages in between time periods. The structure of a spreadsheet does not permit this. Instead you will place the first calculated value alongside 1980 Q3, remembering that strictly it should be half a period earlier.

So go to cell D7 and enter an appropriate formula to calculate the first of the uncentred moving averages. You can actually use the built-in statistical function which takes the form @AVG(range) so in this case enter @AVG(C5.C8). The figure 126.6256 should appear. To get the rest of the moving average series you simply copy this formula down to the cell range D8.D27. (Remember, this is the uncentred moving average so the figure that appears in cell D27 should strictly be half a row up from this position.)

Go back to the top of the column to give it a heading as follows:

Cell	Label
D3	"Uncentred
D4	"Moving Av

Now to get the centred series go to cell E7 and enter the formula @AVG(D7.D8). This will give the first figure in the series of 123.425. Again you can copy down to obtain the average of successive pairs. The value appearing in cell E8 will be the average of D8 and D9, etc., all the way down to cell E26 which is the centred moving average for 1985 Q2 and is found from the average of the values in cells D26 and D27. Every figure in column E is found as the average of the figure next to it in column D and the figure below that in column D. Go back to the top of the column and enter "Centred in cell E3 and "Moving Av in cell E4 to give the column a heading.

Before you go any further there are two aspects of the worksheet which could do with some tidying up. Firstly, the headings for columns D and E run right on to each other. The presentation would be improved if you were to increase the width of these columns by another two or three characters. Secondly, the numbers in the columns show no consistency in terms of how many figures are shown after the decimal point. In computing the averages sometimes 1-2-3 has found a figure which works out exactly to one decimal place, sometimes to two and sometimes to three places. To improve the layout, reformat these columns (and indeed column C as well) to show a specified number of figures after the decimal point. Go to cell D3 and key in the following command sequence:

/Worksheet Column Set-Width 12 <Return>

Then go to cell E3 and type in the same commands (you can do this just by typing */WCS12 <Return>*.

The columns should now be three characters wider than the default width of nine characters and this is big enough to accommodate the column headings with some space in between.

To reformat the columns so as to line up the decimal places choose *Range* from the main menu followed by *Format* and then *Fixed*. You will be required to enter the number of decimal places followed by the range of cells to have the new format. Change the range D7 to E27 to show three figures after the decimal place. Then repeat the procedure to show two figures after the decimal place for the range C5.C28. Your modified worksheet should now look like Table 4.3.

Table 4.3

	A	B	C	D	E	F	G
1	CARS : worksheet for the seasonal adjustment of time series						
2	New registrations of cars (monthly averages in thousands)						
3				Uncentred	Centred		
4	Period	Quarter	Cars	Moving Av	Moving Av		
5	1	1980 Q1	164.40				
6	2	Q2	123.10				
7	3	Q3	137.00	126.625	123.425		
8	4	Q4	82.00	120.225	120.375		
9	5	1981 Q1	138.80	120.525	120.675		
10	6	Q2	124.30	120.825	122.688		
11	7	Q3	138.20	124.550	124.600		
12	8	Q4	96.90	124.650	124.462		
13	9	1982 Q1	139.20	124.275	126.788		
14	10	Q2	122.80	129.300	130.675		
15	11	Q3	158.30	132.050	135.350		
16	12	Q4	107.90	138.650	140.988		
17	13	1983 Q1	165.60	143.325	146.438		
18	14	Q2	141.50	149.550	150.038		
19	15	Q3	183.20	150.525	150.700		
20	16	Q4	111.80	150.875	151.525		
21	17	1984 Q1	167.00	152.175	150.250		
22	18	Q2	146.70	148.325	147.463		
23	19	Q3	167.80	146.600	146.638		
24	20	Q4	104.90	146.675	146.425		
25	21	1985 Q1	167.30	146.175	148.638		
26	22	Q2	144.70	151.100	152.300		
27	23	Q3	187.50	153.500			
28	24	Q4	114.50				

Before proceeding with the calculations add the centred moving-average series to the graph. Call up the graph submenu with the */**Graph** command and press *B* to allow you to enter a second data range. This will be the range E5.E28, which contains the moving average values. Notice that even though the series is shorter than the original series you must include the full range including the blank entries if the points are to be plotted correctly on the graph. Then select *View* and you will be able to see both series shown together.

For the benefit of anyone else who will look at the graph you can identify the two series by giving them *legends*. Choose *Options* from the graph menu and then *Legend*. Press *A* and enter the legend for the original series by typing the words Original series (then *<Return>*). Do the same for B, giving it the legend Moving average.

Let us also change the labelling on the horizontal axis so that instead of simply giving the observation number 1 to 24 the graph shows the years and quarters. From the *Graph* menu choose *X* and put in the range B5.B28 instead of the equivalent range of cells from column A. When you view the graph again the horizontal axis will have changed to show the years and quarters. You will find that there is now too much information to show on the axis without overlapping and the graph looks rather messy. However, if you follow the **/Graph Options Scale Skip** sequence of commands (described in the previous section) with a skip value of 4 you can get 1-2-3 to mark only the year and first-quarter values. Try this and then save the graph with the name CARSMA. (The command is **/Graph Name Create** in case you have forgotten.) Your graph should look like Figure 4.2.

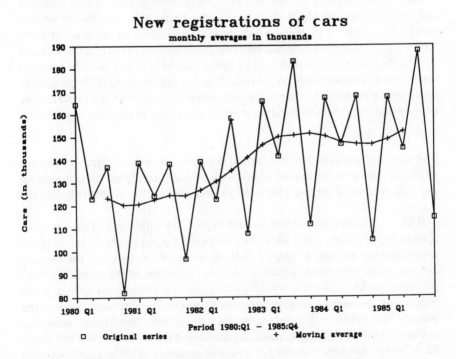

Figure 4.2 Line graph of Figure 4.1 with moving averages

4.4 Isolating the seasonal factor

Now that you have estimated the trend you can remove it from the original series to leave only the seasonal and random factors. If you then separate these two factors you will have isolated the seasonal component.

Before you go any further though you need to consider the way in which the different factors interact. So far all you have needed to do is to say that the actual series can be modelled as some function of the trend, seasonal and random components, i.e. the model has the general form

$$A = f(T,S,R)$$

where A denotes the actual series.

But in order to separate the trend from the rest of the function you need to make some assumption about the form of this function. The simplest model to use is the additive model, which is equivalent to assuming a linear function with

$$A = T + S + R$$

Then you can remove the trend (giving the detrended series) by subtracting the moving-average figures from corresponding values of the actual series.

Such an assumption means that you are content to take it that seasonal influences always result in the actual series being above or below what it would otherwise be by some fixed amount, according to the time of year. The seasonal factors are measured in the same units as the original series and the moving average, in this case in thousands of cars per month. Such an assumption is rather crude. A more reasonable approach might be to assume a multiplicative model, where seasonal factors interact with the trend raising or lowering the values in fixed proportion according to the time of year:

$$A = T \times S \times R$$

The seasonal components here would not be fixed amounts but proportions or ratios, greater than one for seasons where the series tends to be higher on average, and less than one where the season's figures are typically below the trend.

With an additive model you should expect the amplitude of the curve to remain more or less fixed with the distance between peaks in the original series and the moving-average graph, or between troughs and the moving average remaining much the same whatever the value of the trend. A multiplicative model, however, would predict varying amplitudes although the proportion between the gap between the actual series and the moving average in relation to the moving average should stay roughly the same.

Have a look at the graph again. In this case it doesn't look as if too much harm will be done by assuming an additive model. The differences between the third-quarter values and the corresponding moving-average values do show some tendency to rise as the series rises, but the differences are small. We will adopt the additive model and see how we get along with it. It is a little bit easier to work with than the multiplicative model, even with a computer program like 1-2-3 to help you. Remember, whatever choice you make, what you have is only a model which has been adopted to represent the process by which the data have been generated. Neither model is the data-generation process although one might give a better approximation to it than the other. It could be argued that the multiplicative model is always a better model in that in circumstances where the additive model will do, the multiplicative model reduces to virtually the same thing. Against this, the multiplicative model is slightly more awkward to work with.

With the additive model the next step is to obtain the detrended series by simply subtracting the centred moving-average figures from the original series. Go to F7 and enter +C7−E7 and then copy down to F8.F26. You will have to use the /**Range Format** command to tidy up the positions of the decimal points. Put the labels 'Detrended and 'Series in cells F3 and F4 respectively to produce the column heading.

Now the detrended series should represent the sum of the seasonal and random factors, i.e., $D = A - T = S + R$. You can see from the table that the entries for quarters 1 and 3 are positive whereas those in fourth-quarter positions are always negative. Three of the second-quarter values are negative and one is positive, but they are all much closer to zero than in any of the other periods. However, the entries for any particular quarter are not identical: the random disturbances ensure that. You now attempt to eliminate them. The idea is to take all the first-quarter values and to average them. The random disturbances should tend to cancel with one another. Similarly, when we average all the second-quarter, third-quarter and fourth-quarter values we should find the positive and negative disturbances balance each other. To obtain these seasonal averages, first copy down the values from the respective quarters to somewhere below the main table where you can complete your subsidiary calculations. Go to cell B31 and put in a subheading: Calculation of seasonal factors. Now in cells B32 to E32 put in the column headings "Q1 "Q2 "Q3 and "Q4, while in cells A33 to A38 enter the row labels 1980, 1981, . . . , 1985.

You must be careful now. You cannot use the **Copy** command to bring down the numbers from column F because the program would then copy the formula and not the values. The command you need is the /**Range Value** command.

Go to cell F7 and call up the *Command* menu. Select *Range* and then *Value*. When the computer asks for a range to copy from you can just press *<Return>*. The range to copy to will be cell D33 so enter this address (or move the cursor down until this cell is highlighted) and press *<Return>* again. You should find that the value of 13.575 has been copied down. Now do the same with the rest of column F, copying the values into the appropriate places in the new table. (If you need to check what you have in different parts of the Worksheet here use the *<PgUp>* and *<PgDn>* keys.)

In cells A39 and A40 put the labels "Seasonal and "Averages and then use the 1-2-3 @AVG function to work out these averages (e.g. put @AVG(B34.B38) in cell B40 – but be careful in the use of the **Copy** command here since the third- and fourth-quarter columns are shifted up one cell compared with the first and second quarters). You should have the following results:

Seasonal	Q1	Q2	Q3	Q4
averages	17.0225	−4.6325	20.7575	−36.055

However, because the sample is really rather small – you have only four representatives of each season – these simple averages of the seasonal blocks may still contain some residual disturbances. There is a simple check. If all you have are the seasonal factors then their sum should be zero, the negative displacements cancelling out the positive ones. Go to cell F39 and type "Sum. Underneath it in cell F40 enter the formula @SUM(B40.E40). The result is unfortunately not zero but −2.9075. However, if you were to add one-quarter of this number to each of the seasonal averages they would then sum to zero. This is exactly what you must do to obtain the corrected seasonal averages.

In cell B43 you can enter the formula +B40−($F$40/4) and then copy it across for the other quarters. Check that you understand what this formula does. The corrected seasonal averages will then appear in cells B43 to E43. Put a formula into cell F43 to double-check that the sum of the 'corrected' values is zero. The symbols 4.0E-15 will be displayed, which means 4×10^{-15} (1-2-3 uses scientific notation for very small numbers like this), which, although not equal to zero, is near enough to zero to make no difference. Have a look at Table 4.4 to see the full set of calculations for the seasonal factors.

Table 4.4

```
          Calculation of seasonal factors
               Q1         Q2         Q3         Q4
       1980                        13.575    -38.375
       1981    18.125     1.612    13.600    -27.562
       1982    12.412    -7.875    22.950    -33.088
       1983    19.162    -8.538    32.500    -39.725
       1984    16.750    -0.763    21.162    -41.525
       1985    18.662    -7.600
Seasonal                                                   Sum
Averages    17.0225    -4.6325    20.7575    -36.055    -2.9075
Corrected
Seasonal
Averages  17.74937   -3.90562  21.484375  -35.32812    4.0E-15
```

4.5 The seasonally adjusted series

Having estimated the seasonal factors you can now go back and subtract them from the original (or actual) series to get the seasonally adjusted series. You need to copy the values just obtained back into the main table in the worksheet (remember to use the **Range Value** commands, or the formulae rather than the values will be copied). Put these values in appropriate positions in column G of the worksheet, which can be given the heading Seasonal Factors. You can transfer them into all 24 positions in this column since by assumption the relevant seasonal factor appears in every quarter, not just in those used for the calculation. Now subtract column G from column C putting the results in column H (put the formula +C5−G5 in cell H5 and copy down). Put in the column heading "Seasonally Adjusted Series" (spread over cells H2 to H4).

Try using the **Worksheet Column Set-width** command to widen column H. You will discover that if you increase the width of the column to 12 or more characters, the numbers displayed show six figures after the decimal place as opposed to only four when the column width takes the default value of 9. Of course it is spurious to suppose that we have achieved accuracy to this degree – the original series had been rounded to one decimal place only – so use the **Range Format Fixed** command to round the results to two decimal places only. Table 4.5 shows part of the worksheet, including the seasonally adjusted series.

Table 4.5

Quarter		Cars	Uncentred Moving Av	Centred Moving Av	Detrended Series	Seasonal Factors
1980	Q1	164.40				17.749375
	Q2	123.10				-3.905625
	Q3	137.00	126.625	123.425	13.575	21.484375
	Q4	82.00	120.225	120.375	-38.375	-35.328125
1981	Q1	138.80	120.525	120.675	18.125	17.749375
	Q2	124.30	120.825	122.688	1.612	-3.905625
	Q3	138.20	124.550	124.600	13.600	21.484375
	Q4	96.90	124.650	124.462	-27.562	-35.328125
1982	Q1	139.20	124.275	126.788	12.412	17.749375
	Q2	122.80	129.300	130.675	-7.875	-3.905625
	Q3	158.30	132.050	135.350	22.950	21.484375
	Q4	107.90	138.650	140.988	-33.088	-35.328125
1983	Q1	165.60	143.325	146.438	19.162	17.749375
	Q2	141.50	149.550	150.038	-8.538	-3.905625
	Q3	183.20	150.525	150.700	32.500	21.484375
	Q4	111.80	150.875	151.525	-39.725	-35.328125
1984	Q1	167.00	152.175	150.250	16.750	17.749375
	Q2	146.70	148.325	147.463	-0.763	-3.905625
	Q3	167.80	146.600	146.638	21.162	21.484375
	Q4	104.90	146.675	146.425	-41.525	-35.328125
1985	Q1	167.30	146.175	148.638	18.662	17.749375
	Q2	144.70	151.100	152.300	-7.600	-3.905625
	Q3	187.50	153.500			21.484375
	Q4	114.50				-35.328125

You can now construct a graph with the original series and the seasonally adjusted series plotted together. The simplest way to do this is to modify the existing graph. Do not worry about making changes to this graph. Remember you have stored it using the **/Graph Name Create** command with the name CARSMA.

Use **/Graph** to obtain the *Graph* submenu and press B to reset the second data range. Enter the new range H5.H28 and *<Return>*. Select *View* to have a look at the graph. Of course the legend for the B series will have to be changed. Use **/Graph Option Legend** to do that. You will not have room to put 'Seasonally adjusted series', but 'seas. adj. series' will fit. If you want to store this so that it can be recalled again with the worksheet do so now using **/Graph Name Create,** or if you want a printout use the **/Graph Save** command so that you can link it up with the *PrintGraph* program (Figure 4.3 shows you what to expect).

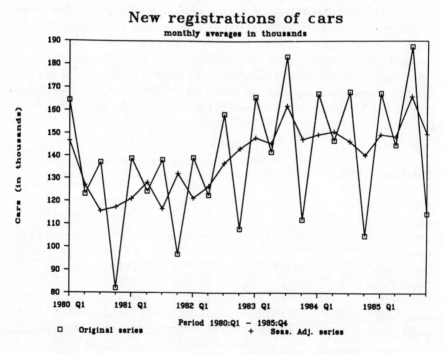

Figure 4.3 Line graph of Figure 4.1 with seasonally adjusted series

Another interesting graph to plot is one with the original series and the seasonal factors on the same graph (see Figure 4.4). The saw-tooth pattern in the original series has been picked up very clearly by the seasonal component series. Notice how 1-2-3 automatically adjusts the scale so it can fit both graphs into the frame. Try constructing this graph on your own.

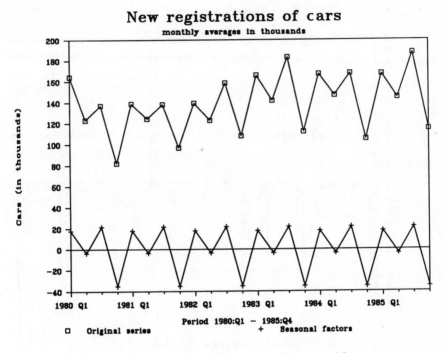

Figure 4.4 Original series of Figure 4.1 with seasonal factors

4.6 Examining the residuals

The random factor R has not yet been isolated. The detrended series is equivalent to $S + R$ so if you subtract all the S values from it the 'residuals' you will be left with should capture the random influences only. So put these residuals in column I (make I7 = + F7 − G7 and copy down). The easiest way to see if these residuals have the kind of pattern you would expect from random disturbances is to plot a graph of them. This time it is easier to start from scratch than to modify the existing graph so call up the *Graph* menu with /**Graph** and select *Reset* and then *Graph* so that you cancel all the previous graph settings. This time construct a bar graph plotting the residuals (cells I7.I26 as the A range) against the time period (cells B7.B26 will be the X range). If you add in a title and label to the axes it should resemble Figure 4.5.

The graph shows that there are some quite large residuals (there was an unexplained increase of just over 11,000 registrations per month in the third quarter of 1983, for example, and similar unexplained downward deviations of nearly 8000 cars per month in the third quarters of 1980 and 1981). It would be worth looking back at those periods to see if there were any specific

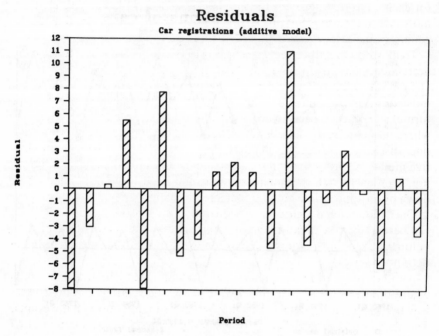

Figure 4.5 Bar graph of residuals

factors which could account for these movements. However, there is no obvious pattern to the residuals.

The deviations do not appear to be associated either with the seasons or with the trend. More formal methods do exist for analysing the randomness of a series such as this, but we shall not explore them here.

4.7 Refinements to the method

In the worked example discussed in this chapter the additive decomposition model gave a reasonably satisfactory disaggregation of the various factors and you were able to use it to seasonally adjust the original series.

However, as noted in Section 4.4, it is sometimes unacceptable to treat the factors as combining additively and you must accept a multiplicative model with the seasonal component raising or lowering the series from the trend by a set of constant proportions, according to the season. With the multiplicative model, instead of subtracting the trend from the original series to obtain the detrended series you must divide by it. The seasonal components would again be found by averaging the detrended series for each set of quarters, but this time it would be appropriate to take the geometric rather than arithmetic mean, i.e. the nth root of the product of all the available values for each quarter, where n is the number of values available. This is rather more difficult to program with 1-2-3 since there is no built-in function for the geometric mean.

To illustrate the procedure, if cells B34 to B38 are assumed to contain the detrended *ratios*, you would put the formula +(B34*B35*B36*B37*B38)^ (1/5) in cell B40. This would give a seasonal ratio for quarter 1, the value indicating how much above the trend quarter 1 figures tended to be. Similar formulae would be used to work out the other seasonal ratios. Quarters where the actual series falls below trend would have seasonal ratios less than one. Just as before, you may need to apply a correction. With the multiplicative model the product of all the seasonal factors should equal 1. If it does not, then each of the seasonal factors would need to be multiplied up or down by an appropriate amount to make this happen.

Once the seasonal factors have been found, the seasonally adjusted series can be obtained by dividing the original series by the seasonal factors. As before, the random factor is found by removing the seasonal factors from the detrended series.

Another point to notice concerns the estimation of the trend. In cases where the trend appears to follow almost a straight-line graph the easiest way to estimate it is to fit a least squares regression line through the points. The actual series is modelled as a constant plus another constant multiplied by time plus a random disturbance, say

$$A = \alpha + \beta t + u$$

where A is the actual series, t is the period number α and β are constants and u is a random error. Estimates for α and β (a and b, say) are obtained from the regression and the trend can then be found from the expression $a + bt$. The extraction of seasonal factors follows on as before or they can be built in to the regression as seasonal dummies. (See Chapter 8 for a discussion of the simple least squares regression model and the 1-2-3 regression commands; and see Chapter 9 for a discussion of the use of seasonal dummies within a multiple regression model.) When using a linear trend it is very easy to predict outside the data sample since all you need to do is to substitute a value for t corresponding to the number of periods ahead plus the original sample size into the estimated equation and then adjust the value by an appropriate seasonal factor.

The Census II method of seasonal adjustment, developed at the US Department of Commerce and now widely used by statistical agencies across the world, is a variant of the model described in this chapter. The method includes a number of refinements not described here, such as making an adjustment to some series for the number of trading days in each period, which can be important for some economic series. Because of these differences in method, officially published seasonally adjusted figures may not correspond to those obtained using the method described in this book. (See Makridakis *et al.* Chapter 4, for further details of the Census II method.)

Exercise 4

For each of Data Sets A and B, set up a Lotus 1-2-3 worksheet and construct a line graph to show the series plotted over time. Obtain the centred four-period moving average and add that series to your graph. Examine the graph and decide whether to use an additive or multiplicative model to estimate the seasonally adjusted series. Then use Lotus 1-2-3 to obtain the seasonally adjusted series and produce a graph showing the original and seasonally adjusted series together. Obtain, plot and examine the residuals from the model and comment on how well the model fits the data. Write a brief report summarising what your results show.

Data Set A UK Consumers' expenditure on energy products (£ million, 1980 prices)

1971	1	2631	1975	1	2813	1979	1	3333
	2	2150		2	2331		2	2519
	3	1984		3	2184		3	2333
	4	2537		4	2799		4	2429
1972	1	2671	1976	1	2942	1980	1	3188
	2	2288		2	2305		2	2371
	3	2229		3	2200		3	2339
	4	2730		4	2900		4	3059
1973	1	2818	1977	1	2936	1981	1	3118
	2	2439		2	2429		2	2484
	3	2317		3	2315		3	2291
	4	2818		4	2853		4	3099
1974	1	2718	1978	1	3044	1982	1	3120
	2	2360		2	2478		2	2488
	3	2341		3	2327		3	2377
	4	2934		4	2910		4	3074

Source: Economic Trends Annual Supplement, 1984, p.281

Data Set B United States money supply (M1) ($ billion)

1982	1	440.9	1985	1	565.0
	2	450.8		2	592.3
	3	461.5		3	609.3
	4	491.9		4	641.0
1983	1	489.2	1986	1	631.3
	2	509.8		2	669.8
	3	516.3		3	691.2
	4	537.9		4	746.5
1984	1	530.4	1987	1	728.9
	2	547.9		2	749.1
	3	548.4		3	749.4
	4	570.5		4	769.1

Source: OECD Main Economic Indicators; various issues

Reference

S. Makridakis, S. C. Wheelwright and V. E. McGee, *Forecasting Methods and Applications* (Wiley, New York, 1983).

Chapter 5

Analysing cross-section data using Lotus 1-2-3

Purpose: To demonstrate how Lotus 1-2-3 can be applied to the quantitative analysis of cross-section data.

Preview: As well as being capable of analysing time-series data the economist must be able to analyse *cross-section* data, that is data recorded over a number of households, firms (or some other reference set) within a particular period or at a single point in time. Such a set of data might have been collected by the economist, by means of a survey, or it might be available from a published source.

This chapter looks at how 1-2-3 can assist the researcher's analysis of such a data set in an effort to extract meaning from it, by computing *summary statistics*, by grouping the data to form a *frequency distribution* and by graphing the distribution to produce such diagrams as *histograms* and *ogives*.

Secton 5.1 concentrates on the analysis of the raw data, using 1-2-3's built-in statistical functions to compute summary measures of average and spread. Section 5.2 shows how the /**Data Distribution** command can be used to group the data into a frequency distribution. Section 5.3 begins with a set of grouped data and uses 1-2-3 to calculate summary statistics. In Section 5.5 the *cumulative frequency distribution* is obtained for the data and 1-2-3 graphics are used to construct an ogive. The spreadsheet formulation is particularly useful where a published frequency table leaves classes open-ended, without giving any explicit indication of appropriate group limits (or mid-points).

Without this information the choice of such values (which can make quite a difference to the calculated mean and standard deviation) has to be a matter of judgement. The flexibility of 1-2-3, with its ability to recalculate instantaneously on the basis of new cell values, allows a researcher to arrive at suitable values by seeing the effects of resetting them.

It is assumed that readers will have a basic knowledge of descriptive statistics so that a full discussion of the measures and diagrams need not be given. This will allow more time to be spent on describing how 1-2-3 can help with the analysis. Readers who do not have a basic knowledge of statistics are advised to consult any standard text on introductory statistics (e.g. Hoel and Jessen, 1982).

1-2-3 features introduced in this chapter: Built-in statistical functions @MIN, @MAX, @COUNT, @STD and @VAR; naming ranges; /**Move** and /**Worksheet Insert** commands; /**Data Sort** and /**Data Distribution** commands; bin ranges; absolute cell references for copying formulae; X–Y graphs.

5.1 Summary statistics for a set of data

Table 5.1 gives figures, derived from the Monopolies and Mergers Commission (MMC) Report on the National Coal Board (now British Coal), on the coal output (in thousands of tonnes) of pits in South Wales and in Nottinghamshire for the financial year 1981–82.

Table 5.1 Coal output (thousand tonnes) from National Coal Board pits in South Wales and Nottinghamshire, 1981–82

South Wales

62	149	116	142	589	76	140	164	263	266
110	74	63	173	448	124	189	132	504	422
165	189	355	261	450	134	237	229	280	245
198	208	255							

Nottinghamshire

527	883	881	615	787	693	773	1048	623	760
831	789	1156	1129	634	438	762	1640	439	821
873	970	501	769	1205					

At a glance it can be seen that there was a fair amount of variation in coal output across the pits in both areas, and that the Nottinghamshire output figures were in general greater than those for South Wales. To see more clearly the extent of the variation in output and the differences on average between areas, one would wish to compute basic summary statistics for each set of data. One might also find it revealing to construct a *frequency table* for each area showing the number of pits with an output between various specified limits. The table could be illustrated visually as a histogram.

Some of 1-2-3's functions and features can be of assistance here, so begin a new worksheet and put the title in cell A1: PITS: Coal output from British pits, 1981/2.

In cell A2 put: '[in thousands of tonnes]

In cell A3 put: Source: Monopolies and Mergers Commission Report on the NCB, 1983.

Draw a dotted line across the worksheet from cell A4 to G4.

Now enter the data for the South Wales pits. Rather than spreading it over a number of columns as in Table 5.1, place it in a single column. This may seem rather wasteful, but there are advantages of arranging the figures this way, as will soon be apparent. Put labels at the top of the columns as follows:

Cell	Label
A6	South Wales Pits
A8	"Pit
B8	"Output

Go to cell A9 and use the **/Data Fill** command to enter numbers into the cell range A9.A41, beginning with 1, with a step of 1 and ending at 33. These numbers will be used to identify the pits. (You could put the names of the pits into the worksheet since they are available in the MMC Report. However, we will not concern ourselves with which pit produced any particular output, only with the variation in the figures.)

Now in cells B9.B41 enter the South Wales output figures, beginning with the first row of figures in Table 5.1, then going on to the second, etc. When this has been done, draw another dotted line across the worksheet in row 43.

Now enter labels as follows:

Cell	Label
A45	Nottinghamshire Pits
A47	"Pit
B47	"Output

Use the **/Data Fill** command again to produce a column of numbers from 1 to 25 in cells A48.A72, and enter the output values in cells B48.B72.

You are now in a position to go on to compute some basic summary statistics. Enter labels as follows:

Cell	Label
E6	Summary statistics
E8	Minimum
E9	Maximum
E10	Mean
E11	Median
E12	Std. Dev.
E13	N

Before proceeding any further, copy the entire block E6.F14 to E45.E53, to save time. Now in Cell F8 enter the 1-2-3 built-in function @MIN(B9.B41). The number 62 should appear. In fact, the first value in the upper part of Table 5.1 is the smallest one. In cell F9 enter @MAX(B9.B41). The number

589 will appear. Now to find the mean value in cell F10 all you need is @AVG(B9.B41). The computer will give you the value 224.6060. The mean (arithmetic mean to give it its full name) is equivalent to the average as defined as the sum of all the values divided by the number of values.

Miss out the median and cell F11 for the moment and go to cell F12. Here we want the *standard deviation* of the output values. This is a measure of the spread or dispersion of the values around the mean value. In fact it is the square root of the variance which is to go in the cell below. The variance takes the deviations of the values from the mean, squares them (which gets rid of the negative signs) and averages these squared deviations by summing them and dividing by the number of observations. In conventional notation, for a series X of N observations,

mean $\bar{X} = \Sigma \, X / N$ variance $= \Sigma \, (X - \bar{X})^2 / N$;
and standard deviation $= \sqrt{(\text{variance})}$

where Σ means 'the sum of'.

These statistics could obviously be found the long way within a worksheet, setting up a column of deviations, a column of squared deviations, summing them, etc., but there is no need. Lotus 1-2-3 has built-in functions to compute these statistics. All you need to do is to specify the range. So in cell F12 put @STD(B9.B41) and in cell F13 put @VAR(B9.B41).

The contents of cell F14, as we know, should be 33. But try another of 1-2-3's statistical functions. It could be useful in a situation where it is not immediately obvious how many values there are in a range. Enter @COUNT(B9.B41) and see the value 33 displayed.

Next obtain equivalent results for the Nottinghamshire pits. This time specify the range in the formulae in a different, but extremely convenient way, making use of the /**Range Name** command. In Lotus 1-2-3 any cell or range of cells can be identified by a *name* and this name can be used in any subsequent formula or operation where the range must be given. It also makes for more readable worksheets since you can see from a formula which range of values is being used in a more literal sense.

First name the range B48.B72 NOTTS by typing

/*Range Name Create* NOTTS ˉB48.B72ˉ

Now type in formulae as follows:

Cell	Formula
F47	@MIN(NOTTS)
F48	@MAX(NOTTS)
F49	@AVG(NOTTS)
F51	@STD(NOTTS)
F52	@VAR(NOTTS)
F53	@COUNT(NOTTS)

The results for the Nottinghamshire pits will then be displayed. If you wish you can change the way that the range is defined for the South Wales pits. Use /**Range Name Create** and call the range B9.B41 by the name SWALES. Notice that the formulae already defined for this range are now automatically respecified to refer to this name.

Turning to the results, as was suspected the average level of output is much greater in Nottinghamshire pits, being between three and four times the South Wales figure. There is also evidence of more variability. The range (used here in the statistical sense of maximum value − minimum value) is over 1000 for the Nottingham pits where there was one pit with an output of 438 thousand tonnes, while at the other extreme there was a pit with an output of 1640. By contrast, in South Wales the largest and smallest output levels were only just over 500 thousand tonnes apart, being 589 and 62 respectively. However, as a percentage of the highest value this is nearly 90% as compared with an equivalent of only about 70% for the Nottingham area.

Unlike the range, which looks only at extreme values, the standard deviation takes account of the positions of all the individual values in relation to the mean in arriving at a single measure of the spread. The Nottingham figure of 264 (to the nearest thousand tonnes) is roughly twice that for the South Wales area. However, where the means differ so markedly, as in this case, one might prefer the *coefficient of variation* as a measure of spread. This is defined as (standard deviation/mean)*100% and is thus unit-free. You can compute these figures here and place them underneath the variance figures in the summary tables. This means moving the number of observations (N) down a cell.

Go to cell E14 and select /*Move* from the main menu. Enter the range to move from as E14.F14 (either by typing in the characters or by pointing to the cells using the expanded cursor). Enter the range to move to as E15.F15 and <*Return*>. The pair of cells moves down a row to accommodate the new input. Type the label "Coef Var in cell E14 and in cell F14 enter the formula +100*F12/F10.

Make the same adjustments and alterations to the table giving the results for the Nottinghamshire area and you will see that, taking account of the much greater average size of pits in this area, this measure of spread shows the dispersion to be relatively greater in South Wales.

Now consider the calculation of the *median*. The median is a different kind of measure of average to the mean. Rather than asking what a pit's output would be if the total output for the area was redistributed on an equal basis (which is effectively what the mean does) it asks what the output is for the pit in the middle of the distribution. In other words, if the 33 pits in the South Wales area were ranked in order of their level of output, what would be the output of the 17th pit on this list? This value can be found using 1-2-3's /**Data Sort** command. When asked for the /**Data-Range** give SWALES. Give the same range for the *Primary key* and select *A* (ascending) as the *Sort order*. Then select *Go*. The outputs for the South Wales pits will be reordered – ranked in ascending order. The pit number has not changed so that the 17th pit in the new order can easily be recognised. Enter +B25 in cell F11 to copy across the output of 189 as the median output value. Doing the same for the Nottingham pits should give a value of 787 (here the median comes from cell B60, the 13th in order when the outputs are ranked).

The differences between the mean and median values gives some idea of how skewed is the distribution. In fact, various measures of skewness can be computed including one which is defined as 3*(mean-median)/st. dev. Distributions where the mean exceeds the median are said to show positive skewness (this is typical of most distributions of income and wealth where a small number of very high values drag up the mean to a value greater than that of the median). There is a small amount of positive skewness in the output of the pits.

5.2 Constructing a frequency table

Another way of seeing more clearly the pattern of a distribution is through the construction of a frequency table showing the number of values falling between specified limits. Without a package like 1-2-3, counting up these values from a block of raw data can be quite a laborious process. However, 1-2-3 enables you to do this automatically using the /**Data Distribution** command. You must first choose the class limits (in 1-2-3 only the upper limits are specified and the range of the worksheet where these figures are held is called the *bin* range) and then identify the range holding the values to be counted into groups (the *values* range). Then 1-2-3 automatically works out the associated frequencies and puts them in the column immediately to the right of the bin range.

Before you begin you should have a good idea of the number of classes you require and how wide each class is to be. Obviously the bin range should start below the minimum value and end at the maximum value (or above), going up in steps to give enough classes to separate different parts of the distribution but not too many so that you get no clearer outline than can be obtained from the raw data. With 33 observations spread between 62 and 589, about six groups should be distinguished. The groups could be 0–100, 100–200, etc., up to 500–600. Lotus 1-2-3 puts any value equal to a class upper limit into that class, so you may prefer to work with upper limits of 99, 199, etc.

Classes do not have to have identical widths. Indeed there may often be very good reasons for taking differing class widths where it is apparent that the *frequency density* varies over the distribution. However, 1-2-3's graphics capabilities are not able to make allowance for differing bar widths in the construction of histograms using the bar chart commands (see below).

Go to cell H6 and type 'Frequency Distribution. Enter column labels as follows:

Cell	Label
H8	"Classes
H9	'(Upper limits)
I8	"Frequencies

(You will need to reset the width of these columns to 14 so that they are big enough to accommodate all the characters.)

Now enter the following numbers in cells H11 to H17 to define the bin range: 0,99,199,299,399,499 and 599.

Call up /*Data Distribution* and give the values range as SWALES (or B9.B41).

When you enter the bin range (H11.H17) the frequencies will be immediately produced. You will discover that 14 of the pits have outputs between 100 and 199, and another 9 between 200 and 299. A zero is shown at the end to indicate that there are no values above 599.

Repeat the procedure for the Nottingham pits, starting in cell H45 with the headings. This time, however, you will have to choose larger class sizes to go up to 1699. Since there is no pit with an output below 399 you could have the limits as 0,399,599,799, etc., up to 1599, but ending with 1699. This classification draws attention to the fact that there is one pit whose output is considerably above even the other quite large values (in fact it is the pit at Thoresby).

You can use 1-2-3's graphics facilities to produce a bar chart to illustrate this table. Unfortunately, it is not possible to construct a proper histogram for two reasons. Firstly, in a genuine histogram the bars showing the frequencies are right up next to each other so that the upper limit of one group and the lower limit of the next group are at the same point on the X-axis. This cannot be achieved using 1-2-3. More seriously, where the class widths differ one would wish to show this in a histogram with bars of differing widths. (The heights of the bars would be adjusted accordingly so as to maintain the relationship between bar area and frequency density.) Since this is also impossible with 1-2-3, we can refer to the graphs produced below as 'pseudo' histograms. To provide more detailed labelling for the South Wales bar chart go to cell J12 and type "<100. Then enter further labels as follows:

Cell	Label
J13	"100–199
J14	"200–299
J15	"300–399
J16	"400–499
J17	"500–599

Now call up the *Graph* menu and construct a bar chart giving cells I12.I17 as the A range and J12.J17 as the X range. With a title added, the diagram should look something like Figure 5.1 (this diagram was actually produced using Quattro, but 1-2-3's graph would be very similar).

Distribution of coal output
South Wales Pits 1981/2

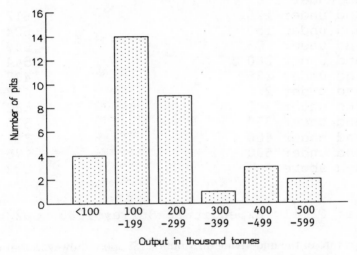

Figure 5.1 Bar chart of South Wales frequency distribution

This shows very clearly that the distribution is bimodal, with a separate cluster of large pits starting with outputs of around 400.

You can produce a similar chart for the Nottinghamshire pits. You will need to be careful in your interpretation of this diagram because the final bar will display the frequency for a class with a smaller width than the others. Unfortunately, as noted earlier, there is no mechanism within 1-2-3 for displaying bars of differing widths.

5.3 Summary statistics for grouped data

In this section we start with a ready-made frequency distribution. Our example comes from the Family Expenditure Survey (1985) and shows the number of households (in a sample of 7012) with normal weekly disposable incomes in specified income classes (see Table 5.2).

The actual incomes of the individual households are not published for reasons of confidentiality, but a classification such as Table 5.2 can give quite

Table 5.2 Normal weekly household income in the UK, 1985

Normal weekly disposable income (£)	Number of households
Under 40	373
40 and under 50	374
50 and under 65	444
65 and under 80	474
80 and under 100	539
100 and under 125	612
125 and under 150	624
150 and under 175	649
175 and under 200	544
200 and under 225	487
225 and under 250	417
250 and under 300	582
300 and under 350	375
350 and under 400	211
400 and under 500	175
500 and above	132

Source: Family Expenditure Survey 1985, pp22-23

a good picture of the underlying distribution. Suppose, however, that one wished to obtain summary statistics on the mean and standard deviation for the purposes of making a comparison with figures for another year. How could one produce the equivalent of the sum of all the households' income, since the individual incomes are not known? What you can do, of course, is to use the mid-point of each class as representative of the values in that class. Total income in a class can then be approximated by the class mid-point multiplied by the number of households in that class. These can then be added up and the result divided by the total number of households (which is the same as the sum of the frequencies). A similar approach can be used when calculating the standard deviation. However, this begs the question as to what values should be used as mid-points for open-ended classes at the top and bottom of the distribution (or what amounts to the same thing, what upper and lower class limits should be assumed). What is required is a figure which is representative of the group.

In the absence of any specific information you must use your judgement, based on your general knowledge of the distribution and on the figures that you have. For example, at the top of the distribution the frequency density shows a reducing pattern going from 7.5 for the £300–£350 class, to 4.22 for the £350–£400 class, to 1.75 for the £400–£500 class (figures calculated by

Table 5.3 Data from Table 5.2 entered into a worksheet

```
                   A          B          C          D          E         F
1 FES :     Distribution of normal weekly disposable income for
2                 households in the UK, 1985
3
4 Normal weekly income              Number of
5            (in £)                 households
6
7               Under  40              373
8       40 and under  50              374
9       50 and under  65              444
10      65 and under  80              474
11      80 and under 100              539
12     100 and under 125              612
13     125 and under 150              624
14     150 and under 175              649
15     175 and under 200              544
16     200 and under 225              487
17     225 and under 250              417
18     250 and under 300              582
19     300 and under 350              375
20     350 and under 400              211
21     400 and under 500              175
22             500 and above          132
23
24
25 Source :  Family Expenditure Survey 1985, Table 7 pp 22-23.
```

taking frequency/(upper limit − lower limit). To maintain this pattern of roughly halving group by group, the upper limit must be well over 600 (which gives a frequency density of 1.32) and near to, say, 650. This would imply a mid-point of 575 for the class.

With the spreadsheet approach to statistical computation, if this number appears to give a distorted picture when the ogive is plotted you can revise it up or down until the ogive slope declines smoothly.

Enter the information from Table 5.2 into a new worksheet as shown in Table 5.3

Notice that column A has been widened to 21 characters to accommodate the class name. Column B is blank at present, but it is to contain the class mid-points, which will be denoted by the letter x in all formulae. Go to cell B6 and enter the label "x. Then enter values as follows:

Cell	Value
B7	30
B8	45
B9	57.5
B10	72.5
B11	90
B12	112.5
B13	137.5
B14	162.5
B15	187.5
B16	212.5

B17	237.5
B18	275
B19	325
B20	375
B21	450
B22	575

Only the first and last of these numbers are in any way controversial and they can be changed if subsequently they appear to be out of line. The number 30 in cell B7 implies an assumed minimum income of £20 per week. Put the label "f in cell C6 since this column holds the frequencies (which will be denoted by the letter f in the formulae).

To compute the mean and standard deviation for grouped data the following formulae are used

$$\text{Mean} = \bar{x} = \Sigma fx / \Sigma f$$
$$\text{Standard deviation} = s = \sqrt{(\Sigma fx^2 / \Sigma f) - \bar{x}^2}$$

(This formula for the standard deviation can be derived from the more basic definitional one.)

We therefore need columns of data for fx and for fx^2 so that they can be summed up. In cells D6 and E6 place the lables "fx and "fx*x. (Superscripts cannot be used in 1-2-3. In any case this way of writing the symbols emphasises that we require f times (x squared) and not (fx) all squared.)

Put the formula +C7*B7 in cell D7 and copy down into D8.D22. Then put +D7*B7 in cell E7 and copy into E8.E22. Now go to cell D23 and enter the formula @SUM(F7.D22). Copy this into cells E23 and B23, adding the label "Totals in cell A23. The real advantages of the spreadsheet (as compared to using just a calculator) can now be identified. The routine only has to be checked at the stage of entering the base formulae. These can then be copied down and will be automatically replicated, leaving no chance of any further errors creeping in. This contrasts with the calculator approach where each product fx (and fx^2) must be entered separately, giving many more chances of making an error by pressing a wrong key.

Notice that some of the results are so large that they cannot be shown in the worksheet as currently formatted. Use the /**Worksheet Column Set-Width** and /**Range Format Fixed** commands to show these columns with 15 characters and 2 figures after the decimal point.

Finally compute the mean and standard deviation. Enter labels as follows:

Cell	Label
A28	Summary statistics
A30	"Mean
A31	"Standard deviation

and then the formulae:

Cell   Formula
B30   +D23/C23
B31   @SQRT((E23/C23)−(B30*B30))

5.4 Cumulative frequencies and the ogive

As yet we have not described how to calculate the median income for the Family Expenditure Survey distribution. Although we do not have the original 'raw' incomes of the households, it is possible to develop a formula which will give the income which divides the distribution into two equal parts, i.e. with 50% of the households with incomes below this level. Indeed it is easy enough to produce a formula to divide the distribution at any chosen percentage point. First it is necessary to work out the *cumulative frequency distribution*. This distribution can be plotted against income in the *ogive* diagram.

It is convenient to place the cumulative frequencies in the column next to the frequencies, so move columns D and E three columns to the right (you will have to reset the widths of the new G and H columns). Now in cell D6 enter the label "cf (short for cumulative frequency). Cell D7 will just have the formula +C7. But cell D8 has the formula +D6+C8. The result (it should be 747) shows the number of households with incomes less than or equal to £50 per week. The column shows the cumulative frequencies, i.e. the number of households with incomes in a particular class or in one below it. So cell D9 will have the formula +D8+C9. The frequency of the class in question is added to the cumulative frequency of the class below. Copy down as far as cell D22 (which should show the total frequency of 7012). The cells in this column now show the number of households with incomes below the upper class limit of the respective classes.

In the next column you will show the percentage cumulative frequency figures, i.e. the cumulative frequency divided by the total frequency expressed as a percentage (the ratio is multiplied by 100). For example, cell E7 would have the formula +100*D7/C23. However, if you were to attempt to copy this formula down the column you would not obtain the values required since the denominator has to be the same for each figure ratio. In Lotus 1-2-3 there is a way of fixing a cell address in a formula (making it *absolute* rather than *relative*), that is, preventing it from being adjusted as the formula is copied down the column. The way to achieve this is to attach dollar ($) signs to the components of the cell address which is to stay fixed. Thus the formula for E7 would be +100*D7/$C$23. This can then be copied into the range E8.E22. Look down the spreadsheet and see how the top of the formula adjusts relative to the cell position but the bottom is fixed at C23.

Put the label "%cf in cell E6 and change the column format to display only two figures after the decimal place. Looking at the figures in this column it can be seen that the median must be very close to £150 per week. This is because 49.06% of the households have weekly incomes less than £150. To obtain an accurate estimate of the median you should use the following formula:

$$\text{Median} = L_M + W_M[(\tfrac{1}{2}\Sigma f - cf_{-1})/f_M]$$

where L_M denotes the lower limit of the median class (here 150); W_M denotes the width of the median class (here 25); $\tfrac{1}{2}\Sigma f$ is half the total frequency (here 7012/2 = 3506); f_M denotes the frequency of the median class (here 4089); and cf_{-1} denotes the cumulative frequency of the class below the median class (here 3440).

The formula tells you what proportion of the median class width needs to be added to the lower limit of the median class width to get to the 50% cumulative frequency point.

If you put the formula +150+25*((7012/2)−3440)/4089) in cell B32 you will obtain a value for the median of £150.40 per week (to the nearest penny).

Now you can plot the ogive. This graph shows the percentage cumulative frequency plotted against the upper class (income) limits. The graph should begin at the origin so go to cell E7 and insert a row (*Worksheet Insert Row* ⁻). An extra row will appear and you should enter the value 0 in cells D7 and E7.

Column F will hold the upper limits of the classes so enter them now as follows:

Cell	Value
F7	20
F8	40
F9	50

etc., all the way down to F23 which has the value 650 (as suggested in Section 5.3).

The ogive is plotted as an X–Y graph with the X range F7.F23 and the A range as E7.E23. With appropriate titles added it should look something like Figure 5.2.

The X–Y graph rather than line graph must be used here because the values plotted on the X-axis are not equally spaced.

The diagram can be used to gauge what percentage of households receive an income at or below a particular percentage figure. Alternatively it can be used to discover what income has a given percentage of households above or below it.

The diagram confirms our choice of mid-points for the open-ended classes. If these had been over- or underestimated we would observe an abrupt change in the slope of the ogive between these and neighbouring classes. If

Cumulative frequency ogive
[FES 1985]

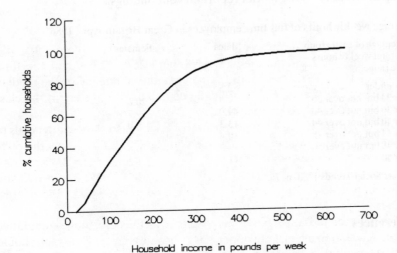

Figure 5.2 Cumulative frequency distribution of household income

this did happen you would need to go back to the worksheet and change the mid-points and class limits.

Exercise 5

(a) The table below gives data on the output of pits in two other NCB areas. Use Lotus 1-2-3 to analyse the figures along the lines described in Sections 5.1 and 5.2. Compare your results with those given for South Wales and Nottinghamshire.

Coal output from NCB pits (in thousand tonnes) 1981–82

Western

451	227	441	854	1240	158	366	1076	515	472
278	379	958	523	1016	457	311	471	355	173
212									

North East

597	140	168	525	1412	254	546	161	890	377
76	1219	1105	264	337	213	231	1291	1061	1763
289	376								

Source: Monopolies and Mergers Commission
Report on the National Coal Board 1983

(b) Construct a Lotus 1-2-3 worksheet with the following data and calculate the mean and standard deviation hours for males and females (choosing suitable mid-points for the open-ended classes). Add columns giving the cumulative percentage frequencies and construct ogive curves for each group of workers. Write a brief report on your findings.

Average weekly hours of full-time employees in Great Britain April 1986

Percentage of each group with total weekly hours in the range:	Males	Females
34 or under	2.5	9.6
Over 34 but not over 36	9.3	20.6
Over 36 but not over 40	49.0	59.7
Over 40 but not over 44	13.3	6.0
Over 44 but not over 48	10.4	2.3
Over 48 but not over 50	3.7	0.6
Over 50	11.9	1.2

Source: Social Trends 1988, p. 75

References

P. G. Hoel and R. J. Jessen, *Basic Statistics for Business and Economics* (Third Edition) (Wiley, New York, 1982).

Monopolies and Mergers Commission, Report on the efficiency and costs in the development, production and supply of coal by the National Coal Board, Volumes I and II [Cmnd 8920] (HMSO, 1983).

Chapter 6

Interest rate and present-value calculations using Lotus 1-2-3

Purpose: To show how Lotus 1-2-3 can be applied to problems of quantitative analysis related to investment and other financial decisions.

Preview: Lotus 1-2-3 and similar packages are often described as *decision-support tools*. Sections 6.2 and 6.3 look at an investment decision-making problem where 1-2-3 can support the decision maker not only in providing the framework for an initial set of calculations, but also by facilitating a quick and easy reassessment of the decision as the background conditions change. A key variable affecting the investment decision is the rate of interest, and 1-2-3 can be a valuable tool for many other problems of financial analysis where the interest rate is crucial. Section 6.1 describes one such problem and introduces the notion of *goal-seeking* which is characteristic of many spreadsheet applications.

1-2-3 features introduced in this chapter: The @IF function and the recalculation (F9) key; setting key parameters in a worksheet; @NPV, @IRR and other financial functions.

6.1 Depositing money in an interest-earning account

Suppose that a sum of money (say £100) is deposited in an interest-earning account paying interest at 10% per annum (10% = 10/100 or 0.1) What sum will have accumulated after one year? The answer is £110. This is £100 + 10% £100, i.e. the principal plus (the principal times the rate of interest). This is the same as the principal times (one plus the rate of interest) if we factorise:

$$100 + 0.1*(100) = 100*(1+0.1)$$

If this sum is left in the account for a further year it is as if £110 had been deposited for that year, so at the end of the second year the account will stand at £110*(1+0.1) = £121. Breaking it down this is

$$100*(1+0.1)*(1+0.1) = 100*(1+0.1)^2$$

In general, if a deposit (or principal) is denoted by the letter P, the interest rate is given by r and the number of years by n, the formula for the accumulated future value after n years is

$$F = P*(1+r)^n \qquad (6.1)$$

We can use the spreadsheet as a framework to produce the value of the accumulated sum, given inputs on the principal, the interest rate and the number of years.

The problem can also be inverted if the user is seeking to find a deposit required to produce a target future sum after a specified number of years, or even the number of years needed for a deposit of a given size to grow to a target sum at the prevailing interest rate.

There are several ways of approaching this kind of problem within a spreadsheet, some based on generating a table of values set up using a recursive formula, and others using equation (6.1) directly. We will explore each of these in turn.

Begin a new worksheet and place the following title in cell A1: 'DEPOST1. Then enter the following labels:

Cell	Label
B3	'Initial deposit
B4	'Interest rate
B7	'Period
D7	'Accumulated sum

Now use /**Data Fill** to enter numbers 0 to 20 in cells B8.B28. In cell D8 put +D3 and in cell D9 put +D8*(1+$D$4). Then copy this formula down to cells D10.D28 (Cell D4 will contain the interest rate, which is assumed unchanged over the period – hence the use of the absolute cell address in the formula.)

At the moment all you will have is a column of zeros because the cells that have been set aside to hold the deposit and the interest rate are currently empty. Go to cell D3 and enter the value 100. The cells D8 to D28 all change to this value; with a zero interest rate the account remains at 100 however long the deposit is left in the account.

Now change cell D4 to 0.1 (which means 10%). The spreadsheet responds to give a growing series of values indicating the accumulated sum after each specified number of years up to 20. You can see that after 20 years the initial deposit has grown by between six and seven times in value. Since you could only draw out a whole number of pence, change the format of column D to display only two decimal places.

Now you can use this worksheet to discover the accumulated value of an initial deposit at a specified interest rate after any number of periods. Change the values in cells D3 and D4 a few times to see what happens. Put 200 in cell D3. Obviously if the deposit is doubled all the future values will double. But if the interest rate is doubled, the future values will grow astronomically. This is because the interest is paid on the previously accumulated sum, i.e. it is compound interest.

This table is all very well, but it would take up a lot of space if the number of periods you wish to consider was to go much above 20. We will turn now to a more compact way of approaching the problem. Save the current worksheet if you wish to keep it and then modify the screen display as follows: edit cell A1 (use the F2 key) to read DEPOSIT2. Use the /**Range Erase** command to erase the table in cells B7.D28.

Now enter the following:

Cell	Entry
B5	"Number of years
B7	"Accumulated sum
D7	+D3*(1+D4)^D5

(this last entry is the equivalent of equation (6.1))

To make the formula easier to interpret use the /**Range Name Create** command to give names as follows:

Cell	Name
D3	DEPOSIT
D4	INTRATE
D5	N

Look in cell D7 and the formula will now appears as

+DEPOSIT*(1+INTRATE)^N

Go to cell D5 and enter a figure for the number of years, say 12. The accumulated value after 12 years is immediately shown in cell D7 (reformat this cell to show only two figures after the decimal place). If you wish, save the worksheet for future reference.

Whereas DEPOSIT1 works recursively, calculating each accumulated sum in terms of the previous year's figure (e.g. cell D9), DEPOSIT2 goes straight to the required year using the formula in cell D7 and shows only this one year's value. In DEPOSIT3 we will make a small adjustment to combine the compactness of DEPOSIT2 with the possibility of seeing the gradual growth as exhibited in DEPOSIT1.

Change the title in cell A1 to DEPOSIT3 and, for the moment, reset the figure in cell D3 to zero. Go to cell D5 and enter the formula: @IF(D3= 0,0,D5+1). (Notice that 1-2-3 will change this to @IF(DEPOSIT=0,0,N+1) if the range names have been set.)

This formula makes use of one of 1-2-3's *logical functions*. The values displayed in cell D5 will be zero (the middle value in the @IF function) if the contents of cell D3 is zero (which it should be at the moment). Otherwise it will add 1 to the value previously displayed.

Go to cell D3 and enter the value 100. The number of years will change to 1 and the accumulated sum will be shown as 110 (provided you still have $r = 0.1$). To change the number of years one step at a time you can use the recalculation key F9. Press it now. The number of years steps up to 2 and the accumulated sum goes to 121. Press F9 again and the values are recalculated once more.

Now try out a small *goal-seeking* exercise. Consider the problem of discovering how many periods it must take for the accumulated value to double. Continue pressing the F9 key until the value in cell D7 passes 200. It should take 8 years.

6.2 Present value and investment decisions

The concept of *present value* is central to the economist's view of investment decision making because it enables an agent to evaluate a series of payments or receipts at different points in time on a common basis. A sum of £500 available in a year's time would not have the same value to an investor as £500 now (quite apart from any problems of inflation). If the rate of interest is non-zero the investor could deposit a sum less than £500 in an interest-earning account which would grow to £500 by the end of the year. For example, the sum of £454.55 ($=500/(1+0.1)$) would need to be deposited if the rate of interest was 10%. The investor would thus perceive the *present value* of the £500 one year from now as £454.55. In general, the present value of a future sum, F, due n years from now at interest rate r, is

$$P = F/(1 + r)^n \qquad (6.2)$$

This is just equation (6.1) cross-multiplied so that it is solved for P rather than F.

When an investor is faced with a series of receipts and payments (costs and benefits) from a variety of investment opportunities, the net present value (NPV) of each project should be evaluated as the sum of the present values of each of the present and future receipts (payments will be regarded as negative receipts). The projects can then be ranked in terms of the NPV and an investment decision can be taken on the basis of these values. Notice that all present values will depend on the rate of interest assumed. Whenever this changes, so will the present values and the ranking of projects could be affected.

Consider the following simple problem (which we shall also use to show how the spreadsheet can be used to support the investment decision maker). An investor may choose between two alternative (mutually exclusive) investment projects A and B.

Table 6.1 Costs and benefits for two alternative investment projects

		Project	
		A	B
Initial cost (in £)		1000	600
Receipts (in £) due at the end of year	1	500	400
	2	700	800
	3	500	0

Project A requires an initial investment of £1000 and is expected to provide a series of payments at the end of each of the next three years, as shown in Table 6.1. Project B costs only £600, but will pay back sums of £400 at the end of one year and £800 at the end of two years. Which of the alternatives should the investor choose if the rate of interest is 6%?

It is not enough simply to add up the receipts and subtract the cost for each project, selecting the one with the largest benefits net of cost. This would be ignoring the point just established that £500 in a year's time is not worth £500 now. (Nor for that matter is £500 in three years' time.) A proper comparison of the project should be based on their net present values calculated as follows:

$$NPV(A) = -1000 + 500/(1+r) + 700/(1+r)^2 + 500/(1+r)^3 \qquad (6.3)$$
$$NPV(B) = -600 + 400/(1+r) + 800/(1+r)^2 \qquad (6.4)$$

These calculations can be evaluated for any specified rate of interest and the decision to invest would be based on choosing the project with the greater (positive) NPV at the specified interest rate. (If neither NPV is positive then neither project would be considered at that interest rate.) This problem can obviously be set up within a spreadsheet so that the cell containing the interest rate can be changed in order to see how sensitive the decision will be to its actual value.

Begin a new worksheet and in cell A1 type in the title

'NPV: worksheet on investment appraisal

Then enter the following labels:

Cell	Label
B4	'Assumed interest rate is
B5	'Implied discount factor
B8	'Undiscounted net benefits
B9	"Project A

D9	"Project B
A10	"Year
A11	0
A12	1
A13	2
A14	3

Enter the formula +1/(1+D4) in cell D5. Enter the values as follows:

Cell	Value
D4	0.06
B11	−1000
B12	500
B13	700
B14	500
D11	−600
D12	400
D13	800
D14	0

(the costs are entered as negative benefits).

This has put the information into the worksheet. Now extend the worksheet to compute NPVs as follows:

Cell	Label/Formula
B16	'Discounted net benefits
A18	0
A19	1
A20	2
A21	3
B18	+B11
B19	+B12*$D$5
B20	+B13*($D$5^2)
B21	+B14*($D$5^3)
D18	+D11
D19	+D12*$D$5
D20	+D13*($D$5^2)
D21	+D14*($D$5^3)
A23	'NPV
B23	@SUM(B18.B21)
D23	@SUM(D18.D21)

The figures on the lower half of the table show the discounted net benefits evaluated at the current interest rate of 6%. The discount factor is simply $1/(1+r)$, and multiplying by this factor is equivalent to dividing by $(1+r)$. The figures are often referred to as discounted cash flows, since when the future cash flows are multiplied in this way they are reduced or discounted by this proportion. The formulae in cells B23 an D23 correspond to equations (6.3) and (6.4), giving the respective NPVs of the projects (in £). With an interest rate of .06 in cell D4 they should work out as 514.51 and 489.36.

On the basis of these results, project A would be selected since, at the 6% interest rate, its (discounted) benefits exceed its costs by the greater amount. However, this decision would not be appropriate at all interest rates. Go to cell D4 and change the value to 0.1 (i.e. 10%). The discount factor becomes smaller and consequently so do the discounted cash flows. The NPVs for both projects fall. However, project B is less affected by the change than project A because it has no benefits in year 3, where the discount factor has its greatest impact. Consequently it should come as no great surprise that the NPV(B) is now greater than the NPV(A). At the rate of interest of 10% project B is preferred on NPV grounds.

6.3 Plotting the graph of net present value against the interest rate

The worksheet as it stands gives a convenient framework for the investment analyst to judge the effects of changing the assumptions about the interest rate. (Indeed, the way the problem has been set up allows a spreadsheet user to see how sensitive the decision would be to a change in any of the costs or benefits in the table.) It is clear that the ranking of the projects can change as the interest rate varies. At low values of r, project A is preferred since the benefit in year 3 is discounted by a relatively small amount, but as the interest rate rises this value is more heavily discounted so that project B becomes preferable. It would be helpful to see the entire picture graphically. This is easily accomplished using 1-2-3's graphics capabilities. First it is necessary to produce a table of values for the NPV against r as the basis for the graph.

Go to cell A26 and enter 'NPV as a function of the interest rate. Then enter labels as follows:

Cell	Label
A28	'Assumed
A29	'interest rate
C28	'Project A
D28	'Project B

Use /**Data Fill** to enter interest rates from 0 to 0.6 in cells A30.A90 (start=0, step=0.01,stop=0.6).

Next enter formulae for the NPV function into cells C30 and D30 which can then be copied down. They are quite long and are as follows:

C30:
> +$B$11+($B$12/(1+A30))+($B$13/(1+A30)^2)+($B$14/(1+A30)^3)

D30:

$$+\$D\$11+(\$D\$12/(1+A30))+(\$D\$13/(1+A30)^{\wedge}2)+(\$D\$14/(1+A30)^{\wedge}3)$$

Now copy these formula down to cells C31.C90 and D31.D90 respectively.

Now you can construct a line graph with the X range A30.A90, A range C30.C90 and B range D30.D90. Use the **/Graph Options Format** to set the graph to *Lines* for ranges A and B so that the symbols do not appear on the graph, and **/Graph Options Scale** to enter a skip factor of 10. Then use the **Titles** command to enter the following labels:

X-axis   Interest rate
Y-axis   NPV
and the title (first line) Net Present Value graphs

We now describe how you can place labels on these graphs. We first plot some dummy points to help find the right position on the graph for the labels. Go to cell E70 (in the row where $r=0.4$) and enter the value -150. In cell F70 put Project A. In E75 (in the row where $r=0.45$) enter the value 100. In cell F75 put Project B. Then identify the C range for the graph as E30.E90. If you now use **/Graph Options Format** to set the format for the C range as *Symbols*. When you view the graph two points will be plotted as $r=0.4,NPV=-150$ and at $r=0.45,NPV=100$.

Now use the **/Graph options Data-Labels** command, selecting C. Give the label range as F30.F90 and align the labels at the centre of the data point. When you view the graph again the curves will have been labelled. If the position is not quite right, change the dummy values until you are satisfied. At that stage you can remove the dummy points themselves with **/Graph Options Format C Neither**.

When you view the graph it should look something like Figure 6.1.

The graph shows how, for each project, the NPV declines as the interest rate rises. With an interest rate of zero the NPV of project A is 700 (just the sum of the undiscounted costs and benefits) and this is well in excess of the comparable figure of 600 for project B. However, as r rises, both graphs fall, with the project A graph falling most steeply. In fact the graphs cross somewhere between the value of $r=0.09$ and $r=0.1$ (see rows 39 and 40 of the worksheet). The graph for project A continues to fall away more steeply and cuts the horizontal axis at an interest rate of about 32%. For interest rates greater or equal to this, project A is not viable, it being better to put any available finance into an account paying that rate. For project B, however, the interest rate would have to reach around 54% before the project becomes financially unsound. This value of r at which the NPV just equals zero is known as the *internal rate of return* (IRR). You sometimes find projects have been ranked according to their IRRs, with those projects for which the IRR is greater than the market interest rate being considered profitable.

However, as the graph emphasises, the ranking of projects is not always

Net Present Value graphs

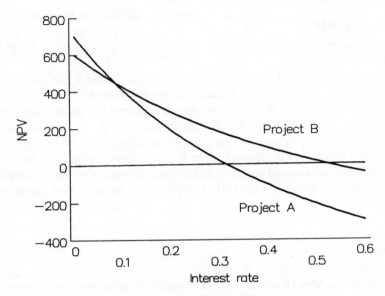

Figure 6.1 Line graph from NPV worksheet

preserved at all interest rates and the NPV is to be preferred as a criterion in investment decision making.

6.4 Using 1-2-3's built-in financial functions

Lotus 1-2-3 does in fact include a number of built-in functions for financial calculations, some of which can be used for the problem discussed in the previous two sections. For example, the function @NPV(rate,series) will find the present value of a series of cash flows (arranged in a consecutive range of cells). Be careful, however, to note that this function only evaluates the present value of the terms which are to be discounted. The initial cost will still have to be deducted (or added in as a negative amount). In our example we could have used the formula +B11+@NPV(D4,B12.B14) in cell B23 instead of identifying individually each of the discounted values in cells B19 to B21 and then adding them up. To find the internal rate of return of a project you can use the @IRR function. This has the format @IRR(guess,range). Confusingly with this function, the first cell in the range must contain the initial cost, so for our example the range would be B11.B14. Notice that you must also provide a guess or estimate of the internal rate of return. This is because 1-2-3 uses an iterative method to compute the IRR. The closer is your guess, the more quickly 1-2-3 will obtain an accurate solution. Add the label 'IRR in cell A24 of the worksheet and in cell B24 enter the formula @IRR(0.3,B11.B14).

The computer will use your initial guess of 0.3 (30%) and come up with a value of 0.318510 (or approximately 31.85%). Copy the formula across the cell D24 and you should get an IRR for project B of 0.535183 or roughly 53.52%.

The financial function @PV is not relevant to our problem but it could be useful in other contexts. It determines the present value of a series of constant payments for a specified number of periods (term) at a specified interest rate (rate). Its format is @PV(payments,rate,term). As in all 1-2-3 @functions, the arguments can be entered as values or as cell ranges (or even range names). A number of other financial functions are available in 1-2-3, but they are beyond the scope of this book (see the *Reference Manual*, pp. 264–74, or look under @FUNCTIONS in the on-line Help facility in 1-2-3).

Exercise 6

(a) The table below shows the initial cost and expected benefits from two mutually exclusive investment projects.

		Project	
		A	B
Initial cost (in £)		500	450
Expected benefits (in £) at the end of year	1	300	0
	2	150	150
	3	100	200
	4	50	250

Create a Lotus 1-2-3 worksheet to enable the net present value of these projects to be evaluated at various interest rates. Compute the NPVs at (i) $r=0.06$, (ii) $r=0.1$, and discuss your results.

(b) Create a Lotus 1-2-3 worksheet to calculate the present value of a stream of future payments of £100 to be made at the end of this year and every year for the next 20 years, assuming an annual interest rate of 10% per annum. Modify the worksheet so that the level of payments, the rate of interest and the term (number of years of payments) are all stored in key cell positions so that they can all be changed conveniently if required.

Chapter 7

Linear programming problems and Lotus 1-2-3

Purpose: To outline the main features of a linear programming problem. To show how Lotus 1-2-3 can be used to help solve such problems.

Preview: In this chapter attention is turned to another type of decision-making analysis – linear programming. It is shown how Lotus 1-2-3 can be used to help analyse and solve such problems. Section 7.1 presents a simple example which is typical of a certain type of linear programming problem, sometimes referred to as a production problem. In this kind of problem a firm must choose what levels of output of its products to produce, given the constraints of the available resources. It is assumed that both the constraints and the profits from the outputs are linear in form – hence the name linear programming. It will be shown how the problem may be set up within the framework of a spreadsheet so that the parameters of the problem can be changed easily if it is wished to see how sensitive the solution is to such values. In Section 7.2 Lotus 1-2-3 is used to construct a graph showing the feasible set of outputs and add to it the profit line showing output combinations which would yield a certain level of profit. By changing the profit value within the worksheet, the profit line can be shifted around until its optimum value is located. Section 7.3 continues with this framework to examine the sensitivity of the solution to changes in the parameters of the problem. Section 7.4 shows how the simplex method, which is the standard method of solution for linear programming problems and which can be used to solve bigger problems than the one described here, can be implemented on a spreadsheet.

1-2-3 features introduced in this chapter: No new features are introduced in this chapter.

7.1 A simple linear programming problem

A small bakery produces two sizes of pizza which it sells wholesale: the standard size which gives a unit profit of 40p, and the large size for which the profit per unit is 60p. Because of restrictions in oven capacity it is only possible to cook 90 standard pizzas per hour or 36 large pizzas per hour, or some equivalent combination of pizzas of the two sizes. Packing is done by hand at the rate of 45 pizzas per hour of either type. How many pizzas of each type should the bakery produce per hour in order to maximise profits and how much profit per hour will be made?

What difference would be made to this conclusion if the bakery was forced to cut the profit on the standard pizzas to 10p per pizza?

This problem is a simple example of a standard type of problem in linear programming where the objective is to maximise a linear function of a number of variables (known as *choice variables*) subject to a variety of linear inequalities involving these variables which set the constraints on the choices available. Here the choice variables are the numbers of pizzas of each type produced per hour. The *objective function* relates the amount of profit to these values – it will be the profit per standard pizza times the number of standard pizzas made, plus the profit per large pizza times the number of large pizzas produced. There are two *constraints*, each of which places limits on the number of pizzas of the different types which can be produced.

Taking the packing constraint first, it is possible to package anything up to but not exceeding 45 pizzas per hour. The constraint is an inequality since it says

> number of standard pizzas　plus　number of large pizzas $\leqslant 45$
> per hour　　　　　　　　　per hour

The oven constraint is a little more difficult to write down since the number of pizzas which can be cooked per hour depends on the precise combination of pizzas of different sizes planned. However, a large pizza evidently needs two and a half times the oven space of a standard pizza (90 divided by 36) so the number of standard pizzas which could be cooked must be less than or equal to $90 - 2.5$ times the number of large pizzas. Alternatively this constraint can be expressed as

> $2 \times$ number of standard pizzas　$+$　$5 \times$ number of large pizzas $\leqslant 180$
> per hour　　　　　　　　　　　per hour

The problem can be written in algebraic form if we introduce symbols to stand for the production levels of the two sizes of pizza and for profit.

Let $X(1) =$ the number of standard pizzas produced per hour
$X(2) =$ the number of large pizzas produced per hour
and $Z =$ the profit generated in £ per hour.
The problem then becomes: choose $X(1)$ and $X(2)$ so as to

$$\text{maximise } Z = 0.4\,X(1) + 0.6\,X(2) \qquad (7.1)$$
$$\text{(objective function)}$$

subject to the constraints

$$2X(1) + 5X(2) \leqslant 180 \qquad (7.2)$$
(oven constraint)
$$X(1) + X(2) \leqslant 45 \qquad (7.3)$$
(packing constraint)

We should also write

$$X(1) \geqslant 0, X(2) \geqslant 0 \qquad (7.4)$$
(non-negativity condition)

since neither production level could be negative.

The inequalities (7.2), (7.3) and (7.4) define the set of Xs (production levels) which are possible. Any combination which satisfies all these conditions is feasible. An optimum combination would be one from this set which could not be improved on in terms of profit.

Because this problem involves only two choice variables the feasible set can be shown graphically in two dimensions and the solution (the optimal numbers of pizzas of each size) can then be established with the aid of the graph. In the next section we shall see how a Lotus 1-2-3 worksheet can be built up to construct a graph showing the feasible set for the pizza problem. We shall see how the optimal solution can be discovered by trial-and-error shifts of profit lines which can also be shown on the graph.

Then in Section 7.3 we will see how the solution is affected by a change in one of the parameters of the problem. (The *parameters* are the numbers in the equations (7.1), (7.2) and (7.3) such as 0.4, which represents the per unit profit on standard pizzas in £.) Lotus 1-2-3 can handle this kind of 'what-if' question very effectively. As soon as the number is changed in the worksheet, the graph will be adjusted automatically.

Unfortunately the graphical approach is not available to us for problems involving more than two choice variables. The standard method for solving such problems is via the simplex algorithm which provides an efficient search procedure through the set of feasible solutions. In Section 7.4 we shall work through the simplex procedure for a simple problem within a 1-2-3 worksheet. For expository purposes we shall use the same pizza example, but we shall indicate how the procedure could be adapted to solve problems with more choice variables or constraints. For problems with more than four or five choice variables or constraints the 1-2-3 application of the simplex method becomes rather cumbersome and it would be better to turn to a specially designed software package or a Lotus 'add-in' (see Chapter 12) for a quick and efficient solution of linear programming problems. Such packages, however, do not always reveal to users the steps involved in reaching the solution and those who wish to appreciate what is going on are advised to work through a simple problem in detail to understand the procedure. Without access to a spreadsheet this would mean a time-consuming and potentially error-laden approach with pencil, paper and calculator. 1-2-3 offers an intermediate position where the grind of calculation can be removed but the relevant steps and formulae will still need to be thought out by the problem solver.

7.2 A graphical solution to the pizza problem

Load Lotus 1-2-3 and begin a new worksheet. Type in a title in row 1: PIZZA PROBLEM : a simple linear programming problem.

Rows 3 to 8 will be used to state the problem. The information will be stored in such a way that parameter values can be changed easily to conduct 'what-if' exercises.

Go to cell A3 and enter Max Z = .

In the rest of the row put

0.4	in cell B3
X(1) +	in cell C3 (leave two spaces in front of the + sign)
0.6	in cell D3
X(2)	in cell E3
In cell F3 type	Objective function
In cell A4 put	subject to

Row 5 will contain information on the oven constraint. Enter the cell contents as follows:

Cell	Entry	
A5	2	
B5	X(1) +	(4 spaces before the + sign)
C5	5	
D5	X(2)<=	($\leqslant$ cannot be used in 1-2-3)
E5	180	
F5	Oven constraint	

Row 6 will contain information on the packing constraint. The cell contents are as follows:

A6	1	
B6	X(1) +	(you can copy from cell B5)
C6	1	
D6	X(2)<=	(you can copy from cell D5)
E6	45	
F6	Packing constraint	

Leave row 7 blank and in cell B8 put X(1), X(2) >=0.

Then move to cell F8 and type Non-negativity condition.

In producing a graph with X(1) on the horizontal axis and X(2) on the vertical axis we will be limited to the positive (top-right) quadrant, but the oven and packing constraints will place further restrictions on the values of X(1) and X(2) which are feasible. We will begin with the packing constraint since this is the more straightforward of the two constraints to translate onto the graph. The inequality

$$X(1) + X(2) \leqslant 45$$

may also be written as

$$X(2) \leqslant 45 - X(1)$$

At the equality X(2) = 45 − X(1) and the points satisfying this equation produce a downward-sloping straight-line graph. The graph starts on the vertical axis at X(2) = 45 and for every unit increase in X(1) the line falls by one unit, reaching the horizontal axis at X(1) = 45. When we look at this line on the graph we must understand that points below the line will also satisfy the inequality since for any X(1) it is not necessary for X(2) to be as much as 45 − X(1).

To get the computer to draw the graph of a function, as we saw in Chapter 6, we create a column of values for the horizontal axis variable (X) and then produce another column with the formula to transform these values into the vertical axis variable (Y).

Go to cell A10 and type in the subheading: Graphical Solution. In cell A12 put " X(1) and in cell B12 (overflowing into C12) type the words Packing constraint.

Column A from row 13 onwards will contain values of X(1) from zero up to a sufficiently large number to calculate all the required X(2) values. Although for the packing constraint the X(1)s need only go up to 45, we will need to go higher for the oven constraint.

So beginning in cell A13 and going up to A113 use the **/Data Fill** command to fill up the cells with numbers from 0 to 100. Now go to cell B13 and enter the formula +($E$6−$A$6*A13)/$C$6. On pressing *<Return>* the number 45 should be displayed. The formula may appear to be unnecessarily complicated, but the results and hence the graph we plot will change automatically if any of the constants in row 6 are changed later.

Now copy this formula down the column from cell B13 to the range B14.B113. The cell values should fall by one unit at a time, reaching zero in cell B58 where the X(1) value is 45.

Leaving the adjoining cells in column C blank for the moment, move across to cell D12 and put the heading Oven Constraint. In cell D13 we need the formula to calculate the value of X(2) when X(1) = 0 where 2X(1) + 5X(2) = 180. Rearranging this equation with X(2) alone on the left-hand side we have

$$X(2) = +(180 - 2X(1))/5$$

To allow for changes in parameter values we enter the formula +($E$5−

$A$5*A13)/$C$5 into cell D13. The value 36 should be displayed when you press *<Enter>*. Use the **Copy** command to replicate the formula for the range D14.D113.

Now call up the *Graph* menu choosing *Type* X–Y, and making A13.A113 the X range, B13.B113 the A range and D13.D113 the B range. Now view the graph. Although it looks rather messy, you should see the line representing the packing constraint crossing the horizontal axis at X(1)=45, the line representing the second constraint crossing the horizontal axis at X(1)=90 and the two lines crossing at X(1)=15 where X(2)=30. You can check this simultaneous solution by returning to the worksheet and going down the rows to row 28 where the X(1) value should be 15 and the numbers in columns B and D should both be 30.

The graph now shows the feasible set as the region enclosed by the two lines and the two axes. A point such as X(1)=0, X(2)=45, although it is on one of the axes and on one of the lines, so satisfying one of the constraints, is above/to the right of the other line and so fails to satisfy the other constraint.

Before turning to the objective function if would be helpful to tidy up the presentation of the graph. From the *Graph* menu select *Options* and *Titles* giving the *First Line* as PIZZA PROBLEM and *Second Line* as FEASIBLE SET.

Give the X-axis the label X(1) Standard pizzas and call the Y-axis X(2) Large pizzas.

To show the lines without the symbols choose *Options* again and then *Format*, choosing *Lines* for both the A and B ranges.

We also want to limit the upper and lower limits shown on the X- and Y-axis to 0 to 100 and 0 to 50 respectively. Select *Options* again followed by *Scale*. Choose *Y Scale* and then *Manual*. Select *Upper* and when prompted *"Enter Upper Limit"* put in 100. Select *Lower* and then simply press *<Return>* because the default figure of 0 is what is required.

Do the same thing again for the *X Scale* but make the upper limit equal to 50.

The labelling on the X-axis is far too crowded so choose *Scale* again from the */Graph Options* menu. Enter a skip factor of 10.

It would be nice to identify the crossing points on the graph more clearly. This can be done using the *Data-Labels* command following *Options* in the *Graph* menu. First, though, we must place labels at key points within the worksheet. Go to cell C13 and type E and then in the following cells enter the letters indicated:

C28	B
C58	C
E13	A
E103	D

Select */Graph Options Data-Labels* and then specify the data labels for the

A range as C13.C113. When you are offered the choice of where to place the labels choose *Above*. Enter the label range for range B as E13.E113 and set the labels *Left* of the data points.

If you look again at the graph you will see that three of the corners of the feasible set are now clearly marked as A, B and C. The other corner is the origin, so the feasible set is all the combinations of $X(1)$ and $X(2)$ on the edges or within the area enclosed by OABC. Unfortunately we cannot use Lotus to shade this area so that it stands out more clearly. Notice that at point E, where $X(1)=0$ and $X(2)=45$, although the packing constraint would be satisfied the oven constraint would not be. Similarly at point D where $X(1)=90$ and $X(2)=0$ the oven constraint could be satisfied, but the packing constraint could not be.

Now we must turn to the objective function and its graphical representation. The function is given by equation (7.1), i.e.

$$Z = 0.4\,X(1) + 0.6\,X(2)$$

This equation links three variables Z, $X(1)$ and $X(2)$, so to show graphically where $X(1)$ and $X(2)$ are on the axes the value of Z must be fixed. For example, if Z were to be fixed at the value of 18, the relationship between $X(1)$ and $X(2)$ would be

$$18 = 0.4\,X(1) + 0.6\,X(2)$$
$$\text{or} \quad X(2) = (18 - 0.4\,X(1))/0.6$$

which simplifies to

$$X(2) = 30 - 2/3\,X(1)$$

The graph of this relationship would start at 30 on the vertical axis, it would be downward sloping with a gradient of (minus) two-thirds, and would eventually cross the horizontal axis at $X(1)=45$. We will add this line to the graph, but do so in a way that allows us easily to change the value of Z.

Go to cell D10 and input "Z = and in cell E10 enter the value 18.

Now go to cell F12 and enter as text Profit line.

In cell F13 enter the formula +($E$10−$B$3*A13)/$D$3.

When you press the <*Return*> key the value 30 should appear (the intercept on the vertical axis). Now use the **Copy** command to replicate this formula all the way down the column in cells F14.F113. Now add this to the graph as range C.

If you now look at the graph you will see the new line has been added in (although it still has the symbols shown – you can get rid of them using *Options Format C Lines*).

All points on this line represent combinations of the two types of pizza which generate profits of £18 per hour. One such point is at C, where 45 standard pizzas and no large pizzas are being produced. This is certainly feasible. However, it is possible to reach a higher profit line and still find a point on the line which is feasible. Go back to the worksheet and cell E10 and change the profit value to 30. Switch back to the graph (just press the function key F10) and see what has happened. The profit line has shifted up and in parallel and now lies entirely outside the feasible region. There is no feasible combination of standard and large pizzas which can generate profits of £30 per hour.

How much higher can profit go while keeping to production levels which are feasible? Experiment with different numbers between 20 and 30 in cell E10 and watch the profit line moving up or down. You will discover that when $Z=24$ the profit line will just pass through the single point B in the feasible set. This is the highest profit that can be earned and the associated production levels are thus the optimal ones. We have already worked out that at B, $X(1)=15$ and $X(2)=30$, so this is the optimum.

Since we now have a graph which indicates where the optimum is as well as simply showing the feasible set, go back to the *Graph* menu and change the second line of the title to OPTIMUM SOLUTION. Your graph should look something like Figure 7.1.

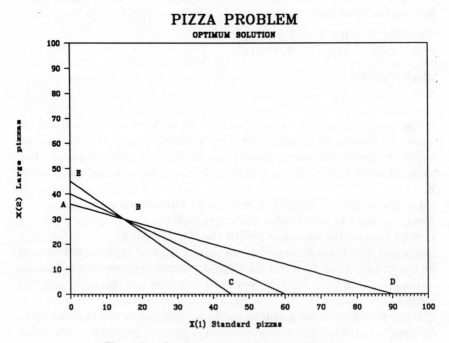

Figure 7.1 Graphical solution of Pizza problem

Save the current worksheet as PIZZA so that you can call it up again if you require it.

7.3 Sensitivity analysis: 'what-if' questions

The analysis of the problem can be usefully extended by considering what would happen to the optimum solution if one of the key parameters were to change. In Section 7.1 we raised the question as to what would be the effect on the outputs and profit if the profit on standard pizzas were to change to 10p per pizza. Go to cell B3 and change the value of 0.4 to 0.1. Notice that the figures in column F will also change, and when you look at the graph you will find that the profit line has become much flatter. It still begins at 40 on the vertical axis, but no longer goes through point B. In fact, none of the points on the line are in the feasible set any more. This level of profit is now unattainable.

Go to cell E10 and gradually reduce the profit level, going backwards and forwards if necessary until the profit line comes down sufficiently to just touch a point in the feasible set. You should find that when Z=21.6 the profit line just touches the feasible set at point A, implying that with these rates of unit profit the bakery would switch production entirely to large pizzas and stop making standard pizzas altogether.

Graphically, as the relative profit on standard pizzas falls, the slope of the profit line becomes flatter. So long as the slope of this line is somewhere between the slopes of the lines defining the constraints then the optimum will continue to occur at B, implying the production of both types of pizza. (Notice, however, that the actual profit attainable will vary.) The moment that the slope of the profit line falls below that of the line AD then the point A becomes the feasible point offering the greatest profit; in other words, the optimum situation is where production is concentrated on large pizzas.

Now try changing some of the other key parameters (first change the profit rate on standard pizzas back to 0.4). For example, change the figure in cell E6 to 66. (This implies a relaxation of the packing constraint; it is equivalent to assuming that pizzas can be packed at the faster rate of 66 per hour). Look what happens to the graph. The EC line moves out to the right by a substantial amount, cutting the AD line at X(1)=50. The profit line is now well inside the feasible set when it passes through the old optimum point. It can now be shifted upwards until Z=29.6, at which value the profit line once again goes through the corner point of the feasible set, which is now at X(1)=50 and X(2)=16.

If you are unclear as to exactly what value of Z gives the optimum (the graph is not all that easy to work from), notice that it will occur at an X(1) value where the X(2) values in columns B, D and F of the worksheet are identical – in this case in row 63. Here with X(1)=50 we find X(2)=16 for both constraints and the objective function.

You can now conduct further sensitivity analysis on this problem, changing other parameters in the resource constraint, to see what effect they will have on the feasible set and on the optimum.

7.4 Using Lotus 1-2-3 to implement the simplex method of solution

The graphical approach to linear programming problems, although instructive, is rather hit-and-miss, and is also limited to problems involving only two choice variables. In fact, linear programming only becomes operational for real-world applications when an algorithm (or set of rules) can be provided which can ensure a step-by-step method of solving problems involving a greater number of choice variables and constraints. The first such systematic approach to linear programming problems was developed in the late 1940s by George Dantzig and is called the *simplex* method of solution. The layout of the simplex tableaux described in this chapter follows that used by Baunol (1972). In this section we show how the simplex method can be implemented using Lotus 1-2-3, illustrating the method by using it to solve the pizza problem. The method is not fully mechanised here in order that the reader can see clearly what is happening at each stage. However, it could be automated using Lotus 1-2-3 macros (see Chapter 12). The approach can easily be extended to problems with more variables and constraints.

We begin by introducing some additional concepts which are required for this method of solution. First, there is the concept of a *slack variable*. A slack variable is a variable which is introduced into a constraint so that it may be written as an equation rather than as an inequality. For example equation (7.2) can be written as

$$2 X(1) + 5 X(2) + S(1) = 180 \tag{7.2a}$$

where $S(1)$ measures the amount of unused oven space associated with a particular output combination. Like $X(1)$ and $X(2)$, the slack variable $S(1)$ must be non-negative. If its value is zero it implies that at that combination of outputs there is no slack or unused capacity in the resource (in this case the ovens).

Similarly equation (7.3) can be written as

$$X(1) + X(2) + S(2) = 45 \tag{7.3a}$$

where $S(2) \geq 0$ gives the unused packing time.

Looking back to the graph, each of the borders of the feasible region defines a situation where one of the variables in the problem is zero. Along the line AD we have $S(1) = 0$, while along the line EC we find $S(2) = 0$. Along the $X(1)$ axis $X(2)=0$ and along the $X(2)$ axis $X(1)=0$. Any point where two of these lines cross, i.e. where two of the variables are zero, is called a *basic* solution. (Two zero values define a basic solution because there are two choice variables, $X(1)$ and $X(2)$.)

Thus the following points are the basic solutions for the pizza problem: O, A, B, C, D and E. However D and E are not feasible – only O, A, B and C are *basic feasible solutions*.

Now it can also be seen from the graph that the optimum must be a basic feasible solution at a corner edge of the feasible set. One possible method of solution might be to identify all the basic solutions, set aside those which are not feasible, and evaluate the objective function at each of the basic feasible solutions. The optimum would be the one giving the greatest value of Z. In the pizza problem this only involves looking at four points, but in general a problem with n choice variables and m constraints will have $^{n+m}C_n$ basic solutions, where this denotes the number of combinations of n items which can be chosen from $n+m$ items. For example, if $n=6$ and $m=10$, this is 8008. Because the number of basic solutions can get so large we require an efficient method of examining basic solutions which ignores non-feasible solutions and only looks at solutions which can generate values of Z at least as great as those already examined. This is what the simplex method does.

Retrieve the PIZZA worksheet and erase all cell entries below row 8. Go to cell C11 and type 'Tableau 1.
Then enter labels as follows:

Cell	Label
A12	Basic
A13	Variables
A14	"Z
A15	"S1
A16	"S2
B13	"Constant
C12	"Zero variables
C13	"X(1)
D13	"X(2)

In cell B14 enter the value zero and then enter formulae as follows:

Cell	Entry
C14	+B3
D14	+D3
B15	+E5
C15	−A5
D15	−C5
B16	+E6
C16	−A6
D16	−C6

The tableau should show the coefficients of the equations in the rearranged form where S(1) and S(2) appear on the left-hand side:

$$Z = \ \ \ 0 \ \ + 0.4X(1) + 0.6X(2) \tag{7.1b}$$
$$S(1) = \ 180 \ - \ \ 2X(1) - \ \ \ 5X(2) \tag{7.2b}$$
$$S(2) = \ \ 45 \ - \ \ \ X(1) - \ \ \ \ X(2) \tag{7.3b}$$

The left-hand-side variables in each equation are indicated in column A, while the right-hand side variables appear in row 13 above their respective coefficients. This tableau reflects the solution

$$X(1)=0, X(2)=0, S(1)=180, S(2)=45 \text{ and } Z=0$$

i.e. the basic feasible solution at the origin.

We must now examine various other basic feasible solutions, exchanging one basic variable for one zero variable at each step, in an attempt to improve the value of Z. This amounts to rearranging and substituting the equations so as to put different variables on the left-hand side of the equation (basic variables) with the remaining variables on the right-hand side) (zero variables). At every step this is done so as to maximise the impact on Z.

For example, introducing X(2) in place of S(1) (moving to point A on the graph) would involve the following in terms of the algebraic manipulations. Write equation (7.2b) with X(2) on the left-hand side, i.e.

$$X(2) = 180/5 - 2/5\,X(1) - 1/5\,S(1)$$
$$\text{or}\quad X(2) = 36 - 0.4\,X(1) - 0.2\,S(1) \tag{7.2c}$$

Now substitute this equation into the right-hand side of equation (7.3b):

$$S(2) = 45 - X(1) - [36 - 0.4X(1) - 0.2S(1)]$$
$$\text{or}\quad S(2) = 9 - 0.6\,X(1) + 0.25\,S(1)$$

Lastly substitute equation (7.2c) into (7.1b) to express Z in terms of $X(1)$ and $S(1)$:

$$Z = 0.4X(1) + 0.6\,[36 - 0.4\,X(1) - 0.2\,S(1)]$$
$$\text{or}\quad Z = 21.6 + 0.16\,X(1) - 0.12\,S(1) \tag{7.1c}$$

Tableau 2 would now be written as:

	Const	X(1)	S(1)
Z	21.6	0.16	−0.12
X(2)	36	−0.4	−0.2
S(2)	9	−0.6	0.2

The same effect could have been obtained by following the procedure outlined in Table 7.1.

Construct this tableau in lines 19 to 24 of the worksheet as follows:

Cell	Entry
C19	'Tableau 2
A20	'Basic
A21	'variables
A22	"Z
A23	"X(2)
A24	"S(2)
C20	'Zero variables
B21	'Constant

Table 7.1 The pivoting procedure

```
Step
1    Examine the Z row and find the largest positive element.
     (If none is positive then the existing solution is the
     optimum.)
     Place a star (asterisk) at the foot of the column in the
     row below the table.
2    Look down this column. Take each negative element and divide
     it into the corresponding element in the constant column,
     putting the results in column F.
     Choose the element in column F with the smallest absolute
     value and place a star (asterisk) next to it in column E.
     The pivot element is now identified as being in the cell where
     the starred row and column intersect.
3    Set up a new tableau several rows below the existing one as
     follows.
     Exchange the starred zero variable for the starred basic
     variable in the row and column headings:
     (i)   replace the old pivot by its reciprocal;
     (ii)  replace the other old pivot row elements by changing the
           sign and dividing them by the old pivot element;
     (iii) replace the other pivot column elements by dividing them
           by the old pivot elements;
     (iv)  for all other elements divide the cross-product by the old
           pivot element (where the cross-product = old element*pivot
           minus the product of the other two elements to complete the
           square.)
```

Cell	Entry
C21	"X(1)
D21	"S(1)
B22	$+(B14*D15-B15*D14)/D15$
C22	$+(C14*D15-C15*D14)/D15$
D22	$+D14/D15$
B23	$-B15/D15$
C23	$-C15/D15$
D23	$-1/D15$
B24	$+(B16*D15-B15*D16)/D15$
C24	$+(C16*D15-C15*D16)/D15$
D24	$+D16/D15$

These formulae are arrived at by following the steps laid down in Table 7.1. The value of Z which results at this basic feasible solution with $X(1) = S(1) = 0$ is 21.6, as shown in cell B22. This is not the optimum, as can be seen from the fact that one of the coefficients of the zero variables in the Z row is still positive. This indicates that introducing this zero variable in place of a basic variable could increase the value of Z. Following the same pivot rules as before we arrive at the following tableau (where C24 is used as the new pivot element):

Tableau 3

Basic variables	Constant	Zero variables	
		S(2)	S(1)
Z	24	−0.26666	−0.06666
X(2)	30	0.66666	−0.33333
X(1)	15	−1.66666	0.33333

The formulae required to obtain these values are the following:

Cell	Formula
B30	+(B22*C24−B24*C22)/C24
C30	+C22/C24
D30	+(D22*C24−D24*C22)/C24
B31	+(B23*C24−B24*C23)/C24
C31	+C23/C24
D31	+(D23*C24−D24*C23)/C24
B32	−B24/C24
C32	−1/C24
D32	−D24/C24

This now identifies the optimum since both coefficients of the zero variables in the Z row are negative (see step 1 in Table 7.1). As we discovered from the

Table 7.2 Worksheet display for the simplex solution of PIZZA

```
 1 PIZZA PROBLEM : simplex method of solution
 2
 3 Max Z =        0.4 X(1)   +        0.6 X(2)     Objective function
 4 subject to
 5        2 X(1)    +      5 X(2)<=      180 Oven constraint
 6        1 X(1)    +      1 X(2)<=       45 Packing constraint
 7
 8        X(1), X(2) >= 0                 Non-negativity condition
 9
10
11                          Tableau 1
12 Basic                    Zero variables
13 variablesConstant        X(1)      X(2)              Ratios
14     Z        0           0.4       0.6
15    S(1)      180         -2        -5  *            -36
16    S(2)      45          -1        -1               -45
17                                        *
18
19                          Tableau 2
20 Basic                    Zero variables
21 variablesConstant        X(1)      S(1)
22     Z       21.6         0.16      -0.12
23    X(2)      36          -0.4      -0.2            -90
24    S(2)      9           -0.6      0.2  *          -15
25                          *
26
27                          Tableau 3
28 Basic                    Zero variables
29 variablesConstant        S(2)       S(1)
30     Z        24 -0.26666 -0.06666
31    X(2)      30 0.666666 -0.33333
32    X(1)      15 -1.66666 0.333333
```

graphical approach, the optimum has $S(1) = S(2) = 0$ (no slack in either of the resources) and $X(1) = 15$, $X(2) = 30$, giving $Z = 24$. Twice as many large pizzas will be produced as standard pizzas.

The final result is shown in Table 7.2.

Exercise 7

A small firm produces two products, bits and bobs. The unit profit rates are £3 and £5 respectively. Each bit requires 5 minutes processing on machine A and 3 minutes on machine B, while each bob requires two minutes on machine A and 3 minutes on machine B. Currently there are 180 minutes of machine A time and 135 minutes of machine B time available each day. The firm wishes to know the production rates of bits and bobs which will maximise profits.

Use 1-2-3 to solve the problem (i) by the graphical method and (ii) using the simplex method.

Reference

W. J. Baumol, *Economic Theory and Operations Analysis* (Third Edition) (Prentice-Hall, London, 1972).

Chapter 8

Simple regression analysis and Lotus 1-2-3

Purpose: To demonstrate the use of Lotus 1-2-3 for simple regression analysis and as an aid to a better understanding of regression concepts and methods.

Preview: Section 8.1 takes a simple example in which it is required to estimate the relationship between two variables. This is used to outline basic regression concepts. The regression equation is obtained using standard spreadsheet functions and formulae. It is shown how the fitted values can be derived and how 1-2-3 can be used to plot a scatter diagram showing the data points and the fitted line. The residuals are also calculated and plotted for diagnostic purposes. Section 8.2 shows how the 1-2-3 **Regression** commands can be used to obtain the regression results, including the standard error and the value of *R*-squared. It is shown how to interpret these values and augment them by computing the *t*-value and a confidence interval for the regression coefficient. Section 8.3 describes the Durbin–Watson statistic and shows how its value can be found within a 1-2-3 worksheet. Emphasis is placed on the use of graphs as an aid to model specification and validation.

1-2-3 features introduced in this chapter: The X–Y graph command; the 1-2-3 regression commands.

Preamble: Regression analysis is probably the most important form of quantitative analysis used by economists. At any rate it is the most used, whether for fitting simple trends, explaining past variations in variables, estimating key parameters (such as elasticities and marginal propensities) or for forecasting the future movement of time series.

Lotus 1-2-3 does not contain the vast array of commands of a dedicated econometrics package such as TSP or RATS, but it does include regression commands in its menu structure. As such it can be a useful tool to use for estimating simple regression models or for learning about the basics of regression analysis. Although the output generated with the regression commands is rather rudimentary, one can use standard spreadsheet functions to augment the results. The simplicity of the graphics features can also to some extent compensate for the lack of a wide range of diagnostic statistics. Another advantage of working with Lotus 1-2-3 is that if it becomes obvious that it would be wise to extend the analysis using a more sophisticated econometrics package, one often finds that these packages will read Lotus files. Thus data can be transferred across to the other software without difficulty. Indeed so simple is the entering and editing of data within a Lotus 1-2-3 worksheet that it may pay researchers engaged on advanced forms of analysis to load their data from a file set up using 1-2-3 (see Chapter 12).

8.1 A simple regression model

The data in Table 8.1 are taken from the *Economic Trends Annual Supplement*, 1986, and show real aggregate consumers' expenditure (C) and real personal disposable income (Y) in the UK, both measured in £ billion at 1980 prices.

Table 8.1 Real consumers' expenditure and real personal disposable income, 1970–84

Year	C	Y
1970	111.0	122.8
1971	114.4	124.3
1972	121.5	134.8
1973	127.7	144.1
1974	125.8	142.2
1975	124.9	143.3
1976	125.3	142.5
1977	124.6	140.8
1978	131.6	150.7
1979	137.6	159.1
1980	137.0	161.2
1981	136.6	157.3
1982	137.6	157.6
1983	143.1	161.3
1984	145.4	164.8

In common with most introductory textbooks on economics (e.g. Begg, D., Fischer, S. and Dornbusch, R., 1987) one might expect that real consumers' expenditure, C, will be an approximately linear function of real personal disposable income, Y, that is,

$$C = \alpha + \beta Y + u \tag{8.1}$$

where α and β are constants (parameters) and u is a disturbance term. α and

β (and hence u) cannot be observed but could be estimated from a set of data such as that given in Table 8.1.

The standard approach is to minimise the sum of the squares of the deviations between the actual and fitted values – that is, to use least squares regression. Distinguishing the fitted value of the dependent variable from its actual value by putting a 'hat' on it (in this case we would have $\hat{C}$) and similarly denoting the estimates of the parameters as $\hat{\alpha}$ and $\hat{\beta}$ we have $\hat{C} = \hat{\alpha} + \hat{\beta} Y$.

The least squares method will choose values of $\hat{\alpha}$ and $\hat{\beta}$ so as to minimise $S = \Sigma (C - \hat{C})^2 = \Sigma(C - \hat{\alpha} - \hat{\beta}Y)^2$.

This is a standard problem in differential calculus and by finding and solving the necessary conditions for minimising S (see any text on regression, such as Koutsoyiannis, 1977) one can arrive at the following equations, which express the estimators in terms of the data:

$$\hat{\alpha} = [\Sigma Y^2 \Sigma C - \Sigma Y \Sigma CY]/[n\Sigma Y^2 - (\Sigma Y)^2] \tag{8.2}$$
$$\hat{\beta} = [n\Sigma CY - \Sigma C \Sigma Y]/[n\Sigma Y^2 - (\Sigma Y)^2] \tag{8.3}$$

where n is the number of observations in the sample.

Even without the built-in regression commands it is possible to obtain values for $\hat{\alpha}$ and $\hat{\beta}$ within the worksheet framework by setting up columns giving the values of Y^2 and the cross-products CY, using the @SUM function to add them up and then defining $\hat{\alpha}$ and $\hat{\beta}$ in terms of these sums.

Begin a new worksheet and put the title in cell A1: CONSUME : a worksheet for the simple regression model. Then enter the data from Table 8.1 as follows:

Cell	Label
A3	"Year
B3	"C
C3	"Y

Cells A4.A18 should contain the dates 1970 to 1984 (you can use /**Data Fill**).

Cells B4.B18 should contain the values for consumers' expenditure and cells C4.C18 should contain the values for disposable income. Now enter labels as follows:

Cell	Label
D3	"Y*Y
E3	"C*Y

(we have to write the square in this way since superscripts cannot be used in 1-2-3).

In cell D4 enter +C4*C4 and copy down to D5.D18, and in cell E4 enter +B4*C4 and copy down to E5.E18.

Now go to A20 and enter the label "Sums, and in cell B20 put the formula @SUM(B4.B18). Copy this across to cells C20.E20. These are the sums needed for substitution into equations (8.2) and (8.3). Go to cell A22 and enter the label 'Alpha Hat and in cell B22 enter the formula:

+(D20*B20−C20*E20)/(@COUNT(A4.A18)*D20−C20*C20)

In cell A23 enter 'Beta Hat and in cell B23 enter the formula:

+(@COUNT(A4.A18)*E20−B20*C20)/(@COUNT(A4.A18)*D20−C20* C20)

You will now see on the screen the results of using the formulae (8.2) and (8.3) to calculate $\hat{\alpha}$ and $\hat{\beta}$. To make the results more readable enter the following labels and formulae into the cells as indicated:

Cell	Label/Formula
A25	'Estimated regression line
A26	'C Hat
B26	+B22
C26	^+
D26	+B23
E26	'Y

Your worksheet so far should look like Table 8.2.

Table 8.2

CONSUME : a worksheet for a simple regression model

Year	C	Y	Y*Y	C*Y
1970	111	122.8	15079.84	13630.8
1971	114.4	124.3	15450.49	14219.92
1972	121.5	134.8	18171.04	16378.2
1973	127.7	144.1	20764.81	18401.57
1974	125.8	142.2	20220.84	17888.76
1975	124.9	143.3	20534.89	17898.17
1976	125.3	142.5	20306.25	17855.25
1977	124.6	140.8	19824.64	17543.68
1978	131.6	150.7	22710.49	19832.12
1979	137.6	159.1	25312.81	21892.16
1980	137	161.2	25985.44	22084.4
1981	136.6	157.3	24743.29	21487.18
1982	137.6	157.6	24837.76	21685.76
1983	143.1	161.3	26017.69	23082.03
1984	145.4	164.8	27159.04	23961.92
Sums	1944.1	2206.8	327119.3	287841.9

Alpha Hat 20.18058
Beta Hat 0.743787

Estimated regression line
C Hat =   20.18058   +   0.743787 Y

Estimated UK Consumption Function
[1974–1980]

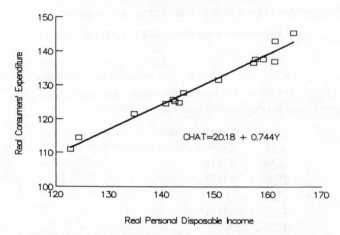

Figure 8.1 Fitted regression line from CONSUME worksheet

The results show an estimated marginal propensity to consume (Beta Hat) of roughly 0.744 and autonomous consumption (Alpha Hat) of roughly 20.18 (£ billion).

You can now get 1-2-3 to work out the C Hat values for each Y, that is the levels of consumers' expenditure which would be predicted simply on the basis of the value of income.

Go to cell F3 and enter "C Hat. Then in cell F4 put +$B$22+$B$23*C4 and copy down to F5.F18. You can see how well the line fits the points when the line and the points are plotted together on a graph. Call up the *Graph* menu and choose the X–Y type of graph. Make the X range C4.C18 (the values of the independent variable, income) and make the A range B4.B18 (the values of the dependent variable, consumers' expenditure).

If you view the graph you will see that the points are joined up. You require a scatter plot of the points so select *Options* followed by *Format* and set the A range to *Symbols*. Look again at the graph and you will see a scatter of points plotted as small squares, following a roughly linear shape from bottom left to top right. Notice that the scaling is automatic and begins at 110 on the vertical axis and 120 on the horizontal axis.

Now you can add the fitted values. Go back to the *Graph* submenu and make the B range F4.F18. View again and you will see the fitted line drawn through the scatter of points. Label the X-axis Real Personal Disposable Income, the Y-axis Real Consumers' Expenditure and give the graph the following title

First line: Estimated UK Consumption Function
Second line: [1974–1980]

You can also add a 'dummy series' to the graph to display the equation itself somewhere on the graph. Your graph should look like Figure 8.1.

Save this graph if you want to print it later with the *PrintGraph* program and store it with the worksheet under the *Graph Name* CFIT.

Looking at the graph it is clear that the line gives a reasonable fit through the points but there is a slight tendency for points to be above the line at either end and below the line in the middle section. You can see this more clearly by calculating and graphing the residuals, which are the differences between the actual values and the fitted values of C.

Go to cell G3 and enter the label 'Residuals. Then in G4 put +B4−F4 and copy to G5.G18.

There is certainly a run of negative residuals for middle values of income, i.e. in those years consumers' expenditure was somewhat less than would have been predicted from the equation (although admittedly the differences are rather small compared with the size of C itself). The pattern can be made more obvious by plotting a graph of the residuals against time. Call up the *Graph* menu and choose *Reset* to clear settings. (Remember, if you want to see the CFIT graph again later you can get it back using the **Name** command). Make the X range A4.A18 and the A range G4.G18.

Give a title 'Residual Plot with the second line [simple UK consumption function]. Label the X-axis Year and the Y-axis u hat.

When you view the graph it should resemble Figure 8.2.

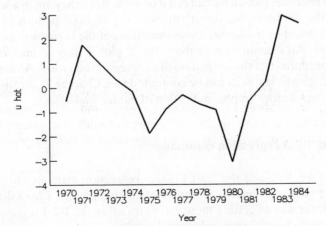

Figure 8.2 Plot of residuals

Certainly there is a tendency for the residuals to be negative for the middle years and positive at either end, which is not what one would wish for since they are supposed to reflect only unpredictable random influences. However, it is hardly surprising that such a simple consumption function with no additional explanatory variables other than income, no allowance for lagged responses and based on such a small data set should have an unsatisfactory residual plot.

In using regression analysis one should keep in mind the assumptions which underly the regression model. These may be stated as follows (for the moment referring to the dependent variables as Y and the independent variable as X).

Assumptions of the simple linear regression model

1. $Y_i = \alpha + \beta X_i + u_i$
   where α and β are parameters, u_i is a random variable. Thus Y is assumed to be a linear stochastic function of X only; it is assumed that the relationship is correctly specified with the correct functional form and the omission of no important explanatory variables.
2. $E(u_i) = 0$;
   the random disturbances are, on average, zero.
3. $\text{Var}(u_i) = \sigma_u^2$;
   the variance of u is a constant.
4. $E(u_i u_j) = 0$ for $i \neq j$;
   the values of u are independent of one another.
5. $E(Xu_i) = 0$;
   the value of the disturbance is independent of the value of X.

Now although we cannot observe the disturbances (the u's), we can see the pattern of the residuals (which we can call $\hat{u}$ or u-hat since they are in a sense estimates of the unobservable disturbances). Any marked pattern in the residuals casts doubt over whether the assumptions of the regression model have been met. An examination of the residual plot is thus an important diagnostic procedure after the estimation of a regression equation. Although a variety of diagnostic statistics can be computed (see Chapter 9), a residual plot literally gives a more graphic indication of model inadequacies.

8.2 Using the 1-2-3 regression commands

In Section 8.1 we obtained the least squares regression estimates for the consumption function by entering appropriate formulae into a worksheet. There is a quicker way of getting these estimates using the 1-2-3 regression commands, which also give some additional results.

Make sure that you have saved the existing worksheet in case you want to look at it again. Then go to cell A1 and edit its contents so that it says:

'CONSUME1 : a worksheet for a simple regression model

In B2 add the text 'using the 1-2-3 regression commands. Next erase everything except these titles and cells A3.C18 which hold the basic data inputs. Now you are ready to use the regression commands. Press the / key and select *Data* followed by *Regression*. The following menu should now appear:

X-Range Y-Range Output-Range Intercept Reset Go Quit

Select *X-Range* and enter this as C4.C18.
Now select *Y-Range* and identify this as B4.B18.
Now you must indicate where in the worksheet you wish to place the regression output. Select *Output-Range* and enter A20. Nothing has happened yet, but if you now press G for *Go* you should get the results as shown in Table 8.3.

Table 8.3

CONSUME1 : a worksheet for a simple regression model
           using the 1-2-3 regression commands

Year	C	Y
1970	111	122.8
1971	114.4	124.3
1972	121.5	134.8
1973	127.7	144.1
1974	125.8	142.2
1975	124.9	143.3
1976	125.3	142.5
1977	124.6	140.8
1978	131.6	150.7
1979	137.6	159.1
1980	137	161.2
1981	136.6	157.3
1982	137.6	157.6
1983	143.1	161.3
1984	145.4	164.8

Regression Output:

Constant	20.18058
Std Err of Y Est	1.659149
R Squared	0.974326
No. of Observations	15
Degrees of Freedom	13

X Coefficient(s)	0.743787
Std Err of Coef.	0.033486

The constant, whose value appears in cell D21, is the estimate of the intercept α (autonomous consumption) and has the same value as we obtained in Section 8.2. The X-coefficient of 0.743787 in cell C27 is the estimate of β, the marginal propensity to consume. (You can use the values in these cells to enter a formula for the fitted values of C, and then to get the residuals, just as you did in Section 8.1.)

The number of observations is shown as 15, while the number of degrees of freedom is the number of observations less 2 (which is the number of parameters to be estimated in the simple regression model). This gives 13 degrees of freedom here. This is really too few to obtain reliable regression results however carefully you specify the model. For research work (as opposed to software demonstrations) you should always try to work with a much larger sample.

The *St(andar)d Err(or) of the Y Est(imate)* is a measure of the spread of the residuals around the regression line, being also an estimator of the standard deviation of the disturbance term σ_u. It is calculated from the residuals using the formula

$$\hat{\sigma}_u = \sqrt{\Sigma \hat{u}^2 / (n - 2)}$$

As an exercise you might like to check this (after first adding the fitted values and residuals to the worksheet).

R Squared measures the goodness of fit of the regression line through the scatter of points. It is defined as the explained sum of squares in the regression divided by the total sum of squares (that is in this case $\Sigma(\hat{C} - \bar{C})^2 / \Sigma(C - \bar{C})^2$, where $\bar{C}$ denotes the sample mean of the dependent variable C). If all the points were to lie exactly on the straight line (so that $\hat{C} = C$) then R^2 would be 1. At the opposite extreme, if all the points are scattered in such a way that the fitted line is perfectly horizontal we would be saying that the fitted (predicted) value of C was always just the sample mean, irrespective of the Y value. Here R^2 would be zero. A value of 0.974326 therefore indicates a pretty good fit, with around 97% of the variations in C around the mean $\bar{C}$ being accounted for (or explained by) variations in Y.

The *St(andar)d Err(or) of (the) Coef(ficient)* is the estimated standard deviation of the sampling distribution of $\hat{\beta}$, the estimator of β. It is used for obtaining confidence intervals for β and for conducting t-tests on the value of β.

Imagine that you had not just one sample of 15 observations, but a great many samples. If you were to run a regression for each of these samples then you would find that the estimates of β would be spread over a range of values (although they would tend on average to be equal to the true value of β). This distribution of estimates is the sampling distribution of $\hat{\beta}$. The smaller is the standard deviation of this distribution, the more confident you could be that an individual estimate is close to the true value of β. Now despite the fact that in practice you will have only one sample available, it will be possible to obtain an estimate of the standard deviation of the sampling distribution (also called the *standard error*) from the sample data. The formula used for the standard error of $\hat{\beta}$ is $s(\hat{\beta}) = \sqrt{\hat{\sigma}_u^2/\Sigma(X - \bar{X})^2}$, where X denotes the independent variable in the regression (here it should be income) and $\hat{\sigma}_u$ is the standard error of the Y estimate as defined above (see, for example Koutsoyiannis, 1977, p. 81).

With this value you can obtain an interval estimate for β within which you can say with a specified level of confidence that the true value of β will lie. Under the classical assumptions the sampling distribution of the estimator $\hat{\beta}$ would have a normal distribution. However, because the standard error has to be estimated, Student's *t*-distribution must be used. (When the number of degrees of freedom is sufficiently large, say 30 or over, the normal distribution can be used as an approximation to the *t*-distribution.)

For a 95% confidence interval with 13 degrees of freedom the confidence interval is $\hat{\beta} \pm s(\hat{\beta})^* t_{13,0.025}$ where $t_{13,0.025}$ is the value from the *t*-tables with 13 degrees of freedom, which leaves 2½% of the distribution in each tail and is 2.16.

Note: Since, whatever the degrees of freedom, the *t*-values are usually close to 2, a rough confidence interval can be found by taking 2 standard errors either side of the estimate of β.

Go to cell A31 and type '95% Confidence Interval for Beta =. Then enter the following:

Cell	Entry
E31	+C27−C28*2.16
F31	ˆ to
G31	+C27+C28*2.16

A more precise 95% estimate could only be obtained if either the model was to be improved so that the estimated standard error could be reduced, or by an increase in the sample size so that a smaller figure from the *t*-distribution could be used.

Many regression software packages produce as part of their output something called the *t*-value for each coefficient estimate. Although this is not given in the 1-2-3 output, it is easy to add to the results. Go to cell A29 and type 't-value. Now in cell C29 put the formula +C27/C28. This will give the ratio of the coefficient estimate to the standard error. Here it works out to just over 22.

This value gives a way of testing the significance of the result. Even in a situation where the regressor (the X variable) has no true influence on the dependent variable (i.e. the true value of β is zero), it is extremely unlikely that the estimated β will also be zero. Thus you will wish to conduct a test to see if the difference from zero of the estimated value is significant. Under the null hypothesis that $\beta = 0$, the ratio $\hat{\beta}/s(\hat{\beta})$ would have a *t*-distribution (with the appropriate number of degrees of freedom). This distribution has a mean of zero but other values can occur. Under the null hypothesis, however, values greater than 2.16 or less than −2.16 could occur only 5% of the time. If values were to be observed in this *critical region* it would be fair to decide that the null hypothesis is unlikely to be true after all. Thus you would reject the null hypothesis and accept that the estimate is not only different, but significantly different from zero. This is equivalent to accepting that the regressor does have an influence on the dependent variable, so sometimes the conclusion is phrased in terms of saying that the X variable is significant (at the specified significance level – significance levels other than 5% could be set by using different values from the tables).

In a case such as you have here where *a priori* a variable is thought to have either a positive effect or no effect at all, you would conduct a *one-tailed* test, with all the 5% being located at one end of the distribution. Thus the 5% critical value (for 13 degrees of freedom) would be 1.771, which, being closer to zero, would be more easily exceeded. So long as the calculated *t*-value exceeds this number from the tables you are able to reject the null hypothesis of no influence of the variable on the dependent variable and conclude that increases in X lead to increases in Y. Notice that a coefficient can be very small but highly significant. The size of the coefficient measures the impact that a one unit change in X has on Y (or here that Y has on C). The *t*-value, however, indicates the statistical significance of the estimated coefficient. A small effect could be highly significant and a large estimate could have very little significance. It is clear from the results in this regression that income has a highly significant effect on consumers' expenditure.

8.3 The Durbin–Watson statistic

Before ending this chapter on the simple regression model we will discuss one other statistic which is usually displayed with regression results and which can easily be calculated within a 1-2-3 worksheet – namely the Durbin–Watson or DW statistic. This statistic is used to assess whether there might be a problem of autocorrelation in a model. *Autocorrelation* means that the disturbance term in any period t, u_t, is not independent of disturbances in other periods as is required by assumption 4 listed at the end of Section 8.1. Instead it is related to past disturbances. In the simplest form of first-order autocorrelation u_t is a proportion of the disturbance in the previous period, u_{t-1}, plus a purely random error ε_t:

$$u_t = \varrho\, u_{t-1} + \varepsilon_t$$

The DW statistic was designed specifically to test the hypothesis $\varrho = 0$ (no autocorrelation) against the alternative that $\varrho \neq 0$.

Although the *u*'s are not observable we may use the residuals (*u*-hats) to compute the statistic which is used in this test using the formula

$$DW = \sum_{t=2}^{n}(\hat{u}_t - \hat{u}_{t-1})^2 / \sum_{t=1}^{n} \hat{u}_t^2$$

The statistic lies in the range 0 to 4 and under the null hypothesis of no auto-correlation is expected to be equal to 2. If the calculated value is close to 2 one may feel able to accept that there is no evidence of autocorrelation. However, if the value is well below 2 one may have to reject this hypothesis and conclude that there is evidence of positive autocorrelation. A formal test can be conducted in which the calculated value is compared with a tabulated value based on the sample size and chosen significance level. If the calculated value is less than the value from the tables, one would reject the hypothesis of no autocorrelation. In the simple regression model with one regressor and 15 observations the critical value (d_L) from the tables at the 5% significance level is 1.08 $(d_u = 1.36)$.

If you have not already done so, add to the worksheet a column to calculate C Hat and another to calculate the residuals (u hat). Put them in the ranges D4.D18 and E4.E18. Now in cell F5 put E4. The residual corresponding to the 1970 observation is placed in the 1971 row where it is interpreted as $\hat{u}_{t-1}$. Copy down to the range F6.F18. At the top of the column (in cell F3) put the label "u hat lag. Notice that you do not have a lagged residual for the first observation. This is why the sum in the numerator of the DW formula goes from $t = 2$ to n. Now to compute the numerator go to cell G5 and enter the formula +(E5−F5)^2. Copy this down to cells G6.G18.

In cell G19 put @SUM(G5.G18). This is the top of the DW ratio. Now go to cell H4 and put +E4*E4 and copy down to H5.H18. In H19 put @SUM(H4.H18).

In cell E27 put the label "DW stat and in cell F27 put +G19/H19. The calculated value of 0.841176 indicates very clearly that there is a problem of positive autocorrelation.

What does this signify and what are the consequences? Autocorrelation can occur for many reasons but all imply some kind of misspecified model. The disturbance term in the regression has to reflect all those influences on the dependent variable other than the independent variable whose influence has been accounted for. Consequently if any important variable was omitted which is itself correlated over time then the errors will have to reflect this. It could also be that the model is too simplistic in terms of its lag structure and that this is reflected in the non-random pattern in the disturbances and hence in the residuals. For example, if consumers adjust their expenditure not to their current income but to variations in their permanent income, this will mean that the disturbance term has to reflect differences between current and permanent income which will be systematic rather than random.

Whatever the source of the problem, any indication that the residuals have a non-random pattern (either from a residual plot or from the DW statistic) should be taken as a signal that the model has been misspecified in some way. Efforts should be made to improve the specification by considering additional explanatory variables suggested by economic theory or by trying out models which include lagged values of the variables to allow for more gradual adjustment to changes in exogenous influences. Indeed, in a properly conducted study the researcher would begin by considering a more general model of this type and would then conduct tests to see if a simpler restricted version of the model could be acceptable. In this chapter it was not our intention to construct a highly accurate model of consumers' expenditure, but simply to illustrate how to use and augment 1-2-3's regression commands. The reader who wishes to know more about recent advances in modelling consumers' expenditure is referred to Davis (1984).

Exercise 8

The table below gives data on United States real personal final consumption expenditure (C) and real personal income (Y). (The figures were derived from *OECD Main Indicators*, various issues, and have been expressed at 1980 prices in billions of dollars.)

	C	Y
1970	1211.89	1581.09
1971	1249.44	1614.31
1972	1313.73	1695.90
1973	1369.31	1796.29
1974	1376.90	1811.78
1975	1383.00	1791.78
1976	1461.32	1874.93
1977	1534.39	1962.29
1978	1597.27	2055.40
1979	1645.31	2130.13
1980	1668.00	2165.30
1981	1697.53	2225.78
1982	1717.07	2223.02
1983	1784.95	2268.07

Use Lotus 1-2-3 to plot a scatter diagram (X–Y graph) of C against Y. Then use the 1-2-3 regression commands to estimate a linear regression equation of C on Y. Calculate the fitted values of C and add the fitted regression line to your graph. Calculate the residuals and plot them against time. Add the calculated t-value and the Durbin–Watson statistic to the regression output by entering appropriate formulae into the worksheet. Write a brief report interpreting your results.

References

D. Begg, S. Fischer and R. Dornbusch, *Economics* (Second Edition) (McGraw-Hill, Maidenhead, 1987).

E. P. Davis, 'The consumption function in macroeconomic models: a comparative study', *Applied Economics*, Vol. 16, No. 6, 1984, pp. 799–838.

A. Koutsoyiannis, *Theory of Econometrics* (Second Edition) (Macmillan, London, 1977).

Chapter 9

Multiple regression analysis with Lotus 1-2-3

Purpose: To show how Lotus 1-2-3 can be used for multiple regression analysis; to describe how the standard 1-2-3 regression output can be augmented and to explain how to interpret the regression results.

Preview: This chapter looks at the use of Lotus 1-2-3 for obtaining the results of a multiple regression using the ordinary least squares (OLS) estimator on data arranged in columns within a worksheet. Real data are used to estimate a model of the demand for alcoholic drink and tobacco in the UK. The objective is to obtain estimates of the price and income elasticities of demand for this range of products. It will first be helpful to consider some relevant theory before specifying the model. This is the subject of Section 9.1. Then the data are assembled within a 1-2-3 worksheet and, as is often the case in empirical work, some preliminary data analysis and transformations are undertaken before moving on to the regression analysis itself. Section 9.2 discusses the data set and all the necessary manipulations that must be made to the raw data. Section 9.3 describes the use of the 1-2-3 regression commands to obtain the OLS estimates and shows how one can add to the regression output to give some additional statistics. Section 9.4 looks at the use of the 1-2-3 framework for conducting *F*-tests on the regression results.

1-2-3 features introduced in this chapter: Automatic scaling of large values in 1-2-3 graphs; manual scale setting; the @LN function.

9.1 Some background theory

Consumer theory predicts that a household's demand for a commodity will depend on the price of that commodity, the price of various other products which might be regarded as either substitutes or complements, and the household's income. For normal goods the demand will respond positively to increases in income (everything else remaining constant).

Empirical analysis of the demand for any particular commodity or commodity group usually focuses initially upon how responsive demand is to these (and possibly some other) influences. In building an empirical model a number of additional theoretical results are available to guide us. For example, neoclassical consumer theory predicts that the sum of the various price elasticities and the income elasticity is zero, that is the demand function is homogeneous of degree zero. The requirements of the constrained maximisation of utility also impose certain restrictions on the form of the utility function (e.g. convexity), which in turn circumscribe the functional forms that can be used for the demand function. However, this still leaves many different formulations available.

In this study we shall assume that the demand function has a multivariate power function (or Cobb–Douglas) form. This is the functional form most often used in empirical work and has two great advantages: although non-linear it is log-linear; and the regression coefficients are the (constant) elasticities. At this level of generality we would write

$$\ln Q = \alpha_0 + \alpha_1 \ln (M/\Pi) + \sum_{j=1}^{n} \beta_j \ln P_j + u \tag{9.1}$$

where Q is the demand for alcoholic drink and tobacco, M is consumers' money income, and the P_j's are the prices of all commodities (from $j = 1$ to n) including P_1 which is the 'price' of drink and tobacco. Π is the overall price index, which is a weighted average of the prices of all consumer goods. u is the disturbance term and the α's and .194's are parameters.

Now we cannot hope to include the prices of all commodities among the regressors and we take the conventional approach of using the overall price index Π as a surrogate for the influences of the prices of all these other goods.

This gives the equation

$$\ln Q = \alpha_0 + \alpha_1 \ln (M/\Pi) + \beta_1 \ln P_1 + \beta_2 \ln \Pi + u \tag{9.2}$$

We then impose the further restriction $\beta_2 = -\beta_1$. This restriction means that we can write the demand for drink and tobacco as a function of real income and the real or relative price of drink and tobacco, that is, its nominal price deflated by the overall price index Π. Changing the notation slightly to put $Y = M/\Pi$, $P = P_1/\Pi$, and α_2 for β_1, we have

$$\ln Q = \alpha_0 + \alpha_1 \ln Y + \alpha_2 \ln P + u \tag{9.3}$$

This model is basically the one we shall use in our empirical work, with a real expenditure series used for Q. We make one further modification because we shall be using quarterly data and consumers' expenditure on drink and tobacco shows a marked seasonal pattern. Rather than using seasonally adjusted data (as described in Chapter 4) we use unadjusted data and add to the regression equation three seasonal dummies S_1, S_2 and S_3. The model becomes

$$\ln Q_t = \alpha_0 + \alpha_1 \ln Y_t + \alpha_2 \ln P_t + \delta_1 S_1 + \delta_2 S_2 + \delta_3 S_3 + u_t \qquad (9.4)$$

S_1 takes the value 1 for every first-quarter observation and zero for all other observations; S_2 takes the value 1 for every second-quarter observation and zero for all other observations; and S_3 takes the value 1 for every third-quarter observation and zero for all other observations. Thus fourth-quarter periods correspond to the basic equation but the regression intercept may be shifted up (or more likely down) by amounts δ_1, δ_2 and δ_3 in each of the other quarters.

This approach is superior to working with seasonally adjusted data for two reasons. First, it means that any seasonal variations in Q which may be accounted for by seasonal movements in P or Y will be attributed to these variables rather than being simply filtered out. Second, rather than merely measuring the size of the seasonal shifts (the values of the deltas), their significance can also be assessed through the regression.

Before moving on to the data you should note some of the ways in which this model differs from some of the more complex models which may be found in the literature of empirical demand analysis.

Aggregation

Our model is a highly aggregated model in terms of the commodity group (we are combining two commodity groups which ought to be analysed separately and possibly even further subdivided into types of drink or tobacco products). We are also aggregating over consumers – some models dealing with such aggregates divide quantity and income variables by population figures to obtain per capita measures.

Lags

There are no lagged variables in this model. Only the current values of Y and P are included and no lagged values of Q enter the regression equation. In their work on consumer demand in the United States, Houthakker and Taylor (1970) included a lagged dependent variable (i.e. last period's consumption figure) when modelling tobacco in an effort to represent the effects of habits and addiction.

Other variables

No variables other than income and price are included in the model. Some researchers have successfully introduced variables measuring the influence of advertising in their models. However, such variables are most likely to be significant at a finer level of commodity disaggregation since advertising appears to influence the market share of individual brands but not the overall consumption of a commodity group.

Functional form

As already commented, this functional form has been adopted as much for convenience and for comparison with previous studies as for strong theoretical reasons. Experimentation with other more flexible functional forms has been a feature of some recent work, but this usually requires more sophisticated estimation techniques than ordinary least squares.

Homogeneity restrictions

The imposition of the restriction $\beta_2 = -\beta_1$ ought really to be tested and not simply imposed. This would certainly be essential for a proper piece of applied econometrics but is omitted here due to space constraints.

Single-equation problems

The model is a single-equation model with the quantity demanded being determined by income and price variables. Even a beginning student of economics knows that the price of a commodity results from the interaction of the forces of supply and demand. The quantity that we observe is the result of the solution of these pressures. Ignoring this may mean that what we obtain from the estimation procedure is not the demand function but some hybrid function which is a mixture of supply and demand. We shall not concern ourselves here with such difficulties but assume that the demand function is 'identified' by our method.

A second problem which may result from using ordinary least squares regression with a single-equation model is that this estimation procedure will give biased results if causation runs not only from price to quantity but also from quantity to price. Since the prices of drink and tobacco products are to a large extent determined by the tax and duties imposed by government, we shall be content to assume that they are exogenous of demand.

All these and other issues would have to be addressed by a full empirical study of drink and tobacco demand (see for example, Duffy (1983)). However, since this is only an introduction to the subject and an illustration of the use of 1-2-3 we shall proceed having given these warnings about the possible deficiencies of the approach which should be borne in mind when interpreting the results.

9.2 Preliminary data analysis and transformations

The data in Table 9.1 are taken from *Economic Trends Annual Supplement*, 1988, and cover the period 1971 Q1 to 1987 Q2.

Table 9.1 Data set for regression analysis

Period		QCURR	TCURR	Q	T	Y
1971	Q1	877	8032	2548	26510	29699
	Q2	1053	8815	3025	28219	30972
	Q3	1116	9203	3212	29118	31148
	Q4	1238	9774	3557	30638	32298
1972	Q1	963	9132	2743	28125	31361
	Q2	1161	9855	3263	29923	34203
	Q3	1212	10353	3365	30830	33598
	Q4	1382	11151	3806	32617	35397
1973	Q1	1058	10649	2904	30718	34233
	Q2	1318	11163	3593	31362	36215
	Q3	1398	11667	3800	32198	36286
	Q4	1587	12605	4248	33485	36452
1974	Q1	1218	11657	3213	29761	34936
	Q2	1489	12765	3548	30827	34850
	Q3	1557	13621	3623	31779	36204
	Q4	1880	15081	4316	33539	36115
1975	Q1	1438	14413	3141	30176	36423
	Q2	1810	15988	3510	31019	35442
	Q3	2008	16804	3602	31341	35757
	Q4	2327	18184	4102	32675	35210
1976	Q1	1683	17262	2900	29908	35241
	Q2	2153	18268	3531	30726	35298
	Q3	2340	19267	3712	31633	36751
	Q4	2630	21076	4129	33334	35454
1977	Q1	2045	19880	2963	29849	33997
	Q2	2517	20967	3485	30276	34094
	Q3	2612	22059	3538	31331	35073
	Q4	2999	23851	4097	33535	36385
1978	Q1	2317	23107	3164	31622	35786
	Q2	2759	24051	3702	32018	37225
	Q3	2820	25626	3753	33398	37957
	Q4	3272	27239	4295	34890	38686
1979	Q1	2522	26258	3257	32659	38113
	Q2	3117	28890	3890	34619	39053
	Q3	3349	30314	3835	34090	39144
	Q4	3911	32899	4360	36120	41721
1980	Q1	3135	32149	3358	33973	39756
	Q2	3537	33167	3542	33324	39748
	Q3	3760	35225	3707	34622	40424
	Q4	4344	36929	4169	35551	40369
1981	Q1	3427	35419	3180	33347	40213
	Q2	4096	37158	3440	33542	39904
	Q3	4265	39121	3515	34544	39220
	Q4	4879	41329	3948	35936	39373
1982	Q1	3816	38963	2984	33064	39362
	Q2	4346	40463	3279	33423	39234
	Q3	4478	42746	3327	35065	39614
	Q4	5244	45427	3908	36895	39516
1983	Q1	4169	42956	3003	34319	39265
	Q2	4660	44158	3274	34802	40188
	Q3	4979	46913	3475	36700	40744
	Q4	5771	49041	4060	38156	41104
1984	Q1	4511	46031	3068	35123	40573
	Q2	5064	47918	3330	35916	41182
	Q3	5285	49316	3445	36825	41303
	Q4	6192	52647	4083	39192	42613
1985	Q1	4854	50034	3053	36234	41370
	Q2	5446	51483	3348	36690	42716
	Q3	5682	54406	3459	38681	42704
	Q4	6807	57769	4201	40896	43334
1986	Q1	5100	54910	3011	37990	42770
	Q2	5782	56848	3361	39088	44419
	Q3	5997	59803	3460	40983	44727
	Q4	7066	62606	4196	43216	45439
1987	Q1	5359	58611	3032	39552	44980
	Q2	6027	60829	3427	40768	46067

Source: Economic Trends Annual Supplement, 1988

The variables are defined as follows:

Q = real consumers' expenditure on alcoholic drink and tobacco in £ million, 1980 prices (p. 28 column 4 (FCCA))

Y = real personal disposable income in £ million, 1980 prices (p. 20 column 6 (CFAG))

QCURR = consumers' expenditure on alcoholic drink and tobacco in £ million, current prices (p. 25 column 4 (CDFH))

T = total consumers' expenditure in £ million, 1980 prices (p. 28 column 1 (CCBH))

TCURR = total consumers' expenditure in £ million, current prices (p. 25 column 1 (AIIK))

Where the page numbers refer to *Economic Trends Annual Supplement 1988* and the four letter code is the CSO identifier for each series.

Enter these data into a new worksheet with general heading and labels as follows:

Cell	Label
A1	DRINK :
A2	a multiple regression analysis of the demand for
A3	alcoholic drink and tobacco in the UK 1971–1987
A4	"Period
B4	"QCURR
C4	"TCURR
D4	"Q
E4	"T
F4	"Y

Then enter the respective variables (beginning with the time periods in column A) into rows 5 to 70 of the worksheet.

To begin the analysis you should examine time series plots of Q and QCURR. Construct a line graph of QCURR using the following command:

/Graph Type Line X A5.A70⁻ A B5.B70⁻

You can also use *Options Scale Skip* with a skip factor of 8 to tidy up the look of the graph.

Lotus 1-2-3 will automatically transform the units on the Y-axis into thousands. If you do not like this (since the data are already in £ millions) you will have to edit the figures so that they are divided by 1000 and you can then give your own axis label with units of £ billion. The graph shown in Figure 9.1 was produced from the 1-2-3 worksheet using Quattro, which does not automatically modify the scale in this way.

The series has a clear upward trend with a pronounced seasonal pattern. Of course, part of the reason for the increases in expenditure in current

UK expenditure on drink and tobacco

[current prices;1971Q1−1987Q2]

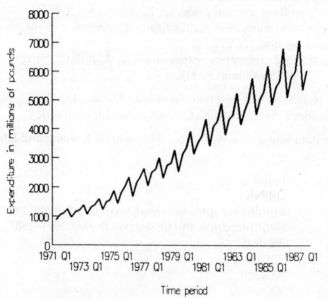

Figure 9.1 Times series plot of expenditure at current prices

prices may be accounted for by general price increases, i.e. inflation. Store this graph as QCURR using the **Name** command and construct a new graph showing how the real expenditure series Q has evolved (just replace range A by D5.D70 and change the titles).

You should see something like Figure 9.2 on the screen.

The graph reveals that real expenditure has not really increased at all, although the seasonal pattern is still very pronounced. It is apparent that the seasonal dummies are likely to play an important role in explaining movements in this series. The series has something of a cyclical pattern to it, with Q first increasing on average up until the end of 1974, and then falling a little for three years, then rising again and so on. If the objective was simply to forecast the series, some kind of decomposition approach with a cyclical factor as well as a seasonal factor might work quite well. However, the object is to measure the responsiveness of Q to changes in real income and the relative price of drink and tobacco using regression analysis. We must first use 1-2-3 to create the variables which will actually be used in the regression.

UK expenditure on drink and tobacco [constant prices;1971Q1−1987Q2]

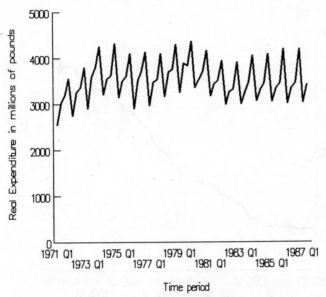

Figure 9.2 Times series plot of expenditure at constant prices

Go to G4 and enter "PNOM (short for nominal price). The range G5.G70 is to hold an index of the nominal price of this group of commodities. As we saw in Chapter 2, this is implicit in the data and can be extracted when series both at constant and current prices are available.

In cell G5 put +100*B5/D5 and copy this down to the rest of the range. If you look at a graph of this series (see Figure 9.3) you will see that, after a slow start, it follows a steady upward trend. Indeed, that much is probably apparent from the figures themselves where you can see that the index goes from just under 35 in 1970 to around 175 in 1987.

However, like QCURR this series has inflation built into it. You can get a good idea of how prices changed overall in the period by constructing an index of the prices of all consumer goods.

Go to cell H4 and put the label "PDEF (short for price deflator). In cell H5 enter the formula +100*C5/E5 and copy down the column. Now you can construct an index of the real or relative price of drink and tobacco, i.e. the nominal price deflated by the price index for all goods. In cell I4 put "PREL and in cell I5 enter the formula +100*G5/F5 (and copy down).

The graph of this series (Figure 9.4) shows an interesting pattern with an

Nominal price of drink and tobacco [1980=100]

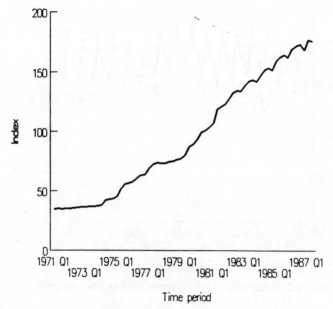

Figure 9.3 Plot of nominal prices

initial fall, then some ups and downs and then a steady increase. At the beginning of the period the (nominal) prices of drink and tobacco products were not increased in line with inflation although in the 1980s they have been rising faster than prices overall. (You can see this even more clearly if you view a graph showing PNOM and PDEF together.)

Now the regression model you are going to use is log-linear in form so you must first generate the logarithms of the relevant variables in the worksheet. Enter column headings as follows:

Cell	Label
J4	"LN(Q)
K4	"LN(Y)
L4	"LN(P)

In Cell J5 put @LN(D5) and copy down to cells J6.J70. @LN is the built-in function which gives the natural logarithm of a (positive) number. In cell K5 put @LN(F5) and copy down, and in cell L5 put @LN(I5) and copy down.

Real price of drink and tobacco

[1980=100]

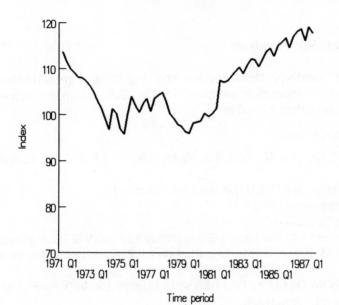

Figure 9.4 Plot of real prices

Now you need to create the seasonal dummies. Enter the following labels:

Cell	Label
M4	"S1
N4	"S2
O4	"S3

S1 will have the value 1 for every first quarter and 0 for every other quarter, S2 will be 1 for every second quarter and 0 otherwise, and S3 will have the value 1 for every third quarter and 0 otherwise. Thus the first part of the set of entries (for 1971) will look like this (cells M5.O8):

1	0	0
0	1	0
0	0	1
0	0	0

Enter these values and then copy this range to cell M9. 1-2-3 will give the values for 1972. Keep copying in this way until all the dummy variable values have been created (at the end you will only copy two rows in for 1987 quarter 1 and 2). (Column M should now have values alternating 1 0 0 0 1 0 0 0, etc.; column N should have 0 1 0 0 0 1 0 0, etc.; and column O should have values 0 0 1 0 0 0 1 0, etc.)

This completes the pre-regression data work and you can now proceed to the regression analysis itself.

9.3 The regression analysis

Go to cell A73 and type 'Drink and tobacco : log-linear regression model. In cell A74 put 'Dependent variable : LN(Q). Then call up the regression commands using the keystrokes

/Data Regression

For the X-range give K5.O70 (i.e. all the LN(Y), LN(P), S1, S2 and S3 values).
For the Y-range give J5.J70 (i.e. the LN(Q) values)
For the Output-range give A75.
Then select *Go*.

After a short wait the basic 1-2-3 regression results will be displayed in cells A75.G83. Before considering what they tell us you can add to them as follows.

Copy cells K4.O4 to C81.G81 (this will add labels for the X coefficients to help in their interpretation).
Then in cell A84 put 't-values.
In cell C84 put +C82/C83 and copy to D84.G84
Then go to cell P4 and put "LN(Q)HAT.
In cell P5 enter the formula

$$+\$D\$76+\$C\$82*K5+\$D\$82*L5+\$E\$82*M5+\$E\$82*N5+\$G\$82*O5$$

This formula will calculate the fitted value of LN(Q) for 1971 Q1. Now copy it down into P6.P70.

In cell Q4 put UHAT and in cell A5 put +J5–P5 and then copy down to Q6.Q70 (these are the regression residuals).
Now compute the DW statistic as follows:

In cell R6 put +(Q6–R6)^2 and copy to S7.S70.
In T5 put +Q5*Q5 and copy to Q6.Q70.
In cell S71 put @SUM(S6.S70) and in cell T71 put @SUM(T5.T70)
Now you can add to the regression results as follows:

Cell	Entry
A86	"DW statistic
D86	+S71/T71

To improve the layout you can insert a row at A79 (/*Worksheet Insert Row* A79⁻) and then move what is now A87.D87 to row 79. Then in cell E80 put '[1970Q1–1987Q2].

Print out the results (Range A73.G85) and they should look like Table 9.2.

Table 9.2

```
Drink and tobacco : log-linear regression model
Dependent variable : LN(Q)
             Regression Output:
Constant                        7.609192
Std Err of Y Est                0.025619       SSR 0.039381
R Squared                       0.958765      Fcal 279.0212
DW statistic                    1.418567
No. of Observations                   66 [1970Q1-1987Q2]
Degrees of Freedom                    60
                       LN(Y)      LN(P)        S1        S2        S3
X Coefficient(s)     0.416887  -0.79400  -0.28185  -0.15371  -0.12507
Std Err of Coef.     0.035599  0.055366  0.009028  0.009006  0.009119
t-values            11.71046  -14.3407  -31.2183  -17.0665  -13.7154
```

Now you can interpret the results. The fitted regression line has the equation

$$LN(Q)HAT = 7.609192 + 0.416887\,LN(Y) - 0.79400\,LN(P) - 0.28285\,S1$$
$$- 0.15371\,S2 - 0.12507\,S3$$

The estimated coefficients all have acceptable signs and magnitudes. The coefficient of LN(Y) is positive and in the range 0 to 1. It provides a point estimate of the income elasticity of demand for drink and tobacco and implies that for every 1% increase in real income, expenditure on drink and tobacco would rise by less than half a per cent.

The coefficient of LN(P) is negative and is consistent with an inverse relationship between demand and price. The coefficient estimate suggests that the price elasticity of demand is around -0.8 so for a 10% increase in price (everything else being equal) the demand for drink and tobacco would fall by around 8%.

The coefficients of the seasonal dummies show that demand is below its fourth-quarter value in every other quarter, declining most severely in quarter 1. For example, the value of Q is predicted to be only approximately 75% of what it would be on the basis of Y and P alone. (Taking antilogarithms, for quarter 1 $QHAT = A\,Y^{0.416887}\,P^{-0.79400}\,S1^{-0.28185}$ where $A = exp(7.609192)$. This is roughly three-quarters of the value you would get by ignoring the seasonal dummy.)

The *t*-values suggest that all the independent variables are easily significant at the 5% level and the high R^2 confirms a good overall fit. However, the DW statistic at 1.418567 is below the critical d_L value of 1.44 (at the 5% level) so the results must still be viewed with some suspicion. A residual plot (see Figure 9.5) suggests some 'tracking' which reinforces this concern. However, as we noted in Section 9.1, the model is a highly simplified one in terms of the level of aggregation of the dependent variable and the lack of any dynamics. We should therefore not be surprised that the results are deficient when we delve beyond the apparently satisfactory coefficient estimates, t-statistics and R^2 values.

Residual plot
[drink and tobacco regression model]

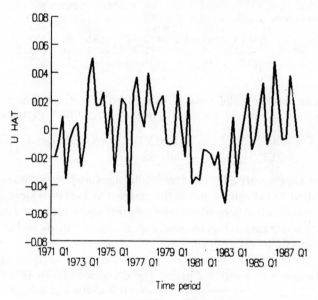

Figure 9.5 Residual plot

9.4 Further regression statistics

Many regression outputs show the calculated F-statistic for testing the overall significance of the regression. In our model this would be used to test the joint hypothesis

$$\alpha_1 = \alpha_2 = \delta_1 = \delta_2 = \delta_3 = 0$$

This contrasts with the t-statistics which are used to test hypotheses about the individual parameters.

The F-test is based on the ratio of two independent estimates of the variance of the u's, σ_u^2. For the denominator we have $\Sigma\, \hat{u}_t^2 / [N - (k + 1)]$, where N is the sample size and k is the number of independent variables (regressors). $N - (k + 1) = N - k - 1$ is then the number of degrees of freedom in the regression. The numerator is $\Sigma\,(\hat{Y} - \bar{Y})_t^2/k$, where $\hat{Y}$ refers to the fitted value of the dependent variable (which in our model is LN(Q)HAT).

Under the null hypothesis the movements in LN(Q)HAT would be purely random, reflecting only movements in the disturbance u, so this expression could also be used as an estimator of σ_u^2.

The ratio of these two variance estimates should have an F distribution with k and $N - (k + 1)$ degrees of freedom. If the calculated value exceeds the value from the tables (at some specified significance level) the null hypothesis of no relationship will be rejected in favour of the hypothesis that some relationship does exist.

The simplest way of calculating the F-value is to use the formula

$$F_{\text{cal}} = (R^2/k) / [(1 - R^2)/(N - k - 1)]$$

Go to cell E78 and put "Fcal. Then in cell F78 put the formula $+(D78/5)/((1-D78)/D81)$. The calculated value of F should work out to be 279.0212, which is easily in excess of the critical value at the 5% significance level with 5 and 60 degrees of freedom (namely 2.37). The null hypothesis of no overall relationship is comfortably rejected.

Although this was not a surprising result in view of the high R^2 and large t-values, we now show how to construct a more discriminating test, the Chow test. In this test we look to see whether observations from two subsamples of the data set can be accepted as coming from the same underlying data-generation process. In fact we must assume that the error variance σ_u^2 is the same for all observations. This allows us to test the hypothesis that the regression parameters in the first subsample take the same values as those in the second subsample.

The procedure is as follows. First run separate regressions for the first n_1 observations, for the remaining n_2 observations and for the full (pooled) sample. Then compute the following statistic:

$$F_{\text{cal}} = \frac{[\text{SSR}_P - (\text{SSR}_1 + \text{SSR}_2)]/(k + 1)}{(\text{SSR}_1 + \text{SSR}_2)/[n_1 + n_2 - 2(k + 1)]}$$

where SSR_P is the sum of squared residuals from the regression based on the pooled sample, SSR_1 is the sum of squared residuals from the regression based on the first subsample and SSR_2 is the sum of squared residuals from the regression based on the second subsample.

Under the null hypothesis this statistic should have a small value so that its calculated value would be less than the critical value at the 5% level (with $k + 1$ and $n_1 + n_2 - 2(k + 1)$ degrees of freedom). If, however, the calculated value was to exceed the critical value we would have to reject the null hypothesis. This would be evidence of either a structural shift in the relationship between the two samples or of misspecification of the model.

Go to cell A87 and type 'First subsample. Then run the regression using only data for 1971–78 (i.e. rows 5 to 36). Put the 1-2-3 results in the worksheet beginning at cell A88.

Now go to cell A98 and type 'Second subsample. Run the regression for 1979–87 (i.e. rows 38 to 70). Put the 1-2-3 results beginning at cell A99.

Now in computing the F-statistic recall the definition of the St(andard) Err(or) of the Y Est(imate) given in Chapter 8, namely $\hat{\sigma}_u = \sqrt{\Sigma \hat{u}^2/(N-2)}$. Now in a multiple regression, instead of using $N - 2$ degrees of freedom in the denominator we require $N - k - 1$ degrees of freedom (in a simple regression $k = 1$ so the number of degrees of freedom simplifies to $N - 2$). Now the 1-2-3 results include a value for $\hat{\sigma}_u$ and by manipulating the formula we can demonstrate a simple way of recovering the sum of squared residuals from it.

Square both sides and multiply across, to give

$$\Sigma \, \hat{u}^2 = (N - k - 1) \, \hat{\sigma}_u^2$$

This means that to get the sum of squared residuals for a regression all you need do is to square the standard error of the Y estimate and multiply by the degrees of freedom. You do not need the actual individual residuals.

Go to cell E77 and enter "SSR, and in cell F77 put +D81*D77*D77. In cell E90 put "SSR, and in cell F90 put +D93*D90*D90; in cell E101 put "SSR, and then +D104*D101*D101 in cell F101.

Then go to cell A110 and type "CHOW TEST. In cell B110 put "Fcal=, and in cell C110 put the formula

$+(F77-(F90+F101))/6/((F90+F101)/(D93+D104)$

The value displayed should be 5.629474, and this is in excess of the critical value of $F(6, 54)$ at the 5% level, which is around 2.30 (the tables do not give a value for 6 and 54 degrees of freedom so the value must be approximated by interpolation). Here again we have evidence of misspecification. Either the original equation has been inadequately specified or some shift has occurred in the demand function since 1979 (in which case this shift should be allowed for in the overall regression model).

Although Lotus 1-2-3 can be used to estimate and test multiple regression models as we have shown here, it is not an ideal framework for thorough econometric analysis. It does not automatically generate the range of diagnostic statistics required for modern econometric analysis. Although it is possible to augment the results within the worksheet to add the t-values, DW statistic and F-values, some of these figures require a considerable number of worksheet manipulations.

Another drawback is faced when one attempts to select regressors from a list of potential explanatory variables (as one might if one was searching for the appropriate form of model within a general class of models). The X variables included in the regression must be in adjacent columns. If they are not, the only way to make progress within 1-2-3 is to move intervening columns to a new position so that the X variables required form a single uninterrupted range. This is a very clumsy approach to regression analysis.

Thus, although 1-2-3 offers a useful framework to assist beginners to understand the basics of regression analysis by enabling them to see how the results are calculated, it is too inflexible for anything much more than the estimation of simple pre-specified models. Nevertheless, a 1-2-3 worksheet does provide a convenient framework for storing data for use with other packages and for conducting some preliminary data analysis.

Exercise 9

The data given below are annual index numbers of manufacturing output, labour and capital in the USA, 1899–1922 (they come from Cobb and Douglas's original 1928 study of empirical production functions). Use Lotus 1-2-3 to perform a regression of log(output) on log(labour) and log(capital). Supplement the results to show *t*-values, the *F*-value and the DW statistic. Write a brief report on your findings.

Year	Output	Labour	Capital
1899	100	100	100
1900	101	105	107
1901	112	110	114
1902	122	118	122
1903	124	123	131
1904	122	116	138
1905	143	125	149
1906	152	133	163
1907	151	138	176
1908	126	121	185
1909	155	140	198
1910	159	144	208
1911	153	143	216
1912	177	152	226
1913	184	154	236
1914	169	149	244
1915	189	154	266
1916	225	182	298
1917	227	196	335
1918	223	200	366
1919	218	193	387
1920	231	193	407
1921	179	147	417
1922	240	161	431

References

C. W. Cobb and P. H. Douglas, 'A theory of production', *American Economic Review*, Vol. 18 (Supplement), 1928, pp. 139–65.

M. Duffy, 'The demand for alcoholic drink in the UK 1963–78', *Applied Economics*, Vol. 15, 1983, pp. 125–40.

H. S. Houthakker and L. D. Taylor, *Consumer Demand in the United States* (Second Edition) (Harvard University, Cambridge, 1970).

Chapter 10

Dynamic economic models: difference equations and Lotus 1-2-3

Purpose: To demonstrate how dynamic economic models (which are described mathematically by difference equations) can be set up and analysed within a worksheet framework. To show how experiments can be conducted by altering the values of key parameters and exogenous variables in order to discover the dynamic properties of the model.

Preview: This chapter shows how a spreadsheet package with graphics capabilities (such as Lotus 1-2-3) can be used to examine the properties of dynamic economic models. With examples from both microeconomics and macroeconomics it is shown how the model's equations can be entered into a worksheet and the time paths of the variables generated. With the model's parameters stored together at the top of the worksheet they can be changed conveniently and the effect on the time paths of the variables can be viewed straight away. In this way a large set of numerical examples can be scrutinised rapidly, allowing the modeller to draw conclusions about which combinations of parameter values give rise to convergent paths and which do not. Rather than replacing formal analysis, the objective of this kind of experimentation is to provide an intuitive base upon which to develop a more formal analytical treatment.

Section 10.1 describes the basic approach to setting up difference equation models on a spreadsheet. Section 10.2 looks at an application in microdynamics – the cobweb model. This is extended in Section 10.3 to allow for random disturbances and a more complex price expectations mechanism. Section 10.4 describes a macroeconomics spreadsheet application; the multiplier–accelerator model. A more flexible version of this model is examined in Section 10.4

1-2-3 features introduced in this chapter: /**Worksheet Global Column-Width**; *ERR* cell display; @RAND built-in function.

This chapter is based on a paper written jointly with Bob Jones of Trent Polytechnic (Judge and Jones, 1988).

10.1 Difference equations on a spreadsheet

Suppose we wish to examine difference equations of the form

$$Y(t) = a + b\,Y(t-1) \qquad\qquad (10.1)$$

for different values of the parameters a and b and for various initial values $Y(0)$. Equation (10.1) is the general form of a first-order linear difference equation, and one frequently encounters equations of this type in economic dynamics.

You can enter both the equation and values of a, b and $Y(0)$ into a spreadsheet as follows. Begin a new worksheet and in cell A1 put

DIFFERENCE : worksheet to analyse first-order linear difference equations

Then enter labels as follows:

Cell	Label
A2	Parameters
A3	a =
A4	b =
C3	'<---
C4	'<---
D2	Initial value
D3	Y(0) =
F3	'<---

(The arrows are used to point to the cells where the parameters will be entered.)

Now add the following entries:

Cell	Entry
B6	Difference equation
A8	Y(t) =
B8	+B3
C8	^+
D8	+B4
E8	Y(t−1)
B10	Equilibrium value
B12	Y* =
C12	+B3/(1−B4)

Row 8 of the worksheet simply displays the difference equation currently being analysed. Go to cells B3 and B4 and enter values of 10 and 0.5 for the respective parameters. The equilibrium value of 20 is now also displayed in cell C12. For the given parameters this is the value which, if it occurs in any particular time period, will generate an identical value for the next time period and so on.

Putting Y^* for both $Y(t)$ and $Y(t-1)$ in equation (10.1) we find

$Y^* = a + b\, Y^*$

Solving for Y^* we obtain $Y^* = a/(1-b)$ (hence the formula in cell C12).

Now consider what happens if Y does not initially have this equilibrium value. Go to cell E3 and enter 12. Then enter the following labels:

Cell	Label
B14	'Time path for Y
B16	"t
C16	"Y(t)

Now use /**Data Fill** to generate values for t going from 0 to 40 in the range B17.B57.

In cell C17 put +E3. The initial value for Y will be displayed. Cell C18 is to show the value of $Y(1)$ which, according to equation (10.1) will be $Y(1) = a + b\, Y(0)$. So enter the formula +\$B\$3+\$B\$4*C17 and the value 16 will be displayed. The \$ signs are needed so that the parameters remain fixed as the formula is copied down. Copy the formula to the range C19.C57.

The evolution of Y over time should now be shown in the worksheet. (Use the $<PgDn>$ key to see the values for the later periods.) With the parameter values given above the time path would show uniform convergence with the $Y(t)$ values steadily approaching the equilibrium value of 20. Indeed, by period 34 the computer finds the value of $Y(t)$ so close to 20 that this figure will be displayed for this and all subsequent periods.

To give a more immediate view of this convergence use the graphics facility to create a line graph with C17.C57 as the A range and B17.B57 as the X range.

After various modifications such as skipping every 5 values on the X-axis, manually setting the Y-axis to go from 0 to 25, removing the markers and adding titles the graph should look something like Figure 10.1

The graph shows how $Y(t)$, while initially below the equilibrium value, converges uniformly towards the equilibrium value. The uniform convergence is because the parameter b is positive but less than 1.

Now try changing its value and seeing the effect on the characteristics of the time path. Go to cell B4 and change the value to 0.9. The equilibrium now changes to 100 and although there is convergence towards this value it is much slower than for $b = 0.5$. Even after 40 time periods it has still not quite been reached. Set the graph scaling back to *Automatic* and look at the graph again. Experiment with different values of b and look to see how the value affects the equilibrium and the time path.

Values between zero and one give uniform convergence, with convergence being faster, the closer b is to zero. Values of b greater than 1 cause the path to diverge so that Y will never reach equilibrium. Negative values lead to oscillations around the equilibrium with the series converging on the

$$Y(t) = 10 + 0.5\ Y(t{-}1)$$

$$Y(0) = 12$$

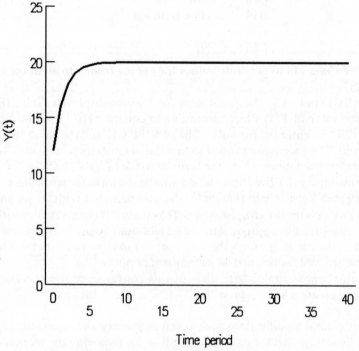

Figure 10.1 Graphical solution of difference equation

equilibrium so long as *b* is less than 1 in absolute value. You can switch backwards and forwards from worksheet to graph just by pressing the GRAPH function key F10. By experimenting in this way (changing the values of *a* and *Y*(0), too) you should get a good idea of the properties of first-order difference equations. Check them in a textbook such as Chiang (1984) or Baumol (1959).

10.2 Microdynamics: the cobweb model

In this section we develop the use of spreadsheets in the analysis of dynamic models by considering a simple microdynamic model based on the familiar cobweb model. The model has the form

$$QD(t) = a - b P(t) \tag{10.2a}$$
$$QS(t) = -e + d P(t - 1) \tag{10.2b}$$
$$QD(t) = QS(t) \tag{10.2c}$$

Equation (10.2a) is the demand function and it shows that for some commodity the quantity demanded is a linear function of the price of the commodity. Equation (10.2b) is the supply function and it shows that the quantity supplied is a linear function of last period's price. Equation (10.2c) is the market-clearing equation which provides the mechanism by which price is determined in each period.

These equations can be reduced to a simple first-order linear difference equation in P:

$$P(t) = (a+e)/b + (-d/b) P(t-1) \tag{10.3}$$

From our discussion in Section 10.1 it is clear that if the market is initially in equilibrium at $P = (a+e)/(b+d)$ then it will remain so (given no outside disturbances). However, if $P(0)$ is not equal to this value then P will oscillate around the equilibrium (the coefficient of $P(t-1)$ is negative) and will converge if $d/b < 1$ (or $d < b$).

Set up a new worksheet as follows

A1   COBWEB1 : simple microdynamics
B2   where supply depends on last period's price

To improve the screen display you should convert all the columns to a 7 character width. The command is

/Worksheet Global Column-Width 7¯

Now enter labels as follows:

Cell	Label
D4	Parameter
A5	Demand :
B5	Intercept a =
E5	'<-:-
F5	Supply :
G5	Intercept e =
J5	'<---
B6	Slope
C6	"b =
E6	'<---
G6	Slope
H6	"d =
J6	'<---
D7	Initial price
D8	P(0) =

F8   '<---
D10   Model equations

Then enter further labels and formulae as follows:

A11   QD(t) =
B11   +D5
C11   ^−
D11   +D6
E11   P(t)
G11   Demand function
A12   QS(t) =
B12   −I5
C12   ^+
D12   +I6
E12   P(t−1)
G12   Supply function
A13   QD(t) =
C13   QS(t)
G13   Market clearing equation

Now before the worksheet is completed use the /**Range Name Create** command to name these cells as follows:

Cell   Name
D5   a
D6   b
I5   e
I6   d
E8   P(0)

This will make the subsequent cell formulae easier to enter and interpret.
    Now add cell labels and formulae as shown:

Cell   Label/formula
D15   Equilibrium
C16   Price =
C17   Quantity =
E16   +(a+e)/(b+d)
E17   +a−b*E16

Do not be concerned at the *ERR* display in these cells. This is because the b and d cells have yet to have values assigned to them so 1-2-3 assumes that they have zero values. The formula (a+e)/(b+d) requires the computer to divide by zero and consequently it returns an error message.

Now enter values as follows:

Cell	Value
D5	15
D6	5
I5	1
I6	3

The model equations will now be displayed in rows 11 and 12 and the equilibrium price and quantity will be shown on cells E16 and E17 (see Table 10.1).

Table 10.1

```
COBWEB1 : simple microdynamics
        where supply depends on last period's price

                        Parameters
Demand:Intercept a =      15 <---    Supply:Intercept e =     1 <---
        Slope    b =       5 <---           Slope    d =     3 <---
                        Initial price
                        P(0) =       1 <---

                        Model equations
QD(t) =      15      -        5 P(t)        Demand function
QS(t) =      -1      +        3 P(t-1)      Supply function
QD(t) =           QS(t)                     Market clearing equation

                        Equilibrium
                Price =            2
                Quantity =         5
```

Now you can produce a table of values to enable you to plot the time series graphs. Enter the following labels:

Cell	Label
A20	"t
C20	"P(t)
E20	"QD(t)
G20	"QS(t)

Use /**Data Fill** to create a column of numbers from 0 to 40 in cells A21.A61. In cell C21 put +P(0) (or +E8 if this cell has not been named). A value of 0 is displayed. Go to cell E8 and enter a value of 1. In cell C22 put the formula +($a+$e)/$b+(−$d/$b)*C21 and copy this down to the range C23.C61.
In cell E22 put +$a−$b*C22 and copy to E23.E61.
In cell G22 put −$e+$d*C21 and copy to G23.G61.
You should now have a table of values showing how the market price and quantity fluctuate over time.

Use the /**Graph Type Line** command sequence to construct a graph plotting the price series against time. It should look something like Figure 10.2.

Time path of PRICE

[COBWEB1]

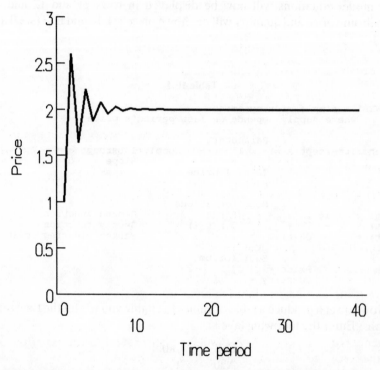

Figure 10.2 Graph of prices series against time for COBWEB1 worksheet

Price begins below the equilibrium and fluctuates around the equilibrium with damped oscillations, converging towards the equilibrium value of 2.

Now try each of the following combinations of b and d and draw some general conclusions about the conditions which must apply in order that equilibrium should be stable (i.e. for price to converge to equilibrium if it is not initially at that level).

b	d
5	4.5
5	0.5
2	3
3	3

You should be able to see that the ratio d/b is crucial and if it is greater than 1 the oscillations will be explosive. If it is less than 1 the oscillations will be damped, with price converging more rapidly when the ratio is small.

This result can also be found by examining the solution to equation (10.3). The equation implies that

$$P(1) = (a+e)/b + (-d/b) P(0) \qquad (10.4)$$

This in turn means that

$$P(2) = (a+e)/b + (-d/b)[a+e)/b + (-d/b) P(0)]$$
$$= (a+e)/b + (-d/b)[(a+e)/b] + (-d/b)^2 P(0)$$

After t substitutions you would arrive at

$$P(t) = (a+e)/b + (-d/b) (a+e)/b + (-d/b)^2 (a+e)/b$$
$$+ (-d/b)^3 (a+e)/b + \ldots + (-d/b)^t P(0)$$

Here, with the exception of the last term, we have a series of terms forming a geometric progression with first term $(a+e)/b$ and common ratio $-d/b$. This means that we can write

$$P(t) = [(a+e)/b] \; \frac{1 - (-d/b)^t}{1 - (-d/b)} \; + (-d/b)^t P(0)$$

After further rearrangement this becomes

$$P(t) = P^* - (-d/b)^t (P^* - P(0)) \qquad (10.5)$$

where P^* denotes the equilibrium price $(a+e)/(b+d)$.

From equation (10.5) it can be seen that oscillations occur because $(-d/b)^t$ changes sign as t moves from odd to even numbers. The condition for convergence is $d/b < 1$ or $d < b$. $P(t)$ will fluctuate around P^* (unless $P(0) = P^*$) but the second term will approach zero as t increases.

Save COBWEB1 on your disk as a worksheet file so that you can retrieve it again when required.

10.3 Extensions to the cobweb model

The first extension to the cobweb model is the addition of a random disturbance $v(t)$ to the supply equation (as might occur in the market for an agricultural commodity where supply is subject to the vagaries of the weather).

In COBWEB2 we will make use of the random number generator within 1-2-3 to add $+\$v^*(-0.5+@RAND)/\$b$ to the formula for P(t) in cells C46.C85. @RAND produces a random number (from a uniform distribution) in the range 0 to 1. By subtracting 0.5 we can centre these values on zero. The parameter v is used to increase or decrease the variance of the disturbance. (Although v is not equal to this variance, it is proportional to it.) As before, the chosen value of v can be held at the top of the worksheet and referenced in the formulae further down the worksheet. If this parameter is set to zero the model will be equivalent to COBWEB1. But if it is given a positive value (say 0.1) the price series will not converge but will continue to fluctuate around it.

Call up COBWEB 1 and edit cell A1 so that it now shows

COBWEB2 : simple dynamics with random shocks

In cell G7 put "Disturbance v = and in cell J7 put '<---. In cell F12 put '+ v(t) and use /**Range Name Create** to name cell I7 as v.

Then edit cell C22 so that it reads

+($a+$e)/$b+(−$d/$b)*C21+$v*(−0.5+@RAND)/$b

Then copy this formula to cells C23.C61.

Enter the value 0.1 for v in cell I7 and watch what happens. A small disturbance is introduced into the price series, causing random fluctuations around the convergent oscillations. The QD and QS series are also affected but you will have to make one further alteration to the worksheet formulae to ensure consistency of these series. Go to cell G22 and change the entry to +E22. Copy this down to G23.G61.

Do not be concerned if, when you do this, the P and QD series also change. Every time an adjustment is made to the worksheet the random numbers will be reset automatically and any formula based on them will be recalculated. A similar effect can be achieved by pressing the recalculation (F9) key.

By experimentation, the value of b as well as the value of v will be found to affect the amplitude of the persistent fluctuations. Formal analysis of the new model shows that the price difference equation has become

$$P(t) = (a+e)/b + (−d/b)P(t−1) + (−1/b)v(t) \qquad (10.6)$$

and this has the solution

$$P(t) = P^* + (−d/b)^t (P^* − P(0)) + (−1/b)w(t)$$

where

$$w(t) = v(t) + (−d/b)v(t−1) + (−d/b)^2 v(t−2) + \ldots + (−d/b)^{t−1}v(1)$$

Two things are revealed by these equations:

1. The disturbance to price from the random supply shocks depends inversely on the size of b.
2. The effects of shocks to supply on the time path of $P(t)$ persist from one period to another, the current price disturbance being a geometrically weighted average of present and past supply disturbances.

These points can be demonstrated graphically by resetting the parameter values in the worksheet (just press the GRAPH function key F10 to see the effect on the graph).

The second extension modifies the model in a different way by replacing the supply equation by

$$QS(t) = -e + d\,EP(t)$$

where $EP(t)$ denotes the expected price for period t as seen by suppliers at the end of the previous period.

COBWEB1 and COBWEB2 effectively adopt the naive expectations hypothesis of $EP(t) = P(t-1)$. In COBWEB3 we have instead

$$EP(t) = h\,EP(t-1) + (1-h)\,P(t-1)$$

This is an adaptive expectations model with the parameter h restricted to the range $0 \leqslant h < 1$. As before, the value of h can be stored at the top of the worksheet so that it can be altered conveniently in the computer-based experiments.

The formula for $P(t)$ in column C will have to change since on reduction the model will now give the price difference equation

$$P(t) = (a+e)(1-h)/b + [hb-d(1-h)]/b\,P(t-1) \qquad (10.7)$$

With $h = 0$ the equation is the same as in COBWEB1, but if $h \neq 0$ the nature of the time path could be rather different because the coefficient of lagged price in equation (10.7) is more complex than in the simple model.

Save COBWEB2 and retrieve COBWEB1. Then modify the worksheet as follows:

Cell	Entry
A1	COBWEB3 : simple microdynamics
B2	where supply depends on expected price [adaptive expectations]
G7	Adaptive h =
J7	'<---
E12	EP(t)
A14	EP(t) =
B14	+I7
C14	EP(t-1)
D14	^+
E14	+(1-I7)
F14	P(t-1)

Use **/Range Name Create** to name cell I7 as h.

In cell C22 put +($a+$e)/$b+(1/$b)*($h*$b-$d*(1-$h))*C21, and copy to C23.C61. So far $h = 0$ and the table and graph as they were in COBWEB1.

Now try different values for h (in cell I7) and study the effect that it has on the time path. You will discover that for low values of h there will still be oscillations before equilibrium is reached, but convergence will be quicker than in the naive expectations case. The response to the last movement in price is balanced by a sensitivity to previous ups and downs in prices.

For high values of h convergence will be uniform. This is because, depending upon the values of h, b and d, the expression $[hb-d(1-h)]/b$ can now be positive (although it remains less than 1).

It is interesting to try a value of $h=d(b+d)$ since this leads to a value of zero for $[hb-d(1-b)]/b$ and price shoots straight to the equilibrium value.

Further extensions to the model are now possible. For example, you could add unpredictable disturbances to both equations and even introduce (predictable) shift variables into the equations, making the model

$$QD(t) = a - b\,P(t) + c\,Z(t) + u(t)$$
$$QS(t) = -e + d\,\mathrm{EP}(t) + f\,W(t) + v(t)$$
$$QD(t) = QS(t)$$

where u and v are random disturbances, Z and W are trending shift factors (representing, say, income and technological progress causing the demand curve to shift up and the supply curve to shift down over time).

We do not pursue any of these extensions here, but you may like to try modifying your worksheet to incorporate them.

10.4 Macrodynamics: the multiplier–accelerator model

In this section we turn to an application of difference equations in macro-economics and show how 1-2-3 can be used to examine a variant of the well-known multiplier–accelerator model first decribed by Samuelson (1939). The model is made up of a simple consumption function, a 'naive accelerator' investment function and product market equilibrium conditions. These equations combine to give rise to a second-order difference equation in income, whose properties are linked to the values of the two parameters of the model, the marginal propensity to consume and the accelerator coefficient. Usually this kind of model is analysed mathematically, but here we show how its properties can be explored numerically. The results of the numerical experiments can then be checked against the analytical results.

Begin a new worksheet and use **/Worksheet Global Column-Width** to make all columns 7 characters wide. In Cell A1 put

MULAC1 : simple multiplier–accelerator model

Then enter labels, values and formulae as follows (using the **/Range Name Create** command to name cells as indicated):

Cell	Entry	Name
D3	Parameters	
A4	Consumption	
C4	b =	
D4	0.75	B
E4	'<---	
A5	Investment	
C5	'v =	
D5	0.85	V
E5	'<---	
A6	New value of A =	
D6	610	A
E6	'<---	
F6	'[Original A =	
H6	600	A0
I6	']	

These cells give the values which can subsequently be changed. Now identify the model equations by entering the following information:

Cell	Entry
D8	Model equations
A9	C(t) =
B9	+B
C9	Y(t)
F9	Consumption function
A10	I(t) =
B10	+V
C10	'[Y(t)−Y(t−1)]
F10	Investment function
A11	AD(t) = C(t) + I(t) + A(t)
F11	Aggregate demand
A12	Y(t) = AD(t−1)
F12	Output

Your screen should now look like Table 10.2.

The equations appearing in rows 9 to 12 have the following form:

$$\begin{aligned}
C(t) &= bY(t) \\
I(t) &= v[Y(t) - Y(t-1)] \\
AD(t) &= C(t) + I(t) + A(t) \\
Y(t) &= AD(t-1)
\end{aligned} \tag{10.8}$$

The first equation is a simple consumption function with consumption being given as a proportion ($b = 0.75$) of current income. The second equation determines investment as a proportion ($v = 0.85$) of the change in income

Table 10.2

```
A1: MULAC1 : simple multiplier-accelerator model
                                                          READY

        A       B       C       D       E       F      G      H
 1 MULAC1 : simple multiplier-accelerator model
 2
 3                              Parameters
 4 Consumption    b =        0.75 <---
 5 Investment     v =        0.85 <---
 6 New value of A =           610 <---     [Original A =     600 ]
 7
 8                          Model equations
 9 C(t) =     0.75 Y(t)                    Consumption function
10 I(t) =     0.85 [ Y(t) - Y(t-1) ]       Investment function
11 AD(t) = C(t) + I(t) + A(t)              Aggregate demand
12 Y(t) = AD(t-1)                          Output
13
14
15
16
17
18
19
20
25-Aug-88    11:13 AM
```

since last period. This is equivalent to requiring a constant capital–output ratio v such that $K(t) = vY(t)$ since $I(t) = K(t) - K(t-1)$.

The last two equations determine output as adjusting to last period's aggregate demand, which is the sum of consumption, investment and any additional autonomous expenditure.

In this model income will tend to fluctuate around its equilibrium value through the combination of the multiplier (operating via the marginal propensity to consume, b) and the accelerator (operating through the accelerator coefficient, v). The equilibrium itself is that level of income which is consistent with the system reaching a static condition with

$$Y(t) = Y(t-1) = \ldots = Y^*$$

(assuming that A remains fixed).

With $A = 610$ and $b = 0.75$, $Y^* = 2440$.

Go to cell D14 and enter 'Equilibrium income. In cell C15 put 'Y* = and in cell D15 put +A/(1−B)

The model equations (10.8) reduce to the following second-order difference equation in Y:

$$Y(t) = (b+v) Y(t-1) - v Y(t-2) + A(t) \tag{10.9}$$

The equation itself will produce various patterns over time for Y according to the values of b and v. For the values $b = 0.75$ and $v = 0.85$ the graph will show damped oscillations with convergence to equilibrium.

Now you can add a table of values so that the variables can be plotted against time. Enter the column headings as follows:

Cell	Label
A17	"t
C17	"Y
E17	"C
F17	"I
G17	"A
H17	"AD

Use **/Data Fill** to place values from −2 up to 40 in cells A18.A60. Then enter the first two rows of the table as follows:

Cell	Formula
C18	+A0/(1−B)
E18	+$B*C18
F18	0
G18	+A0
H18	+E18+F18+G18
C19	+H18
E19	+$B*C19
F19	+$V*(C19–C18)
G19	+A0
H19	+E19+F19+G19
G20	+$A

Now use the **Copy** command as follows:

Range to copy FROM	Range to copy TO
C19	C20.C60
E19	E20.E60
F19	F20.F60
H19	H20.H60
G20	G21.G60

Autonomous demand begins at its old level (A0) or 600, but in period zero it changes to 610. This increase in demand starts the cycle and leads to a change in output and income in the following period when consumption (via the marginal propensity to consume) and investment (via the accelerator coefficient) also increase. As time passes, income rises and falls through the interaction of the multiplier and accelerator effects. Because investment is related to changes in income it falls when the increase in income slows and even becomes negative when income falls. After a while the reduction in income also slows and this leads to a lower level of disinvestment. Demand starts to rise again and the cycle continues. However, the cycles are damped and each has a smaller amplitude than the one before.

The pattern can be seen more clearly from a graph. Use the 1-2-3 Graph commands to construct a line graph showing $Y(t)$ plotted against t (for $t = -2, -1, \ldots, 40$).

Give the graph a title and label the axes and use the **/Graph Options Scale Skip** command to relabel the X-axis, and you will get a graph something like Figure 10.3.

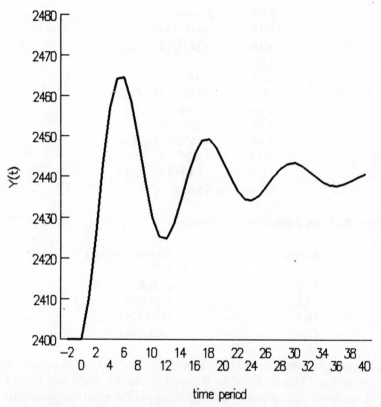

Figure 10.3 Graph from multiplier–accelerator model MULAC1

Save the worksheet with the name MULAC1.

You can now try out some 'what-if' experiments. First try changing the old value of A in cell H6. Try it at 550 and then at 700 (use F10 to switch between the worksheet and the graph). You will see that although the initial value of A will affect where the graph begins, it will not change the basic pattern of damped cycles. (The only exception is if you make A0 = 610. In this case Y begins at its equilibrium value and so remains unchanged over time.)

Now return A0 to 600 and make some changes to b and v. Try each of the following pairs, noting the kind of pattern which emerges:

B	V
0.75	0.7
0.75	1
0.75	1.2
0.9	0.85
0.9	0.75
0.5	0.85

You should attempt to draw some conclusions about the relationship between the combination of parameter values and the properties of the series plot. These conclusions can then be checked by analytical methods (see, for example, Chiang, 1984).

10.5 A flexible multiplier–accelerator model

In this section we modify the multiplier–accelerator model to allow for more flexible consumption and investment functions. We show how spreadsheet simulations can permit an examination of the properties of such a model which might otherwise be rather inaccessible.

The multiplier–accelerator model described in Section 10.4 and captured in MULAC1 has oversimplistic and restrictive consumption and investment functions which imply a rigid, mechanistic reaction by economic agents to the most recent changes in income. This contrasts with contemporary theories of consumption and investment behaviour which are based on the notion that agents respond to perceived changes in the 'permanent' value of income. It is not surprising therefore, that if b and v are interpreted as the long-run values of the marginal propensity to consume and the capital–output ratio, then plausible values of b and in particular v give rise to unrealistic time paths for income. For a capital–output ratio in excess of unity the time path of income is unstable unless a smoother response of consumption and investment to changes in income is allowed for.

In MULAC2 the equivalent equation in MULAC1 is replaced by a permanent income/adaptive expectations consumption function of the form.

$$C(t) = b\, Y_{\mathrm{P}}^{\mathrm{C}}(t) \tag{10.10}$$

Consumption is assumed to depend on consumers' permanent income and this is taken to be a geometrically weighted sum of present and past incomes where h gives the weight on last period's income:

$$Y_{\mathrm{P}}^{\mathrm{C}}(t) = (1-h)\sum_{i=0}^{\infty} h^{i}\, Y(t-i)$$

This is equivalent to assuming that agents' expectations are formed adaptively. By substitution and the application of the Koyck transformation one arrives at the equation

$$C(t) = b(1-h)\,Y(t) + h\,C(t-1) \tag{10.11}$$

If h is set to zero the equation reverts to the one used in MULAC1.

Similarly, investors look at changes in what they view as permanent income (where a different weight m may be used):

$$Y_P^1(t) = (1-m)\sum_{i=0}^{\infty} m^i\,Y(t-i)$$

This leads to an investment equation of the form

$$I(t) = v(1-m)\,Y(t) - (1-m)\,K(t-1) \tag{10.12}$$

Again, if $m = 0$ this is equivalent to the simpler equation in MULAC1.

Substituting equations (10.11) and (10.12) into the aggregate demand and output equations, the model can be condensed to the following equation for Y:

$$Y(t) = [b(1-m) + v(1-h)]\,Y(t) - h\,C(t-2) - (1-h)\,K(t-2) + A(t-1) \tag{10.13}$$

Now it is rather more difficult to establish what types of time path are associated with different parameter values for this equation by analytical means. However, by experimenting with different values of the parameters in a spreadsheet framework the pattern can be discovered.

Recall MULAC1 and modify it as follow:

A1	MULAC2 : flexible multiplier–accelerator model
D4	0.9
F4	h =
G4	0.65
H4	'<---
D5	2.5
F5	m =
G5	0.65
H5	'<---

and use /**Range Name Create** to name cells G4 and G5 as h and m respectively. Then continue with the following alterations:

B9	+B*(1−H)
C9	Y(t) +
D9	+H
E9	C(t−1)
B10	+v*(1−m)
C10	Y(t) −
D10	+(1−m)
E10	K(t−1)

Table 10.3 shows how rows 1 to 15 should now appear.

Table 10.3

```
MULAC2 : flexible multiplier-accelerator model
                          Parameters
Consumption    b =        0.9 <---    h =       0.65 <---
Investment     v =        2.5 <---    m =       0.65 <---
New value of A =          610 <---    [Original A =    600 ]

                        Model equations
C(t) =   0.315 Y(t) +    0.65 C(t-1) Consumption function
I(t) =   0.875 Y(t) -    0.35 K(t-1) Investment function
AD(t) = C(t) + I(t) + A(t)           Aggregate demand
Y(t) = AD(t-1)                       Output

                        Equilibrium income
              Y* =       6100
```

Now add the label "K in cell I17 and put +$v*C18 in cell I18. Then modify the formulae in the table as follows:

```
E19     +($B*(1−$H)*C19)+($H*E18)
F19     +($V*(1−$M)*C19)+(1−$M)*I18)
I19     +I18+I19
```

The formula in cell E19 defines consumption according to equation (10.11). Copy it down to the range E20.E60.

The formula in cell F19 defines investment according to equation (10.12). Copy it down to the range F20.F60.

The formula in cell I19 defines capital as last period's capital plus current investment. Copy it to the range I20.I60.

Before proceeding, the appearance of the worksheet can be improved as follows. Use /**Range Format Fixed** to show one figure after the decimal point in all columns except G, and widen column I to 8 characters. Table 10.4 shows the first few rows of values as they should now appear on the screen.

Table 10.4 Part of screen display from MULAC2

t	Y	C	I	A	AD	K
-2	6000.0	5400.0	0.0	600	6000.0	15000.0
-1	6000.0	5400.0	0.0	600	6000.0	15000.0
0	6000.0	5400.0	0.0	610	6010.0	15000.0
1	6010.0	5403.2	8.8	610	6021.9	15008.8
2	6021.9	5408.9	16.1	610	6035.0	15024.9
3	6035.0	5416.9	22.0	610	6048.8	15046.8
4	6048.8	5426.3	26.3	610	6062.7	15073.2
5	6062.7	5436.9	29.2	610	6076.1	15102.4
6	6076.1	5447.9	30.7	610	6088.7	15133.1
7	6088.7	5459.1	31.0	610	6100.1	15164.1
8	6100.1	5469.9	30.1	610	6110.1	15194.2
9	6110.1	5480.1	28.3	610	6118.4	15222.6
10	6118.4	5489.4	25.7	610	6125.1	15248.3

Now press the F10 key to view the graph. With these values there will be a smooth pattern of convergence (see Figure 10.4).

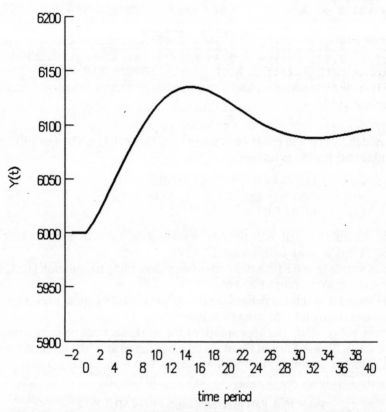

Figure 10.4 Graph from flexible multiplier–accelerator model MULAC2

However, if the h and m parameters are set to zero the pattern is quite different. Income grows exponentially. This is what you should have discovered for the same values in MULAC1 since MULAC1 is now contained within MULAC2 (for h and $m = 0$).

It appears that values of 0.9 for b and 2.5 for v (which are plausible values) only produce damped cycles if consumption and investment are made to respond only gradually to income changes.

At this point save the worksheet with the name MULAC2. Try choosing some other values for h and m to explore their dynamic consequences. You will discover that the nature of the time path is quite sensitive to the combination of parameter values.

This worksheet gives an extremely effective way of illustrating the macroeconomic implications of different assumptions about the underlying behaviour of economic agents. Further extensions such as incorporating random disturbances (as described in connection with the cobweb model) could now be attempted.

Exercise 10

The version of the multiplier–accelerator model described in Chiang's book (1984) is slightly different from the one given in this chapter. Chiang's equations are:

$$C(t) = b\,Y(t-1) \qquad (0 < b < 1)$$
$$I(t) = a[C(t) - C(t-1)] \qquad (a > 0)$$
$$Y(t) = C(t) + I(t) + G(t)$$

which can be condensed to

$$Y(t) = b(1+a)\,Y(t-1) - ab\,Y(t-2) + G(t)$$

Construct a worksheet to show the equations, equilibrium Y and the time-series values of Y, C, I and G, and to allow simulation experiments with the values of a and b. Write a brief report comparing the two variants of the multiplier–accelerator model and their properties.

References

W. J. Baumol, *Economic Dynamics* (Macmillan, London, 1959).

A. C. Chiang, *Fundamental Methods of Mathematical Economics* (Third Edition) (McGraw-Hill, New York, 1984).

G. Judge and R. H. Jones, 'Using spreadsheets in the teaching of dynamic models', *CALECO Discussion Paper 6*, School of Economics Portsmouth Polytechnic, 1988.

P. A. Samuelson, 'Interactions between the multiplier analysis and the principle of acceleration', *Review of Economics and Statistics*, 1939 (May), pp. 75–8.

Chapter 11

Input–output analysis: an application of the matrix commands of Lotus 1-2-3

Purpose: To introduce the 1-2-3 matrix commands and to demonstrate their application to input–output analysis and the study of industrial interdependence.

Preview: This chapter deals with the use of Lotus 1-2-3 as a framework for input–output analysis. Using highly aggregated data from the UK to illustrate the method, Section 11.1 shows how the industry-by-industry flow matrix may be laid out within a worksheet, and how the elements of this matrix may be interpreted. An example is introduced of the kind of analysis which can be conducted with the input–output model, which is re-examined in a later section. Section 11.2 outlines the assumptions of the input–output model, introduces the basic notation and equations of input–output analysis and shows how the input–output coefficient matrix and the Leontief inverse may be computed. In Section 11.3 the Leontief inverse matrix is used to simulate the effect on output of various changes in the pattern of final demand. Finally Section 11.4 provides comments on other applications of input–output analysis and the commodity-by-commodity form of the model.

Lotus 1-2-3 features introduced in this chapter: 1-2-3 matrix commands, **/Data Matrix Multiply** and **/Data Matrix Invert**; **/Worksheet Window**.

11.1 Industry-by-industry flows

Input–output analysis is used to study the economic interdependence between industrial sectors. It provides a method for the empirical investigation of how changes in one sector would be likely to lead to changes in other sectors. It can be used either as part of a forecasting exercise where changes in demand in different sectors are projected forward and the consequences for output and employment are predicted, or for simulation exercises where possible changes in demand or technology can be experimented with to see what quantitative effects may be expected to follow.

The basis of input–output analysis is the input–output flow matrix which records the value of sales and purchases between production sectors in an economy in a particular year. The first tables of this type were produced in 1941 for the United States economy in 1919 and 1929 by Wassily Leontief. Such tables are now produced on a regular basis by the governments of most countries, who also use them as a means of checking the internal consistency of their national accounts statistics.

Table 11.1 shows a highly aggregated version of the industry-by-industry flow matrix for the UK economy in 1974. All figures are in £ million. Sector 1 consists of agricultural and extraction industries, sector 2 includes all manufacturing and construction industries, and sector 3 is made up of Services, Transport and Distribution. The figures are derived from *Business Monitor* PA 1004 (1983).

Table 11.1 Aggregated industry-by-industry flow matrix for the UK in 1974 (£ million)

	Sector 1	Payments Sector 2	Sector 3	Final demand	Total output
Sector 1	2243.6	3880.3	805.1	5098.9	12027.9
Sector 2	3054.7	31086.8	5974	47053.8	87169.3
Sector 3	1374.4	8307.5	20750.3	42554	72986.2
Primary inputs & value added	5355.2	43894.7	45456.8		
Total inputs	12027.9	87169.3	72986.2		

Reading across a row one can see how much an industry (sector) received from selling its output to firms in other industries (and even to firms in the same industry) and to final demand (for consumption, exports and other final uses). Reading down a column one can see what payments were made by industries in exchange for this output, as well as to the providers of primary inputs, such as labour. Allowance is also made here for imports, expenditure taxes and subsidies and for value added, so that the sum of a sector's payments and sales balance exactly.

As we have observed, this table is in highly aggregated form. In fact published tables in the UK distinguish 101 separate industrial groups and with that level of disaggregation there are quite a number of entries in the flow matrix which are zero or too small to record. Nevertheless a considerable number of *direct* links between industries can be observed in such a table with firms purchasing outputs from other firms to be used as inputs in their own production process.

In our table all these entries are positive and of considerable size, most notably the figure showing payments of over £31 billion by firms in the manufacturing and construction sector to other firms in that sector.

To enable us to make use of the 1-2-3's commands in analysing this data it must first be entered into a new worksheet. Begin by entering labels as follows:

Cell	Label
A1	INOUT : worksheet for input–output analysis
A3	Aggregated industry by industry flow matrix for the UK, 1974
A4	– (and copy to B4.G4)
B5	Sector 1
C5	Sector 2
D5	Sector 3
F5	Final
G5	Total
F6	demand
G6	output

At this point use **/Worksheet Column Set-Width** to increase the width of column A to 12. Then continue as follows:

Cell	Entry
A7	Sector 1
A8	Sector 2
A9	Sector 3
A10	Primary
A11	inputs and
A12	value added
A13	Total
A14	inputs

Enter the flows between the sectors in the range B7.D9 and the final demand in the range F7.F9. Put the payments for primary inputs in cells B11.D11.

Then use the @SUM function to add across the rows and down the columns. Notice that you can include the empty column E and the empty row 10 in the sum ranges.

Now consider the following hypothetical changes in demand. Suppose that the pattern of demand was to change so that there was a shift away from manufacturing towards services of £1 billion. What implications would this have for the production levels in the different sectors? There are good reasons to suppose that production would fall in sector 2 and rise in sector 3, but the effect would go beyond the immediate direct impact because of the underlying demands which are implicit in the flow matrix. Indeed the in-direct effects of this change in the pattern of final demand would be felt even in sector 1. We can provide an answer to our question using the simple input–output model. This model has the fundamental assumption of con-stant input–output ratios and these can easily be found within a 1-2-3 worksheet as the ratio of two cells. The model's equations are most easily manipulated in matrix form and the steps required are straightforward within 1-2-3 using the program's matrix commands.

11.2 The equations of the input–output model and the calculation of the input–output coefficient matrix and the Leontief inverse matrix

In input–output models it is assumed that the various industrial sectors produce output for sale to both consumers (i.e. to meet final demand) and to other industries (to meet intermediate demands). Intermediate demands reflect the fact that in producing its own output, as well as using primary inputs a firm may need to use inputs produced by industry (either in a different industrial sector or by a firm in its own sector). More specifically it is assumed as a rough approximation that intermediate demands arise in proportion to the outputs they help to produce. To give an example, if sector 2 were to require £20 worth of the output of sector 3 in order to produce £100 worth of its own output, then we assume that it would need £40 worth of these inputs to produce £200 worth of its output. The per-unit input–output ratio here would be $20/100 = 0.2$. So if industry 2 was producing some unspecified amount of its output, x_2 say, then the intermediate demand it would place on industry 3 would be for $0.2x_2$.

This assumption can also be stated by describing the production process as exhibiting constant returns to scale. In order to scale up the output of a sector by a given factor, the inputs must be scaled up by the same factor. We also assume that there are no substitution possibilities between sectors or, to put it another way, the production process has rectangular isoquants. Nor is there assumed to be any substantial delay in the production process so that inputs purchased within any (annual) period may be assumed to be used to produce output sold that year.

Although these assumptions may appear to be rather crude, they do permit us to make progress on the basis of one year's figures and without too many computational difficulties. Provided that the model is only used for projections or simulations over a relatively short time period when the input–output ratios may be taken to remain roughly constant, the predictions of the model will be reasonably good.

We must now introduce some notation so that the model assumptions can be stated more formally, and so that the model equations can be laid out and manipulated. Let x_{ij} denote the sales by industry i of its output to industry j. Let y_i denote the sales by industry i to final demand and let x_i denote the value of total or gross output produced and sold by industry i. Then, by definition (assuming n industries)

$$x_i = \sum_{j=1}^{n} x_{ij} + y_i \qquad (11.1)$$

for every i ($=1$ to n); that is, for each industry

total output = intermediate demand + final demand

The assumption of constant input–output ratios means that each of the following is taken to be constant:

$$a_{ij} = x_{ij}/x_j \qquad \text{for all } i, j \tag{11.2}$$

For every x_j units produced by industry j it requires x_{ij} units of industry i's output as an input.
Thus

$$x_{ij} = a_{ij} x_j \qquad \text{for all } i, j$$

The a_{ij}'s are the input–output coefficients.

In terms of our three-sector model we have

$$\begin{aligned}
x_1 &= a_{11} x_1 + a_{12} x_2 + a_{13} x_3 + y_1 \\
x_2 &= a_{21} x_1 + a_{22} x_2 + a_{23} x_3 + y_2 \\
x_3 &= a_{31} x_1 + a_{32} x_2 + a_{33} x_3 + y_3
\end{aligned} \tag{11.3}$$

In order for each sector to produce exactly the right amount of output to ensure that it can meet both the intermediate and final demands for its product, these equations (which may be described as the structural form of the model) must all be satisfied.

With a larger number of industries (n) there would be a corresponding number of equations each with n terms relating to intermediate demand plus the final demand term. Such equations can be written more compactly using matrix algebra. Denoting the set of sectoral outputs by the (column) vector $\mathbf{x}$, the set of final demands by the vector $\mathbf{y}$ and the set of input–output coefficients by the matrix $\mathbf{A}$, we can write equation (11.3) as

$$\mathbf{x} = \mathbf{Ax} + \mathbf{y} \tag{11.4}$$

With a little rearrangement this can be solved for $\mathbf{x}$:

$$\begin{aligned}
\mathbf{x} - \mathbf{Ax} &= \mathbf{y} \\
(\mathbf{I} - \mathbf{A})\mathbf{x} &= \mathbf{y} \\
\mathbf{x} &= (\mathbf{I} - \mathbf{A})^{-1}\mathbf{y}
\end{aligned} \tag{11.5}$$

Equation (11.5) is the reduced form of the model, expressing the gross outputs in terms of the (exogenous) final demands. For any postulated set of final demands, $\mathbf{y}$, it is now simple to translate this into a set of gross outputs by premultiplying by the matrix $(\mathbf{I} - \mathbf{A})^{-1}$. The $(\mathbf{I} - \mathbf{A})$ matrix is sometimes called the *Leontief matrix*, so that its inverse is known as the *Leontief inverse*.

All this presupposes that we know the matrix of coefficients, $\mathbf{A}$. If we have available the industry-by-industry flow matrix for any recent year we can use it, along with the definition given by equation (11.2) to compute the $\mathbf{A}$ matrix.

We now illustrate using the 1974 data in the worksheet. Go to cell A18 and enter the following label:

'The A matrix (input–output coefficient matrix)

Then enter the following formulae

B20	+B7/$B$14
C20	+C7/$C$14
D20	+D7/$D$14

Then copy the range B20.D20 to the range B21.D22. The following numbers should be displayed:

0.186532	0.044514	0.011030
0.253967	0.356625	0.081851
0.114267	0.095303	0.284304

Use the **/Range Name Create** command to call this matrix **A**. The elements are, of course, all less than 1. An industry must necessarily pay only a part of the value of its gross output to its suppliers. Indeed the sum of the figures in any column must also be less than 1.

Next we need to generate the elements of the Leontief matrix $(I - A)$. The **I** here denotes the identity matrix which is a square matrix with ones down the main diagonal and zeros elsewhere. For a 3×3 matrix we have

$$I = \begin{bmatrix} 1 & 0 & 0 \\ 0 & 1 & 0 \\ 0 & 0 & 1 \end{bmatrix}$$

$I - A$ will thus have diagonal elements which are $1 - a_{ii}$, where a_{ii} is in row i, column i of **A**, and off-diagonal elements of $-a_{ij}$, where a_{ij} is in row i, column j of **A** $(i \neq j)$.

Go to cell A24 and type 'The I − A matrix (Leontief matrix). Now enter the formulae for the elements as follows:

Cell	Formula
B26	+1−B20
C26	−C20
D26	−D20
B27	−B21
C27	+1−C21
D27	−D21
B28	−B22
C28	−C22
D28	+1−D22

Now use the **/Range Name Create** command to call the range B26.D28 by the name **I − A**.

To find the Leontief inverse you must use one of the 1-2-3 matrix commands. In cell A30 put the label 'I−A inverse (Leontief inverse). Then move to cell B32 and key in /*Data Matrix invert*. The range to invert should be given as either B26.D28 or by the name $I - A$. Just press <*Return*> for the output range to start at B32. The Leontief inverse should then be displayed as follows:

1.262162	0.091764	0.029948
0.532895	1.619833	0.193466
0.272477	0.230350	1.427785

These values relate the gross output levels in each sector to (per unit) final demand values.

For example, in order to sustain one unit of final demand for sector 2's output it is necessary to produce 0.091764 units of output in sector 1, 1.619833 units of output in sector 2 and 0.230350 units of output in sector 3. The figures down the main diagonal must be at least one because they include the output which goes to final demand itself. All the figures are greater than the equivalent ones in the **A** matrix because they not only represent the direct output supplied to industries, but also take account of the indirect requirements. For example, the **A** matrix indicates that firms in sector 2 purchase 0.044514 units of output from sector 1 for every unit that is produced in sector 2. But that is not enough to support a unit of final demand. Sector 2 also requires an input from sector 3 and since this in turn needs inputs from sector 1 this must be allowed for. In fact a whole series of such effects must be considered. The $(I - A)^{-1}$ matrix captures all such effects.

Now before you move on to use the Leontief inverse in a simulation there are a number of checks which you can do which will also help to reinforce ideas. According to equation (11.5) the original total output vector should be equal to the Leontief inverse times the original final demand vector. Use the /**Range Name Create** command to assign the name LINV to the range B32.D34.

Now in cell A36 type 'Gross Output check. Then move to cell B38. Call up the menu and select *Data* followed by *Matrix* and then *Multiply*. For the first range to multiply give LINV (or B32.D34). For the second range give F7.F9 and just press <*Return*> for the output range. The following figures (which are identical to the original gross outputs) will be displayed:

12027.9
87169.3
72986.2

Next you can approach the Leontief inverse by a longer route than that taken in equation (11.5) but one which is quite interesting. Recall equation (11.4) and substitute it into itself:

$$x = Ax + y$$
becomes $x = A(Ax + y) + y$
$$= Ax^2 + Ay + y$$

Now repeat the process ad infinitum:

$$x = A^2(Ax + y) + Ay + y$$
$$= A^s x + A^{s-1} y + A^{s-2} y + \ldots \ldots + Ay + y$$

Now for sufficiently large s the matrix $A^s \to 0$ (the null matrix) since all the elements of A are less than 1. At the same time, reordering terms on the right-hand side we can write

$$x \simeq y + Ay + Ay^2 + \ldots + A y^{s-1} + \ldots$$
i.e. $\quad x \simeq (I + A + A^2 + A^3 + \ldots)y$

Thus we can see that the matrix $(I - A)^{-1}$ can be approximated by the sum of the series of matrices $I + A + A^2 + A^3 + \ldots$.

This can be interpreted as follows: the total output requirements needed to sustain a unit vector of final demands is

I (to meet final demand)
plus A (the direct input requirements)
plus A^2 (indirect requirements one stage removed)
plus A^3 (indirect requirements two stages removed)
etc.

(In ignoring the further removed indirect requirements we are assuming that they quickly become negligible.)

We can use the worksheet to see how close an approximation is provided by $I + A + A^2 + A^3$. Go to cell A42 and put

'The approximation of the Leontief inverse by series expansion

In cell A44 put 'I (identity matrix) and enter the following values:

Cell	Value
B45	1
C45	0
D45	0
B46	0
C46	1
D46	0
B47	0
C47	0
D47	1

In cell A49 put 'A and in cell B50 select /*Range Value*. Give the range to copy from as A and just press *<Return>* to confirm the range to copy to. (*Question* – why was it not possible to use the usual **Copy** command here?)

Now go to cell A54 and enter 'A squared. Then use the /**Data Matrix Multiply** command to multiply **A** by itself, giving the output range as B55.

Lastly, in cell A59 put 'A cubed and use /**Data Matrix Multiply** to multiply **A** by **A** squared, putting the result in the range beginning B60. Notice how, as **A** is multiplied by itself again and again, the elements in the resulting matrix become smaller and smaller. Now you are ready to add up the series of matrices. However, as you may have noticed, although there is a matrix multiply command there is no addition command (or for that matter a command for the subtraction of matrices). The reason for this is that it is not really necessary because matrix addition can be achieved using a simple formula for one element followed by the use of the **Copy** command to replicate this for all other elements.

Go to cell A64 and type 'I + A + A^2 + A^3. Then in cell B65 enter the formula +B45+B50+B55+B60. Copy this across to C65.D65 and then copy B65.D65 to B66.D67. You will now be able to see how close an approximation this is to LINV. Actually it would be better if you could see both the range which holds LINV and the range which holds the approximation on the screen together. This is possible using 1-2-3's *Windows* feature.

With the cursor in cell A64 select /*Worksheet Window*, followed by *Horizontal*. A new border appears above this cell with the cursor now flashing in cell A63. Use the arrow key to move the cursor upwards until it reaches A23. By that time the exact Leontief inverse will be on the screen just above the position where the screen was split. Table 11.2 shows what you should now see on the screen.

Table 11.2 Screen display of matrix calculations

A23:   [W12]

READY

	A	B	C	D	E	F
23						
24	The I-A matrix (Leontief matrix)					
25						
26		0.813467	-0.04451	-0.01103		
27		-0.25396	0.643374	-0.08185		
28		-0.11426	-0.09530	0.715695		
29						
30	I-A inverse (Leontief inverse)					
31						
32		1.262162	0.091764	0.029948		
33		0.532895	1.619833	0.193466		
34		0.272477	0.230350	1.427785		
35						
	A	B	C	D	E	F
64	I+A^2+A^3					
65		1.250144	0.081692	0.024968		
66		0.472208	1.566906	0.166423		
67		0.233900	0.197108	1.406027		
68						
69						

Although the matrix giving the sum of the first four terms of the series is not equal to the exact inverse LINV, the elements are quite close.

To remove the split screen display just select /*Worksheet window* again followed by *Clear*.

11.3 Simulating changing patterns of demand

You are now ready to find the answer to the question posed in Section 11.1, namely what would be the consequences for the output of the three sectors of a simultaneous decrease of £1 billion in sector 2 and an increase of the same amount in sector 3?

There are several ways in which you can tackle the problem. First, you could set up a range of cells to hold the new final demands which would be respectively

+F7
+F8–1000
+F9+1000

(remember the figures in the table are all in £ million). You could then pre-multiply this vector by LINV to produce a new output vector.

Go to cell I4 and type 'Simulation results. Then enter labels as follows:

Cell	Label
I5	New final
I6	demand
J5	New total
J6	output

and the formulae

Cell	Formula
I7	+F7
I8	+F8–1000
I9	+F9+1000

Now use the /**Data Matrix Multiply** command with the first range to multiply as LINV (B32.D34); the second range to multiply as I7.I9 and the output range as J7.J9 (just J7 would do).

The projected gross output figures should now be seen in cells J7 to J9. As expected, the output of sector 3 would have to increase, and by more than 1000. The output of sector 2 would decrease, also by more than 1000. This is because the change in output following the changes in demand include those induced by a fall in intermediate demand. Notice that output in sector 1 would fall too. On balance, sector 1 is more dependent on (because it supplies) sector 2, where demand has fallen, than on sector 3, where demand has risen.

In this case, with only three sectors, perhaps this pattern was not hard to predict (although without 1-2-3 the computation of the quantitative effects would have been tiresome). However, in a model with many more sectors the indirect effects are harder to pick up without the aid of Lotus 1-2-3 (or a program like it).

Now it might be helpful to see explicitly what change there is between the old and new outputs. Of course now that you have the output projections you could simply subtract the original values from them. However, suppose you had not yet found these values. We can demonstrate a slightly different approach to the original problem based on the equation

$$\Delta x = (I - A)^{-1} \Delta y$$

Here Δx and Δy denote respectively *changes* in gross output and final demand. It follows from the original equation (11.5) that changes as well as levels must be linked in this way.

Go to cell L4 and put 'Changes in, and then copy cells F5.G6 to L5. Now enter values as follows:

Cell	Value
L7	0
L8	−1000
L9	+1000

Then use the /**Matrix Multiply** command with LINV as the first range, L7.L9 as the second range and M7.M9 as the output range. The changes in output will now be displayed.

In a final approach to the problem we will separate out the effects of the increase in the demand in sector 3 from the decrease in sector 2. Enter the following labels and values:

Cell	Label/Value
O4	Fall in
O5	Sector 2
O6	Demand
O7	0
O8	−1000
O9	0
P4	Change in
P5	Total
P6	Output

Then use the /**Matrix Multiply** command with LINV as the first range, O7.O9 as the second range and P7.P9 as the output range. These results show the partial effects of the fall in demand in sector 2.

Now enter labels and values for the calculation of the partial effects of the increase in demand in sector 3, as follows:

Cell	Label/Value
R4	Rise in
R5	Sector 3
R6	Demand
R7	0
R8	0
R9	+1000
S4	Change in
S5	Total
S6	Output

Again use the **/Matrix Multiply** command, this time with cells S7.S9 as the output range.

From the results you can see how the net reduction in the output of sector 1 would be the result of a small increase in output due to the expansion in demand in sector 3 being swamped by a fall in output of about three times that amount caused by the reduction in demand for sector 2's output.

The results can be seen more strikingly on a bar chart. Defining the x range as A7.A9, the A range as P7.P9, the B range as S7.S9 and the C range as M7.M9, you get the graph shown in Figure 11.1 (after adding appropriate titles and legends).

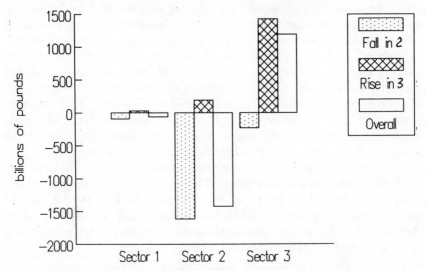

Figure 11.1 Bar chart showing results of input–output analysis

11.4 Other applications and manifestations of input–output analysis

In this chapter we have only been able to examine the basic concepts and applications of input–output analysis. The reader is referred to O'Connor and Henry (1975) for a full treatment of the topic. O'Connor and Henry show how the input–output approach can be extended to examine price changes. They also describe the techniques which have been developed to enable the coefficients to be updated on the basis of survey results (so that it is not necessary to wait for the next tables based on a full Census of Production). One of the big problems with this kind of work is that it takes so long to assemble the data and it is usually four years or more before the input–output tables for a particular year are published. In fact, the tables for 1984 have only recently been published (CSO, 1988). An interesting development for users of Lotus 1-2-3 is that this time the publication was accompanied by a floppy disk containing data files and instructions on how to read the data into a 1-2-3 worksheet.

Readers turning to this source will discover one important difference between the tables supplied for 1984 and those described in this chapter. The 1984 tables are given on a commodity-by-commodity basis rather than on an industry-by-industry basis. This distinction arises because, no matter how far one pursues the disaggregation of industries, one can never really assume that each industry produces one and only one commodity. Producing units are classified to a particular industry according to which commodity they mainly produce. Most producing units will produce only one commodity, or at least if they produce more than one commodity these commodities will have similar characteristics and can be classified within the same industrial group. In some cases, however, a producing unit will be found which, in addition to its main commodity, produces a commodity which is the characteristic product of another industry. Thus there is not an exact one-to-one correspondence between industries and commodities. With the industry-by-industry model one effectively assumes that all the commodities produced within an industry have the same input requirements. Or, to put it in a different way, one is assuming that commodities will actually have different input requirements according to the industry in which they are produced. It would appear to make more sense to assume that a commodity has the same structure of inputs no matter which industry produces it. To make the adjustment one would need to know how much of each industry's characteristic products were produced elsewhere. This information is available in the *make matrix* (one of the published Input–Output Tables). With it one can convert industry-by-industry tables into commodity-by-commodity tables (or vice versa). The algebra showing how the two sets of tables are related is given in the Introduction to the 1984 tables.

Table 11.3 Input–output tables for the UK national economy for 1979

A MATRIX	1	2	3	4	5	6	7
1	0.18046	0	0	0.00006	0.0001	0	0
2	0.02253	0.13789	0.305	0.07222	0.05009	0.01469	0.00971
3	0.01311	0.01674	0.02137	0.046	0.03874	0.02491	0.01179
4	0.00566	0.00874	0.01603	0.13735	0.01798	0.19011	0.07974
5	0.04365	0.002	0.00468	0.01375	0.0739	0.0175	0.00993
6	0.00217	0.00826	0.01302	0.0206	0.02096	0.06043	0.06067
7	0.00471	0.01142	0.01419	0.02073	0.0136	0.01048	0.09509
8	0.00047	0.00368	0.01595	0.00684	0.00279	0.00843	0.03448
9	0.00038	0.00016	0.001	0.0048	0.00086	0.00077	0.0009
10	0.00321	0.00011	0.00008	0.00211	0.00013	0.00064	0.00011
11	0.17971	0.00053	0.00025	0.00096	0.01712	0.00051	0.00045
12	0.00519	0.00037	0.00109	0.00179	0.00405	0.00192	0.00367
13	0.00792	0.00542	0.00893	0.00691	0.01712	0.01214	0.01484
14	0.00735	0.00142	0.00676	0.01337	0.02003	0.01431	0.01072
15	0.00735	0.019	0.03682	0.00179	0.00206	0.0023	0.00158
16	0.05544	0.0131	0.02655	0.08515	0.03158	0.06337	0.05282
17	0.01056	0.02558	0.01161	0.05463	0.0333	0.03513	0.02523
18	0.01131	0.00126	0.00885	0.01842	0.01267	0.0152	0.01823
19	0.04771	0.00663	0.01812	0.02361	0.05626	0.02926	0.04041

8	9	10	11	12	13	14	15
0.00017	0	0	0.24878	0.00271	0.00631	0.00039	0.00015
0.00866	0.01567	0.01123	0.00831	0.01151	0.00712	0.01066	0.00303
0.01316	0.01663	0.01399	0.01176	0.01471	0.01849	0.01686	0.00281
0.06503	0.07834	0.03993	0.01003	0.00145	0.02795	0.0063	0.11354
0.01409	0.00193	0.01031	0.00894	0.04054	0.07502	0.01754	0.01164
0.04109	0.10056	0.03754	0.02356	0.00745	0.0239	0.00765	0.01836
0.0225	0.03348	0.06478	0.00764	0.00861	0.00947	0.00824	0.01459
0.07394	0.02157	0.06294	0.00191	0.00039	0.0055	0.00136	0.01067
0.00042	0.06257	0.00018	0.00133	0.00068	0.00099	0.00145	0.00026
0.00008	0.00011	0.05263	0.00008	0	0.00036	0.00029	0.00004
0.00068	0.00043	0.00018	0.13155	0.00261	0.00162	0.00242	0.00048
0.00204	0.00622	0.00478	0.00204	0.20395	0.01533	0.00436	0.00465
0.02411	0.05108	0.00902	0.01215	0.00803	0.08584	0.01153	0.03003
0.01655	0.00751	0.00662	0.03206	0.01529	0.02786	0.16481	0.00569
0.0017	0.00236	0.00239	0.0018	0.00213	0.00171	0.00281	0.2272
0.04601	0.04733	0.03441	0.03951	0.03764	0.03553	0.04389	0.03786
0.02521	0.03177	0.01104	0.03673	0.02883	0.03093	0.0498	0.01991
0.01469	0.00848	0.01251	0.01584	0.01219	0.01704	0.02073	0.00573
0.03523	0.02232	0.01932	0.03559	0.02564	0.02994	0.07209	0.01097

16	17	18	19		
0.00353	0.00012	0	0	1	Agriculture
0.00974	0.03929	0.00189	0.00165	2	Coal
0.02089	0.00792	0.00671	0.00358	3	Public Utilities
0.00095	0.00568	0	0.00034	4	Mining
0.00462	0.00257	0.00698	0.01086	5	Chemicals
0.00351	0.00158	0.00298	0.00055	6	Metal goods n.e.s.
0.00323	0.00133	0.00032	0.00014	7	Mechanical Engineering
0.00815	0.02004	0.00374	0.00371	8	Electrical & Inst Eng
0.00656	0.01079	0.00839	0.00117	9	Vehicles
0.00069	0.01672	0	0	10	Other transport
0.04447	0.00083	0.00027	0.00028	11	Food,drink & tcbac
0.01963	0.0017	0.00384	0.00344	12	Textiles & clothing
0.01524	0.0256	0.01218	0.0152	13	Other manf
0.02332	0.02809	0.05143	0.02578	14	Paper & print
0.01164	0.00328	0.04748	0.00928	15	Construction
0.03609	0.02514	0.0163	0.01389	16	Distribution
0.07562	0.05327	0.10184	0.02351	17	Transport & communication
0.05362	0.03634	0.05344	0.03644	18	Banking & finance
0.0284	0.01394	0.04234	0.0163	19	Misc services

Source: OPCS Business Monitor, 1985

Exercise 11

You are provided with an estimated input–output coefficient matrix for the UK in 1979, where the industries have been grouped together to give a 19-sector model (Table 11.3). Construct a 1-2-3 worksheet to hold this matrix and use 1-2-3 to compute the Leontief inverse matrix. Trace the effects on the output of all sectors of a switch of £1 billion in final demand from the mechanical engineering sector (7) to banking and finance (18). (*Note*: You are looking only at changes so you do not need to know the original levels of output or demand.)

References

R. O'Connor and E. W. Henry, *Input–output Analysis and its Applications* (Griffin, 1975).

W. W. Leontief, *The Structure of the American Economy, 1919–1939* (Second Edition) (New York, 1951)

'Input–output tables for the United Kingdom 1979', *OPCS Business Monitor 1983* (PA 1044) (HMSO, London, 1983).

CSO, *Input–output Tables for the United Kingdom 1984* (HMSO, London, 1988).

Chapter 12

Further 1-2-3 features and applications

Purpose: To review briefly some of the 1-2-3 features and applications covered in this book. To indicate some other 1-2-3 features which might be found useful for quantitative analysis in economics and to suggest some of the other applications where the package could be utilised.

Preview: This book has shown how Lotus 1-2-3 can be used in a number of applications of quantitative analysis in economics. It would be idle to pretend that all possible types of application have been illustrated; the fact that the package is so flexible means that the types of application are legion. Nor, in fact, have we examined all of the commands of 1-2-3's command structure or all of the built-in functions available. No book could attempt to do this *and* provide full-blown applications within a reasonable number of pages. However, this chapter provides a partial solution to the problem, filling in a few gaps by indicating some of the other 1-2-3 functions and features which could be of value to economics users and suggesting some further ways in which the program could be applied for quantitative analysis.

Lotus 1-2-3 features discussed in this chapter: 1-2-3 macros; cell **Protection** and **Hidden** commands; 1-2-3 'Add-Ons' and 'Add-Ins'; stacked bar charts; further built-in financial functions; transferring data to and from 1-2-3 and other packages; the **/File Import**, **/File Xtract**, **/File Combine** and **/Print File** commands and the Translate utility.

12.1 The use of macros, templates, add-ons and add-ins

In the Introduction it was suggested that Lotus 1-2-3 could be used to support three types of quantitative analysis in economics: statistical (or data) analysis, problem-solving or decision-making analysis and model analysis. Examples of each of these have been provided in the book.

We began in Chapter 2 with a simple business application. Cost and revenue figures were provided for a hypothetical firm and we showed how they could be entered, manipulated and displayed within a 1-2-3 worksheet. Basic program features were introduced and in addition a very important way of working with spreadsheets was suggested, namely through worksheet templates. A template is a worksheet file which is a kind of application shell. Labels, formulae and perhaps some basic data associated with a particular type of application are entered into the worksheet and saved in a file for further use, perhaps by someone else. Such a template could be valuable where a similar type of application with a common structure is encountered again and again. It might, in fact, be relevant to any of the applications dealt with in this book.

One 1-2-3 concept which we have not as yet introduced could be very helpful in such a context – namely that of the Lotus 1-2-3 'macro'. A Lotus macro is a set of instructions, stored together in part of the worksheet, which can allow a user to automate a sequence of keystrokes and commands so that they can be activated by a single keyboard action which calls up the macro. For example, suppose the designer of a worksheet template wished a user to be taken automatically to a particular cell and prompted to enter data on a particular item, and after that to be taken to another cell for further data inputs, etc. This procedure could be automated using a Lotus macro. In this way one can avoid the need for the template user to know anything about the underlying instructions, formulae and cell movements.

Lotus 1-2-3 has a full macro command language and it can allow experienced users to program instructions as they might in any high-level computer language, but with the added benefit that they can call upon all 1-2-3's built-in functions and graphics. The instructions are entered in a cell or column of cells and this range is given a name. The macro is also assigned a label such as A, B, etc., which is placed in the cell to the left of the macro. The macro may then be invoked by pressing the macro key (the <*ALT*> key) together with the letter in the macro label (e.g. <*ALT*> and A together would activate the macro labelled A). It is even possible to have a macro which is invoked immediately upon loading the worksheet by giving it the label O. A full discussion of macros is beyond the scope of this book. See the *Reference Manual*, Chapter 3, and Le Blond and Cobb (1985, Ch. 12) for details on 1-2-3 macros and how to use them.

Further features which could be useful to 1-2-3 programmers designing a template to be used by non-experts are the cell protection and cell hidden commands. /**Worksheet Global Protection**, /**Range Protect** and /**Range Unprotect** enable a programmer to prevent all but specified cells from having their entries changed. The cell hidden commands (/**Worksheet Global Format Hidden** and /**Range Format Hidden**/ can be used to hide the contents of a range of cells from the screen.

For some types of application it is possible to buy ready-made worksheet templates which have been programmed in this way using 1-2-3 macros and which can be used with 1-2-3. Examples include 'Ivy-Calc' from Ivy

Software, which gives worksheet templates for financial analysis and discounted cash flow problems, and '1-2-3 Forecast!' from 4-5-6 World which links together a number of files with templates for a variety of forecasting methods.

A software package which is file-compatible with 1-2-3 and designed to work in conjunction with it is sometimes referred to as an 'add-on'. An example which would be of interest to economists is 'What's Best!', a package from General Optimization which enables 1-2-3 users to solve large linear programming applications without the need to construct a worksheet containing the steps of the simplex method of solution within it.

Also available are a number of 1-2-3 'add-ins'. These include a number of useful utilities such as 'Sideways' from Funk Software, which can print 1-2-3 worksheet files sideways down the paper, and SQZ from Turner Hall, which can compress worksheet files so that they take up less space on disk. Add-ins work differently to add-ons since they attach directly to 1-2-3's core code. They have been written using the Lotus Developers' Tool Kit and they can be added in permanently to the Lotus directory using the 1-2-3 Add-In Manager program. Further information on these and other products can be obtained from the Lotus User Group at 79–80 Peascod Street, Windsor SL4 1DH.

12.2 Further examples of statistical and data analysis with 1-2-3

Chapters 3, 4 and 5 all dealt with applications of 1-2-3 to problems of descriptive statistics, and Chapters 8 and 9 showed how best 1-2-3 can be used for regression analysis. A number of other types of statistical application for which 1-2-3 can be used are briefly outlined here.

In descriptive statistics various pie charts and bar charts can be used to display data. One form of chart which 1-2-3 can produce which we have not discussed is the stacked bar chart. This chart enables you to see both how a variable compares in overall size over time (or between places) and at the same time allows you to see the shares of the component parts. It could be used instead of a line graph or a series of pie charts.

Although 1-2-3 is restricted to five basic types of graph it is possible to adapt the commands to produce a variety of types of graph which an economist might require. For example, just as we have seen in Chapter 5 how an ogive can be constructed using cumulative frequency data from a worksheet, in a similar way one could construct a Lorenz curve to illustrate inequality patterns (see Soper and Lee,1988).

The biggest disappointment, as we have noted, is that proper histograms cannot be constructed where the width of the bars can be varied according to the size of the classes and where the bars have no gaps between them.

The range of graphs available to a 1-2-3 user can also be extended by using an add-in program like 3D Graphics. As its name suggests, this program enables you to see 1-2-3 data plotted in three dimensions. This could be useful not only for viewing a bar chart in three dimensions, but also for seeing a three-dimensional perspective of a production or utility function with two independent variables.

With a colour monitor the graphs can also be displayed in a variety of colours (depending on the graphics adapter available) and you can also get an add-in to print graphs straight from the worksheet (this feature is standard in Quattro). 1-2-3 can also be tricked into providing a screen dump of a graph using the *<Shift>* and *<PrtScr>* keys if the DOS command **GRAPHICS** is issued before 1-2-3 is loaded.

As we saw in Chapters 8 and 9, Lotus 1-2-3 can be used to help improve the understanding of regression analysis as well as merely for generating the results. For econometrics students this understanding can be further improved if they were to make use of the 1-2-3 matrix commands to compute the least squares vector and the variance–covariance matrix (from which the standard errors could be extracted).

Regression analysis is by no means the only form of statistical inference which 1-2-3 can help with. Analysis of variance, chi-squared tests and the use of Bayes' theorem can all be illustrated and applied within a worksheet. Probability distributions (such as the binomial and normal) can also be explored and approximate tables of values generated (see Soper and Lee, 1987).

The availability of the random number generator (@RAND) makes possible all kinds of sampling and Monte Carlo experiments with 1-2-3.

12.3 Further problem-solving and decision-making applications of 1-2-3

Two types of decision-making application were illustrated in this book: investment and interest rate problems in Chapter 6 and linear programming problems in Chapter 7.

1-2-3 does have a number of built-in financial functions which could be of use for working out such things as the future value of an investment (@FV), the size of regular loan payments such as a mortgage (@PMT) and the number of payment periods required for an annuity to accumulate a target value (@TERM). Another type of application of interest to economists is decision making in conditions of risk (where the probabilities of the outcomes of the different options as well as the payoffs can be quantified). The payoffs could be stored together in one range, the probabilities of the outcomes in another, so that the expected payoff associated with each alternative could be computed. Problems of insurance and portfolio selection can be dealt with in this way (see Begg *et al.*, 1987, Ch. 13).

In the discussion of investment decision-making problems and the computation of the IRR we noted that such problems must be solved by an iterative method with initial solutions being adjusted according to a rule or algorithm until certain conditions are satisfied which guarantee that a reasonable approximation to the solution has been found. For built-in functions like @IRR this has all been internalised, but a 1-2-3 user could devise and implement his own algorithm to solve a problem using 1-2-3's macro 'language'. The language has branching and conditional commands and could be used for producing specialised computational routines for use, say, in finding consistent forward-looking (rational) expectations to replace the adaptive expectations assumptions used in Chapter 10.

12.4 Further examples of model analysis with 1-2-3

The 'what-if' potential of Lotus 1-2-3 has been exploited on a number of occasions in the applications described in this book. It is particularly effective if the 'key' parameters in a model or problem are stored together in a separate part of the worksheet so that they can easily be reset. Used with the **/Range Name Create** command this can make worksheet applications transparent in their meaning.

One type of application of this idea which should prove valuable to students of economics is in the investigation of the properties of various mathematical functions and models. Indeed, this was essentially what lay behind the discussion of dynamic models in Chapter 10. A similar approach could be used to investigate the properties of different functional forms to see how the graph is affected by the values of the parameters or for the comparative static analysis of an economic model expressed in matrix equation form.

In the first type of application one would use the **/Data Fill** command to generate a set of values for the independent variable and then the **Copy** command to replicate a formula entered for the first cell in the range for the dependent variable. A graph could be constructed and viewed to see how changes in parameter values would affect its shape and position.

In the second type of application, if the equations of the model are linear in form the analysis would be most efficiently conducted in the worksheet if the model's structural and reduced-form equations were to be expressed and manipulated in matrix terms.

12.5 Transferring data to and from Lotus 1-2-3

At the end of Chapter 9 it was noted that although Lotus 1-2-3 may not be the ideal package for regression analysis it is a very useful package for data-entry and data-storage purposes. This is because a number of econometrics packages can recognise 1-2-3 worksheet files. RATS, for example, will read a 1-2-3 worksheet file provided that it satisfies certain conditions. Briefly these are as follows. Variable values should be organised in rows or columns at the top of the worksheet (with no empty intervening rows or columns) and with variable labels and dates confined to the first row and column, entered as right justified text (i.e. preceded by "). The series themselves should be values only (i.e. not generated by formulae) and all cells outside the data range should be completely empty – no characters, no spaces. If you do have data in a worksheet which do not correspond exactly to this format you can use the /**Range Value**, the /**File Xtract** or the/**File Combine** commands to transfer ranges of values from one worksheet to another.

Even just working with 1-2-3 this can be useful with one initial worksheet being set up as a data bank to hold all the data to be used in the subsequent analysis. If a particular series or group of series is required it can be extracted to another file for further work.

Now suppose that you wish to transfer data in the other direction, from a file produced by some other program for use with 1-2-3. Files created from many 1-2-3 'clones' or 'workalikes' such as Quattro and VP-Planner can be retrieved and used by 1-2-3 provided that they do not contain any functions or macros which differ in form from those in 1-2-3. This means that data transfer is completely trouble-free, and many templates can also be exchanged.

It is also possible to import files into 1-2-3 which are not of worksheet form, provided that they are in ASCII format. ASCII stands for American Standard Code for Information Interchange and you can easily tell if a file is in ASCII format because you will be able to read ordinary letters, numbers and punctuation marks on the screen when you enter the DOS command **TYPE FILENAME.EXT**. ASCII files can be transferred between software applications because most packages have programs to read and write ASCII files. In 1-2-3 you should use the /**File import** command. If, in addition, the file you are importing is in the correct form required by 1-2-3 with individual cell inputs identified between double quotation marks and separated by commas, you can use the choice *Number* from the *File Import* menu to read the file directly in its required form. If the file is not laid out in this manner you would need to choose *Text* from the *File Import* menu and then use the /**Data parse** command to break up the single labels which would be put into the worksheet rows in blocks for the individual cells (see the *Reference Manual*, pp. 97–8 and pp. 157–63).

If you wish to be able to use a 1-2-3 file with another package which can only import ASCII files (and not worksheet .WK1 files) you should use the *File* option from the 1-2-3 *Print* menu. This saves the file in ASCII format with extension .PRN (see the *Reference Manual*, pp. 99–110).

Finally, the Lotus 1-2-3 package has a Translate utility which can be used to move files between 1-2-3 and some other well-known packages such as dBase III. If you require this utility select *Translate* from the *Access* menu or place the 1-2-3 Utility disk in the current drive and type TRANS at the DOS prompt. Follow the on-screen instructions or press the HELP (F1) key (see also the *Reference Manual*, p. 302.

References

D. Begg, S. Fischer and R. Dornbusch, *Economics* (Second Edition) (Macmillan, London, 1977).

G. T. Le Blond and D. F. Cobb, *Using 1-2-3* (Que Corporation, Indianapolis, 1985).

J. B. Soper and M. P. Lee, *Statistics with Lotus 1-2-3* (Chartwell-Bratt, Bromley, 1987).

J. B. Soper and M. P. Lee, 'The Lorenz curve and Gini index with spreadsheets – some details', *Discussion Paper 64*, Department of Economics, University of Leicester, 1988.

Selected 1-2-3 commands

Main menu

Worksheet Range Copy Move File Print Graph Data System Quit

Changing the appearance of the worksheet
(**/Range** and **/Worksheet** commands)

/Worksheet Global Format
[to change worksheet format from default settings]
/Worksheet Global Column
[to change default column width]
/Worksheet Column Set-width
[to change width of a specific column)
/Range Format
[to change the format of a selected range]
/Range Erase
[to erase specific range]
/Worksheet Erase
[to erase the entire worksheet]
/Worksheet Column Hide
[to hide columns in a worksheet]
/Range Format Hidden
[to hide a specific range in the worksheet]
/Worksheet Insert
[to insert new rows or columns]
/Worksheet Window
[to split the screen into two windows]
/Range Format Text
[to display formulae instead of values]
/Worksheet Delete
[to delete specified rows or columns]

/Range Justify
[to change the justification of text in a specified range]

File handling

/File Retrieve
[to retrieve a worksheet file]
/File Save
[to save entire worksheet, including current settings]
/File Combine
[to incorporate data from another worksheet file]
/File Xtract
[to save specified data in a separate worksheet file]
/File Erase
[to erase a file in the current directory]
/File List
[to display the names of the files in the current directory]
/File Import
[to import data from an ASCII (text) file]
/File Directory
[to change the current directory]
also **/Graph Save**
     [to save a graph for later printing]
and **/Print File**
     [to save work as an ASCII (text) file]

Printing from a worksheet

/Print Printer Range
[to print specified range]
/Print File
[to save work as an ASCII (text) file]
/Print Printer (or **File**) **Options**
[to change current print settings]

To print a graph, save the graph as a .PIC file and use the *PrintGraph* program.

Copying cell contents

/Copy
[to copy number, text or formula from one range to another]

/Range Value
[to translate formula into value]
/Range Transpose
[to copy entries, switching row and column positions]
/Move
[to move cell entries to a new range leaving cells in original range empty]

Graphing data

/Graph Type
[to specify type of graph]
/Graph X, A–F
[to select data ranges for graph]
/Graph Options
[to modify the appearance of the graph]
/Graph Name
[to create or use a named graph with given settings]
/Graph Save
[to save a graph as a .PIC file for printing with PrintGraph]

Data commands

/Data Fill
[to enter a series of equally spaced numbers into a range]
/Data Sort
[to sort rows of data]
/Data Distribution
[to calculate the frequency distribution of a range of numbers]
/Data Matrix Multiply
[to multiply two matrices in specified ranges (must be conformable)]
/Data Matrix Invert
[to invert a matrix in specified range (must be square)]
/Data Regression
[to perform linear regression]
/Data Parse
[to break up lines of data into individual cell entries]

Other commands

/Quit
[to leave Lotus 1-2-3 and return to DOS or the Access system]

/System
[to go temporarily to DOS (type EXIT to return to where you were in the worksheet]
/Worksheet Global Protection
[to turn on or off global protection of cells]
/Range Protect
[to remove protection from specified cells]
/Range Name Create
[to assign a name to a cell or block of cells]
/Worksheet Status
[to display the amount of memory remaining]

See the *Reference Manual*, Chapter 2, for a full list of commands.

Appendix B

Frequently used built-in functions in 1-2-3

Mathematical functions

@ABS(x)	the absolute (positive) value of x
@EXP(x)	the number e raised to the power x
@INT(x)	the integer part of x
@LN(x)	the natural logarithm (base e) of x
@LOG(x)	the common logarithm (base 10) of x
@PI	the number π
@RAND	a random number between 0 and 1
@ROUND(x,n)	x rounded to n places
@SQRT(x)	the square root of x

Statistical functions

@AVG(range)	the average of the values in the cell range
@COUNT(range)	the number of non-blank entries in the cell range
@MAX(range)	the maximum value stored in the cell range
@MIN(range)	the minimum value stored in the cell range
@STD(range)	the standard deviation of the values stored in the cell range
@SUM(range)	the sum of the values stored in the cell range
@VAR(range)	the variance of the values stored in the cells in the range

Financial functions

@NPV(interest,range)	the present value of the series of future cash flows stored in the cells in the range, discounted using specified interest rate

@IRR(estimate,range)	the internal rate of return for a series of cash flows stored in the cell range (first cell contains present cost as a negative flow) based on initial estimate
@PV(payment,int,*n*)	the present value of a series of *n* equal payments discounted at the specified int(erest) rate
@FV(payment,int,*n*)	the future value of a series of *n* equal payments earning int(erest) as specified
@PMT(principal,int,*n*)	the periodic payment needed to pay off the principal at the specified int(erest) rate over *n* periods
@TERM(payment,int, future value)	the number of periods necessary to accumulate a future value if equal payments are placed in an account paying the specified int(erest) rate

Other functions

@IF(condition,*x*,*y*)	*x* if the condition is satisfied, *y* if not
@@(cell address)	the value in the cell referenced by the cell address

Lotus 1-2-3 contains many other built-in functions including some for string handling and for database management (see *Reference Manual*, Chapter 4).

Appendix C

Cursor movement keys

←[LEFT ARROW]	moves cursor one column to the left
→ [RIGHT ARROW]	moves cursor one column to the right
↑ [UP ARROW]	moves cursor one row up
↓ [DOWN ARROW]	moves cursor one row down
|←[BIG LEFT]	moves cursor one screen to the left
→| [BIG RIGHT]	moves cursor one screen to the right
<PgUp> [PAGEUP]	moves cursor up one screen
<PgDn> [PAGEDOWN)	moves cursor down one screen
<HOME>	moves cursor to cell A1
<END>	moves cursor to the extreme end of a block of filled cells (when entered before one of the other cursor movement keys)

Appendix D

Function keys in 1-2-3

F1 [HELP]   Displays 1-2-3's Help screens

F2 [EDIT]   Switches 1-2-3 into EDIT mode, allowing the contents of cells to be altered without retyping all the characters

F3 [NAME]   Displays a menu of range names

F4 [ABS]   Changes a relative cell address to an absolute cell address (and vice versa)

F5 [GOTO]   Moves cursor to specified cell

F6 [WINDOW]   Moves cursor to other side of split screen

F7 [QUERY]   Repeats most recent /**Data Query** operation

F8 [TABLE]   Repeats most recent /**Data Table** operation

F9 [CAL]   Recalculates all formulae in worksheet

F10 [GRAPH]   Displays the graph defined by the current settings

Appendix E

Some useful DOS commands

Internal DOS commands (from COMMAND.COM)

DIR	displays a directory of files in the specified directory
COPY	copies a file from one directory (disk) to another
ERASE	erase a file or files from the specified directory
RENAME	changes the name of a file
(or **REN**)	
DATE	displays or sets the date for systems that use an internal clock
TIME	displays or sets the time for systems with clock
MKDIR	make directory – used to create a new directory or sub-
(or **MD**)	directory
RMDIR	remove directory (directory must be empty of files)
(or **RD**)	
CHDIR	change directory – makes the specified directory or sub-
(or **CD**)	directory active
VER	displays MS–DOS version number
TYPE	displays the contents of a specified (text) file

External DOS commands (requires DOS disk)

DISKCOPY	to copy entire contents of disk onto blank disk (which need not be formatted) – useful for backup copies
CHDSK	check to see how much space available on disk
FORMAT	format floppy disk
EDLIN	command utility to edit (or create) text files
DISKCOMP	compares two floppy disks
TREE	to display directories with subdirectories
LABEL	to give a label to a floppy disk

Index